Multi-Agent Programming

Languages, Platforms and Applications

Multiagent Systems, Artificial Societies, and Simulated Organizations
International Book Series

Series Editor: **Gerhard Weiss**, *Technische Universität München*

Books in the Series:

- **CONFLICTING AGENTS:** *Conflict Management in Multi-Agent Systems*, edited by Catherine Tessier, Laurent Chaudron and Heinz-Jürgen Müller, ISBN: 0-7923-7210-7
- **SOCIAL ORDER IN MULTIAGENT SYSTEMS**, edited by Rosaria Conte and Chrysanthos Dellarocas, ISBN: 0-7923-7450-9
- **SOCIALLY INTELLIGENT AGENTS:** *Creating Relationships with Computers and Robots*, edited by Kerstin Dautenhahn, Alan H. Bond, Lola Cañamero and Bruce Edmonds, ISBN: 1-4020-7057-8
- **CONCEPTUAL MODELLING OF MULTI-AGENT SYSTEMS:** *The CoMoMAS Engineering Environment*, by Norbert Glaser, ISBN: 1-4020-7061-6
- **GAME THEORY AND DECISION THEORY IN AGENT-BASED SYSTEMS**, edited by Simon Parsons, Piotr Gmytrasiewicz, Michael Wooldridge, ISBN: 1-4020-7115-9
- **REPUTATION IN ARTIFICIAL SOCIETIES:** *Social Beliefs for Social Order*, by Rosaria Conte, Mario Paolucci, ISBN: 1-4020-7186-8
- **AGENT AUTONOMY**, edited by Henry Hexmoor, Cristiano Castelfranchi, Rino Falcone, ISBN: 1-4020-7402-6
- **AGENT SUPPORTED COOPERATIVE WORK**, edited by Yiming Ye, Elizabeth Churchill, ISBN: 1-4020-7404-2
- **DISTRIBUTED SENSOR NETWORKS**, edited by Victor Lesser, Charles L. Ortiz, Jr., Milind Tambe, ISBN: 1-4020-7499-9
- **AN APPLICATION SCIENCE FOR MULTI-AGENT SYSTEMS**, edited by Thomas A. Wagner, ISBN: 1-4020-7867-6
- **METHODOLOGIES AND SOFTWARE ENGINEERING FOR AGENT SYSTEMS:** *The Agent-Oriented Software Engineering Handbook,* **edited by** Federico Bergenti, Marie-Pierre Gleizes, Franco Zambonelli
- **AUTONOMY ORIENTED COMPUTING**: *From Problem Solving to Complex Systems Modeling,* Jiming Liu, XiaoLong Jin, and Kwok Ching Tsui, ISBN 1-4020-8121-9
- **EXTENDING WEB SERVICES TEHCNOLOGIES**, edited by Lawrence Cavedon, Zakaria Maamar, David Martin, Boualem Benatallah, ISBN 0-387-23343-1
- **AGENT INTELLIGENCE THROUGH DATA MINING,** Andreas L. Symeonidis, Pericles A. Mitkas, ISBN 0-387-24352-6

Multi-Agent Programming

Languages, Platforms and Applications

Edited by

Rafael H. Bordini
University of Durham

Mehdi Dastani
Utrecht University

Jürgen Dix
Clausthal University of Technology

Amal El Fallah Seghrouchni
University of Paris IV

 Springer

Edited by
Rafael H. Bordini
University of Durham, USA

Mehdi Dastani
Utrecht University, NETHERLANDS

Jürgen Dix
Clausthal University of Technology, GERMANY

Amal El Fallah Seghrouchni
University of Paris VI, FRANCE

Library of Congress Cataloging-in-Publication Data

A C.I.P. Catalogue record for this book is available
From the Library of Congress

ISBN-10: 0-387-24568-5 (HB)   e-ISBN 10: 0-387- 26350-0

ISBN-13: 978-0387-24568-3 (HB) e-ISBN-13: 978-0387-26350-2
Printed on acid-free paper

Printed in the United States of America

9 8 7 6 5 4 3 2 1   SPIN 11372691

springeronline.com

Contents

6
Jadex: A BDI Reasoning Engine   149
Alexander Pokahr, Lars Braubach, and Winfried Lamersdorf

7
JACK^{TM} Intelligent Agents: An Industrial Strength Platform   175
Michael Winikoff

List of Figures

Contributing Authors

Fabio Bellifemine is a senior project manager at Telecom Italia Lab. His research interests are in multi-agent systems and platforms, and their applications to mobile VAS. He received a degree in Computer Science from the University of Torino in 1998 and, before joining Telecom Italia, he held a researcher position at the Italian National Research Council since 1988 to 1994. In 2000 he launched the JADE project and, since 2003, he is the president of the JADE Governing Board. Since last year, he chairs the sub-group Systems Architecture of the "Distributed Intelligent Systems" Technical Committee of IEEE Systems, Man, and Cybernetics (SMC).

Federico Bergenti is a Lecturer of Software Engineering courses at the University of Parma. His research interests are centred mainly on agent-based interoperability, agent-based software reuse, and more generally on foundations of agent-oriented software engineering. He participated to various European-scale research projects, most notably, LEAP (IST-1999-10211) and Collaborator (IST-2000-30045). He received a Ph.D. in Information Technology from the Department of Information Engineering of the University of Parma in 2002.

Rafael H. Bordini is a Lecturer in Computer Science at the University of Durham. His research interests are centred mainly on agent-oriented programming languages, verification of multi-agent systems through model checking, and applications of multi-agent systems to social simulation. He received a PhD in Computer Science from the University of London (University College London) in 1999. Before moving to Durham in 2004, he was a Research Fellow at the Department of Computer Science, University of Liverpool. Previous to moving to Liverpool (in 2002), he was invited lecturer at the Federal University of Rio Grande do Sul, Brazil.

Lars Braubach received his diploma in computer science in January 2002 at the University of Hamburg. Since then, he is research assistant at the University of Hamburg. In the course of the DFG funded priority research program "Intelligent Agents in Real-World Business Applications", he is investigating the foundations of multi-agent systems, as well as practically exploring the applicability of this technology in the Jadex Open Source project.

Giovanni Caire is a senior project manager in the Mobile Platforms division of Telecom Italia Lab. His interest is in the field of Java-based mobile distributed applications. In particular he led the porting of JADE into MIDP environments within the framework of the IST LEAP project and, currently, he is the technical leader of the JADE Governing Board, he represents Telecom Italia Mobile in the Java Workstream of the OMTP (Open Mobile Terminal Platform) initiative and he is also member of the JSR 232 – Mobile Device Management – Expert Group. He received a degree in Engineering from "Politecnico di Torino" in 1992 and joined Telecom Italia Lab in 1993.

Mehdi Dastani studied computer science and philosophy at university of Amsterdam. He obtained his Ph.D. in formal analysis of visual perception and information visualization in 1998. From 1998 to 2001 he was research Associate at the department of artificial intelligence, Vrije Universiteit Amsterdam, working on automatic and dynamic configuration of a multi-agent system for electronic commerce. From 2001 until 2002 he was research associate at the institute of information and computing sciences, Utrecht University, where he was responsible for a project on methodology for agent-oriented software design. From 2002 he is a lecturer at the Intelligent Systems Group of Utrecht University. His research focus is agent theories and agent applications, in particular the topic of specification and implementation languages for cognitive agents. He is member of program committees of various international conferences and workshops and has organized various workshops and events.

Jürgen Dix heads the chair for Computational Intelligence at Clausthal University of Technology since 2004. Previously he was Reader for Knowledge Representation and Reasoning at The University of Manchester, United Kingdom (2000-2003) and visiting Professor at the University of Maryland, College Park, USA (1999). His research covers various areas of Computational Logic, Planning and Multi-agent Systems. He is on the editorial boards of several journals, member of various steering committees and coordinating node of CologNet and Agentlink. He organised 8 conferences and workshops, published more than 140 papers, co-authored two monographs and co-edited 10 books and 6 special journal issues.

Amal El Fallah Seghrouchni is a professor at University Paris X, Nanterre and member of LIP6-OASIS. Her research interests focus upon Multi-Agent Systems as a cognitive approach that helps developing distributed and co-operative systems based on intelligent agents. This involves the specification and verification of such complex systems that take into account concurrency, interaction and cognition. She has a background on Formal specification, Distributed Observation, Distributed Planning, Petri Nets, True concurrency semantics and verification. She published more than 60 papers in the major conferences in the area of multi-agent system, co-edited 3 books and co-organised several international events dedicated to Multi-Agent Systems. She also has been invited professor and gave talks in international seminars and courses for post-graduate students about multi-agent planning, coordination, interaction protocols, etc. (For more details, please see: http://www-poleia.lip6.fr/~elfallah). She is also leader of the Multi-Agent Systems group (Collège SMA) of the French Artificial Intelligence Association (AFIA); see http://sma.lip6.fr.

Jomi Fred Hübner is a lecturer at the University of Blumenau, Brazil, where he teaches courses on Artificial Intelligence and Programming since 1996. He obtained his PhD from the University of São Paulo, Brazil, in 2003. The subject of his thesis was the modelling of multi-agent organisations and the process of reorganisation in multi-agent systems. His research interests are on models of organisation in multi-agent systems and tools to support the development of BDI-based multi-agent systems.

Winfried Lamersdorf is full Professor in the Department of Computer Science of Hamburg University and head of the "Distributed and Information Systems" (Verteilte Systeme und Informationssysteme, VSIS) unit. In 1985 he received his doctorate form the University of Hamburg. From 1983 to 1990 he was a staff-member in the "Distributed Applications" research group at the IBM Scientific Center (WZH, 1983/84) and in the IBM "European Networking Centre" (ENC, 1984-90) in Heidelberg. In the past 15 years, he has lead several research projects financed from various sources.

J.P. Lewis is a computer graphics researcher. His current research interests include facial animation, computer vision, and machine learning topics. He has worked in both academic research labs and in the movie special effects industry, and his algorithms have been incorporated in several leading graphics software packages.

Agostino Poggi is full professor of Computer Engineering at the Dipartimento di Ingegneria dell'Informazione of the University of Parma. His research focuses on agent, Web and object-oriented technologies and their use to develop distributed and complex systems. In these research areas, he cordinated and is coordinating the research of its Department inside different projects funded by national and international, public and private organizations. He is author of more than 150 technical papers in refereed journals and conferences and his scientific contribution has been recognized through the "System Research Foundation Outstanding Scholarly Contribution Award" in 1988 and through the "Innovation System Award" in 2001.

Janusz Marecki is a PHD student of Computer Science at University of Southern California (USC). His research areas are primarily autonomous agents and multi-agent systems. He earned a Bachelor of Science degree at Academy of Computer Science and Management (Poland) and a Master of Science degree at the Jagiellonian University (Poland). He was awarded the Erasmus scholarship to study at Universite Monpellier II in France. He also worked for the European Laboratory for Nuclear Research (CERN).

John-Jules Ch. Meyer studied mathematics with computer science and digital signal processing at Leyden University. In 1985 he obtained his Ph.D. from the Vrije Universiteit in Amsterdam on a subject in theoretical computer science. From 1988 to 1993 he was a professor at the computer science department at the VU Amsterdam holding a chair in "Logic for distributed systems and artificial intelligence". From 1989 to 1993 he also was a professor of theoretical computer science at the Katholieke Universiteit Nijmegen. Since 1993 he has been a professor at the computer science department of Utrecht University (UU). At the moment he is heading the Intelligent Systems Group of the Institute of Computing and information Sciences of the UU. Prof. Meyer is the scientific director of the national graduate school in Information and Knowledge-based Systems (SIKS). He is a member of the editorial boards of the Journal of Applied Non-Classical Logics, Data and Knowledge Engineering and the Journal of Intelligent Agents and Multi-Agent Systems. His current research interests include intelligent agents, cognitive robotics and logics for AI.

Alexander Pokahr received his diploma in computer science in January 2002 at the University of Hamburg. Since then, he is research assistant at the University of Hamburg, with a focus on software architectures and development tools for intelligent agents and distributed multi-agent systems. In conjunction with Lars Braubach, he is developing the Open Source agent system Jadex.

M. Birna van Riemsdijk is a Ph.D. student at Utrecht University, The Netherlands. She is doing research under supervision of prof. dr. John-Jules Meyer, dr. Frank de Boer and dr. Mehdi Dastani. The main topic of her research is semantics of cognitive agent programming languages. In particular, she has worked on the semantics of the cognitive agent programming language 3APL. Further, her research involves developing logics for specification and verification of 3APL. She has published work in a number of agent (programming) workshops and conferences such as ProMAS, DALT, CLIMA and AAMAS.

David Sadek is director of the research program on Intelligent Agents and Natural Interactions, at the R&D division of France Telecom. He is also head of the industrial leverage unit for advanced human-computer dialogue based services. His work on formal models of reasoning and interaction is at the basis of the first effective technology of rational agents and natural dialogue systems, throughout the world. Today, this edge technology enters the industrial process for large-scale commercial applications. In 2002, David Sadek received Medal Blondel for his work in Cognitive Science and Artificial Intelligence and, in 1999, the France Telecom Innovation Award for the Artimis rational dialogue agent technology.

David Sadek is director of the research program on intelligent agents and natural interactions, at the R&D Division of France Telecom. He is also head of the industrial leverage unit for advanced human-computer dialogue based services. His work on formal models of cognitive agents and natural communication is at the basis of the first world-wide effective generic technology of rational agents and dialogue systems, which he has created with his team. Currently, this leading edge technology is entering an industrial process for large-scale commercial applications. Also, his work on the semantics of communicative actions gave birth to the FIPA ACL standard for an inter-agent communication language. In 1999, he received, together with his team, the France Telecom Innovation Prize for the Artimis rational dialogue agent technology. In 2002, he was awarded Medal Blondel for his contribution to Cognitive Science and Artificial Intelligence.

Paul Scerri is a Systems Scientist at Carnegie Mellon University's Robotics Institute. His primary research interests is on coordination of large teams and human interaction with such teams, specifically via the use of adjustable autonomy. He received his PhD from Linkopings University in Sweden in 2001. Before moving to Carnegie Mellon, he worked at the University of Southern California's Information Sciences Institute.

Nathan Schurr is a PhD candidate of Computer Science in the Viterbi School of Engineering at University of Southern California. His research interests are in human interaction with multiagent systems. He was awarded the Viterbi School of Engineering Homeland Security Center Doctoral Fellowship. He served on the Program Committee for AI Technologies for Homeland Security session at the American Association of Artificial Intelligence (AAAI) Spring Symposium 2005.

Alexandru Suna is a 3rd year Ph. D. student at the University "Pierre et Marie Curie", Paris, member of the LIP6 laboratory, OASIS group and lecturer at the University Paris X – Nanterre. In 2001 he obtained an Engineer Diploma in Computer Science at the "Politehnica" University of Bucharest and in 2002 a Master Diploma in Artificial Intelligence and Combinatorial Optimisation at the University Paris XIII. His research interests focus on multi-agent systems in general, on developing distributed systems, on mobile agents and platfors and on programming intelligent and mobile agents (for more details, `http://www-poleia.lip6.fr/~suna/`).

Milind Tambe is an Associate Professor of Computer Science at University of Southern California(USC). He received his Ph.D. from the School of Computer Science at Carnegie Mellon University. He leads the TEAMCORE research group at USC (`http://teamcore.usc.edu`), with research interests in multi-agent systems, specifically multi-agent teamwork, adjustable autonomy and distributed negotiations. His research on these topics has led to some of the most highly cited papers in the field, as well as the ACM SIGART Agents Research award (at AAMAS 2005), the Okawa foundation research grant award (2003), AAMAS best paper award (2002), selection in the "best of" papers of Agents'99 and ICMAS'98 conferences, and the RoboCup scientific challenge award (1999). He was general co-chair for the International Joint Conference on Agents and Multiagent Systems (AAMAS) 2004, and program co-chair of the International conf on multi-agent systems (ICMAS) 2000. He is also currently associate editor of the Journal of Artificial Intelligence Research (JAIR), and on the editorial board of the Journal of Autonomous Agents and Multi-agent Systems (JAAMAS). A current member of the board of directors of the International foundation for multiagent systems, he has also served on the board of trustees of RoboCup, the RobotWorld Cup Federation.

Renata Vieira received a PhD in Cognitive Science from the University of Edinburgh in 1998. Since then she has been a lecturer at the Post-Graduate Programme in Applied Computing, Universidade do Vale do Rio dos Sinos, Brazil. Her research interests are mainly related to natural language processing, intelligent agents, and Semantic-Web technologies.

Michael Winikoff is a senior lecturer in Computer Science at RMIT University. His research interests concern notations for specifying and constructing software. In particular, he is interested in agent oriented software engineering methodologies and is co-author of the book *Developing Intelligent Agent Systems: A Practical Guide*, published by John Wiley and sons in 2004. He received a PhD in Computer Science from the University of Melbourne in 1997, and then spent a little over a year as a research fellow at the University of Melbourne before joining the Institute for Software Research in the USA. Michael returned to Australia in mid-1999 to join RMIT University as a research fellow, then in 2000 he left RMIT to do industrial software development, finally returning to RMIT University in 2001.

Yingqian Zhang is currently a PhD student in the School of Computer Science at the University of Manchester. Her research interests are mainly on logic based multiagent systems, multiagent security and survivability, negotiation and cooperation among agents. She expects to graduate this Autumn.

Preface

Agent technology, in particular multi-agent systems, is beginning to play an important role in today's software development at industrial level. Until recently, the main focus of the multi-agent systems community has been on the development of concepts, architectures, interaction techniques, and general approaches to the analysis and specification of multi-agent systems. However, these contributions, which are sometimes formal but often informal, have been quite fragmented, without any clear way of "putting it all together", and thus completely inaccessible to practitioners. Clearly, the success of agent-oriented system design and implementation can only be guaranteed if we can bridge the gap between analysis and implementation, and thus develop expressive programming languages and well-developed platforms so that the concepts and techniques of multi-agent systems can be easily and directly implemented.

The idea for this book evolved over several years, when the editors started the ProMAS workshop (http://www.cs.uu.nl/ProMAS/) series as well as an AgentLink III Technical Forum Group on Programming Multi-Agent Systems (http://www.agentlink.org/activities/al3-tf/). One of the driving motivations for promoting these activities is the observation that the area of autonomous agents and multi-agent systems has grown into a promising technology, offering sensible alternatives for the design of distributed, intelligent systems. Several efforts, originating from academia, industry, and several standardisation consortia, have been made to provide new tools, methods, and frameworks aiming at establishing the necessary standards for a wide use of multi-agent systems techniques. For this, it is essential that such technology can be incorporated into existing practices in the software industry, and not seen simply as a promising new paradigm. We are convinced that the next step in furthering the achievement of the multi-agent systems project is irrevocably associated with the development of programming languages and tools that can effectively support multi-agent programming, including the implementation of key notions in multi-agent systems in a unified framework. We hope this book will turn out to be a useful contribution in that direction.

While there exist many collections of papers and proceedings on (multi-) agent systems, there are no books presenting in a coherent way the frameworks that can be used for designing and implementing large-scale multi-agent systems. In most of the available books on this subject, the chapters are only very loosely related, which makes it very difficult to compare and evaluate different approaches and to get an idea of their suitability for particular applications.

In this book we have invited several research groups to report on their work on programming languages and platforms, or large-scale multi-agent systems applications. Most importantly, we have explicitly asked them to follow a particular chapter structure, according to templates we provided. More than that, we asked them to answer several key questions providing a summary of the main features of each framework (these can be found in the appendices of this book).

With this structure, we aimed at providing the reader with a good basis for comparison among the reported frameworks. The result is a book that can be used to guide the choice of a particular framework for developing real-world multi-agent systems or for teaching purposes and assigning practical coursework when teaching multi-agent systems. This book has a sufficient level of detail to introduce the reader to the use of some of the most prominent working agent frameworks currently available.

The Structure of Contributed Chapters

Chapters describing *Programming Languages and Platforms* discuss the functionality of the languages, the communication mechanisms they provide, their underlying execution model or interpreters, their expressiveness and verification possibilities, and the software engineering principles that they follow. These chapters discuss also the characteristics of the platforms that correspond to the programming languages. The issues related to the platforms are: system deployment and portability, any standards with which they comply, their extensibility, the tools they provide, their technical interoperability, and their performance. Finally, each of these chapters explains which applications can be supported and implemented by the presented languages and their corresponding platforms. They discuss the typical application examples and their target application domains.

In turn, chapters describing *Applications* present the application domains and explain the added values of multi-agent systems for those domains, also describing how they have designed and specified multi-agent systems for the presented application domain. Moreover, they discuss which main features of agents were used in the applications, which architecture was used to design the agents, and how the designed agents were implemented. An essential issue in the development of multi-agent systems are agent organisations, which can help coordinate the behaviour of individual agents. These chapters also discuss how the interaction between agents and their external shared environment are modelled and implemented. Finally, they explain which platforms are used to develop and execute the multi-agent system being described, and discuss issues related to the deployment of the multi-agent systems, such as fault tolerance and security.

The Selected Frameworks and the Structure of the Book

The selection of the agent programming languages and platforms in this book is, of course, a matter of taste and reflects our own viewpoint. One important characteristic that we used to select the frameworks is that all of them have working implementations that users can download and use to develop their own applications. We also selected two applications that help showing important areas in which agent-oriented programming techniques can have a significant impact.

Unfortunately, we could not incorporate all frameworks and applications we consider interesting: that would be an encyclopaedic task, and there was a limited number of pages we could use for this particular book. However, we aim to produce a sequel for this book, in which we plan to overview and compare other existing agent programming languages and their platforms, as well as other industrial-strength applications. Rather, we hope to have started with some useful material for researchers, students, and practitioners interested in theoretical aspects of agent frameworks as well as their application for practical purposes.

The book is structured in three parts. In Part I of the book, there are four chapters describing approaches that rely heavily on computational logic or process algebra. All programming languages described in these chapters have formal semantics and use heavy machinery based on formal methods, but also provide working platforms for the development of multi-agent systems.

In the first chapter of Part I, Rafael Bordini, Jomi Hübner, and Renata Vieira present their work on *Jason*, an interpreter for a programming language based on the BDI architecture (an extension of AgentSpeak). Implemented in Java, *Jason* allows multi-agent systems to be easily configured and distributed over a network. The platform has an explicit notion of multi-agent environment, and allows for easy customisation of the way agents interact with each other and the environment, amongst other things. The IDE provides a tool that allows the inspection of agents' mental attitudes, which is useful for debugging.

Mehdi Dastani, Birna van Riemsdijk, and John-Jules Meyer introduce *3APL*, which is a programming language for implementing multi-agent systems. It has been developed over the last eight years in Utrecht and it is still subject of ongoing research. The *3APL* programming language supports direct implementation of BDI agents and provides programming constructs to implement interaction among agents, and between agents and their shared environment. The development of multi-agent systems is facilitated by the 3APL platform through which multi-agent systems can be programmed, edited, debugged, and executed.

Jürgen Dix and Yingqian Zhang report on *IMPACT*, an agent language and platform developed in Maryland and extended in Austria, Israel, and Germany. IMPACT has a declarative semantics that is closely related to deductive database technology and logic programming, but it is entirely implemented in JAVA. Its main feature is to agentise arbitrary legacy code, i.e., to transform given code into an agent by wrapping several layers around it.

Amal El Fallah Seghrouchni and Alexandru Suna describe their work on the *CLAIM* language and the distributed platform *SyMPA*. *CLAIM* is a high-level agent-oriented programming language that combines both cognitive aspects of intelligent agents and constructs to deal with communication, mobility, and concurrency. Based on process algebra (Ambient Calculus specifically), *CLAIM* has an operational semantics and is suitable for distributed MAS that require mobility and hierarchical topology. The *SyMPA* platform is compliant with the specifications of the MASIF standard from the OMG, and offers the necessary mechanisms for secure execution of distributed multi-agent systems.

Part II comprises three chapters describing agent languages and platforms that extend or are based on Java. Although they have no formal semantics, the languages are well documented, and the platforms in general provide a variety of tools that have been extensively and widely used in practice.

The first chapter of Part II reports on *JADE*, a well-known agent framework implemented in Java by Agostino Poggi and colleagues. It provides a middleware that complies with the FIPA specifications, and offers several graphical tools that support the debugging and deployment phases of multi-agent programming. A variety of applications has been developed with JADE and it has a considerable large user group.

Lars Braubach, Alexander Pokhar, and Winfried Lamersdorf introduce their work on *Jadex* which extends the *JADE* platform with BDI concepts. The *Jadex* programming language is a combination of XML and Java. The XML notation allows programmers to specify individual agents in terms of BDI concepts. The BDI concepts are then implemented as Java programs. The development of multi-agent systems is facilitated by the *Jadex* platform which facilitates the editing, debugging, and execution of multi-agent systems.

Then, Michael Winikoff describes *JACK*, a commercial agent platform that aims at meeting industrial standards with respect to familiarity, scalability, and integrability. It is being developed and used commercially for a number of years, and available free of charge for researchers and students. Also based on the BDI-based reactive planning systems, *JACK* programs use a particular notation for agent constructs that are added to Java code. The platform includes an IDE with various graphical tools and extensive documentation.

After these seven agent programming languages and their platforms, two industrial-strength applications are described in Part III. There is a huge variety of areas of application (mentioned throught the book) for which multi-agent programming is suitable, and we aimed at providing two significant examples.

In the area of disaster management, Milind Tambe's group has developed a system, called *DEFACTO*, that enables teams of agents and humans to interact for effective disaster response. The system combines various artificial intelligence techniques, and is based on a 3D visualization system and a software proxy architecture.

The last chapter, written by David Sadek, describes a rational agent technology called *ARTIMIS* that has been designed, developed, and recently commercially deployed by France Telecom. It provides a generic framework to instantiate intelligent dialogue agents that are able to engage in rich interactions with human users as well as with other software agents.

Finally, we provide, as appendices, the summaries of each of the seven agent programming languages presented in the book. Appendix A in particular shows the criteria we consider appropriate for comparing agent platforms; they are introduced in the form of objective questions we posed to the authors. Each of the appendices after that contains the short answers, provided by the contributing authors, relative to each of the programming languages and platforms presented in the book.

RAFAEL H. BORDINI
MEHDI DASTANI
JÜRGEN DIX
AMAL EL FALLAH SEGHROUCHNI

Foreword

The design and evaluation of programming languages is the heart and soul of computer science. It first became possible to make practical use of high-level programming languages in the 1950s. Since then, successive programming languages innovations such as subroutines, procedural and functional abstraction, data structures, abstract data types, objects, and components have made it progressively easier and more natural for programmers to manage the difficult task of producing correct, efficient, manageable software solutions.

Programming language design has progressed hand-in-hand with our understanding of what kinds of problems we might tackle using computer-based solutions. Thus as graphical user interfaces and the window-icon-mouse-pointer paradigm began to emerge, so did object-oriented programming as a natural way to conceptualise and build such interfaces. Similarly, as distribution and concurrency became the norm, threads and synchronised communication mechanisms were deployed to make it possible to easily build distributed and concurrent systems. As such features evolved, and programming languages became richer, the importance of a proper theoretical foundation for programming languages also became apparent, and a host of mathematically rich formalisms were developed in an attempt to gain a clear understanding of how programming languages could and should behave. And yet, for all these technical developments, every programmer knows that what makes a "good" programming language is at least in part a kind of magic: there is an indefinable "rightness" to the best languages, that make them somehow easier, more fun, more natural, just *better* to use.

This book is about programming languages for a relatively new class of computer systems, called multi-agent systems. Much has been written about multi-agent systems and why they are an important idea, and this foreword is not the place to add to this mountain of words. Suffice to say that the key feature of a multi-agent system is that it contains multiple, interacting computing elements, called agents, where these agents are capable of "rational" autonomous (i.e., independent) action — making independent decisions about what actions to perform in the furtherance of their goals. From the programming language point of view, the key issue is what is the "right" way to program such agents. In particular, the issue is what kinds of programming language constructs should an "agent-oriented programming language" contain in order to reflect the desire to build these autonomous, interacting components? In short, what is the best (most convenient, most natural, most succinct, most efficient, most comprehensible, ...) way to program agents?

The term "agent-oriented programming language" was coined by Yoav Shoham from Stanford University in the late 1980s. In a highly influential paper [206], he presented both the concept of agent-oriented programming, and a prototype programming language, called AGENT0, which embodied some of the ideas that he felt would be central to this new programming paradigm. Since the early 1990s, Shoham's ideas have been taken up, refined, and modified by many researchers, in the search for that elusive "rightness" which characterises a good programming language.

The present volume contains a comprehensive survey of the state of the art of such languages. The articles it contains describe all the major contenders for the status of agent programming language *du jour*. Some of these languages (in particular, 3APL) can trace their heritage more-or-less directly from Shoham's early vision — although they are of considerably more refined, both in terms of features and their semantic/theoretical foundation. Other languages, by contrast, share some similar ideas but can claim a rather different heritage. The various BDI systems described herein (Jason, Jadex, Jack) all stem from a common root in the AI planning tradition of reactive planning, as embodied in the Procedural Reasoning System developed in the mid-1980s. Yet other languages (CLAIM, SyMPA) come from the very radically different traditions, of mobile processes and process calculi, and these languages have only a very slight intellectual debt with respect to the original agent-oriented programming vision. Still other languages (IMPACT, JADE) are focussed on different issues, and address different concerns in different ways. Of course, all the languages described in this book are different; sometimes in subtle ways, and sometimes in rather substantial ways. Readers must decide for themselves which has that elusive "rightness" when it comes to programming multi-agent systems.

Is this book the final word on agent-oriented programming? I doubt it. Just as our ideas evolve with respect to what can be done with computers, and how it can be done in terms of programming languages, so our ideas about agents and how to program them will evolve. But this book, capturing as it does the state of the art in such a comprehensive and comprehensible way, will make a fundamental and lasting contribution to this fascinating area.

Michael Wooldridge
Department of Computer Science
University of Liverpool
Liverpool L69 3BX, U.K., April 2005

Acknowledgments

We would like to thank Gerhard Weiss, series editor of the "Multiagent Systems, Artificial Societies, and Simulated Organizations" international book series, for his encouragement when we decided to edit this book. We are also grateful to all the Programme Committee members of ProMAS'03, ProMAS'04, and ProMAS'05, as their careful work has done a great service to the area of Programming Multi-Agent Systems in general. Finally, we thank Peter Novak, Tristan M. Behrens, Alexandru Suna, and Yingqian Zhang for various help with either this book or the workshop series.

We dedicate this book to all the enthusiasts of this exciting new approach to programming.

I

LOGIC- OR PROCESS ALGEBRA-BASED AGENT PROGRAMMING LANGUAGES

Chapter 1

JASON AND THE GOLDEN FLEECE OF AGENT-ORIENTED PROGRAMMING

Rafael H. Bordini,[1] Jomi F. Hübner,[2] and Renata Vieira[3]

[1] *Department of Computer Science, University of Durham*
Durham DH1 3LE, U.K.
R.Bordini@durham.ac.uk

[2] *Departamento de Sistemas e Computação, Universidade Regional de Blumenau*
Blumenau, SC 89035-160, Brazil
jomi@inf.furb.br

[3] *Programa Interdisciplinar de Pós-Graduação em Computação Aplicada,*
Universidade do Vale do Rio dos Sinos, São Leopoldo, RS 93022-000, Brazil
renata@exatas.unisinos.br

Abstract   This chapter describes *Jason*, an interpreter written in Java for an extended version of AgentSpeak, a logic-based agent-oriented programming language that is suitable for the implementation of reactive planning systems according to the BDI architecture. We describe both the language and the various features and tools available in the platform.

Keywords: Logic-Based Agent Programming, Beliefs-Desires-Intentions, Operational Semantics, Speech Acts, Plan Exchange, Java-based Extensibility/Customisation.

> *Now was remaining as the last conclusion of this game,*
> *By force of chaunted herbes to make the watchfull Dragon sleepe*
> *Within whose eyes came never winke: who had in charge to keepe*
> *The goodly tree upon the which the golden fleeces hung.*
>
> *...*
>
> *The dreadfull Dragon by and by (whose eyes before that day*
> *Wist never erst what sleeping ment) did fall so fast asleepe*
> *That Jason safely tooke the fleece of golde that he did keepe.*
>
> *P. Ovidius Naso, Metamorphoses (ed. Arthur Golding), Book VII.*

1.1   Motivation

Research on Multi-Agent Systems (MAS) has led to a variety of techniques that promise to allow the development of complex distributed systems. The importance of this is that such systems would be able to work in environments that are traditionally thought to be too unpredictable for computer programs to handle. With more than a decade of work on Agent-Oriented Programming (AOP) — since Y. Shoham's seminal paper [206] — it has become clear that the task of putting together the technology emerging from MAS research in a way that allows the practical development of real-world MAS is comparable, in mythological terms, to the task of retrieving the Golden Fleece from the distant kingdom of Colchis, where it hang on a tree guarded by a sleepless dragon. Of course, this is not a task for *Jason* alone, but for the greatest heros of the time, who became known as the Argonauts (a selection of "whom" is described throughout this book).

The work described here is the result of an attempt to revive one of the most elegant programming languages that appeared in the literature; the language was called AgentSpeak(L), and was introduced by A. Rao in [180]. AgentSpeak(L) is a logic-based agent-oriented programming language, which is aimed at the implementation of reactive planning systems (such as PRS [98]) but also benefited from the experience with more clear notions of Beliefs-Desires-Intentions (BDI) as put forward in the work on the BDI agent architecture [182, 181] and BDI logics [183, 237]. However, AgentSpeak(L) was not but an abstract agent programming language. The work we have done, together with various colleagues, was both on extending AgentSpeak so that it became a practical programming language (allowing full integration with what we consider the most important MAS techniques) as well as on providing operational semantics (a standard formalism for semantics of programming languages) for AgentSpeak and most of the proposed extensions.[1]The driving force of all work reported here is to have a programming language for MAS which is practical (in the sense of allowing the development of real-world applications), yet elegant and with a rigorous formal basis.

Jason is the interpreter for our extended version of AgentSpeak, which allows agents to be distributed over the net through the use of SACI [115]. *Jason* is available *Open Source* under GNU LGPL at http:// jason.sourceforge.net [22]. It implements the operational semantics of AgentSpeak originally given in [24, 152] and improved in [229]. It also implements the extension of the operational semantics that accounts for speech-act based communication among AgentSpeak agents, first proposed

---

[1]We shall use AgentSpeak throughout this chapter, as a general reference to either AgentSpeak(L) as proposed by Rao or the various existing extensions.

in [153] and then extended in [229] (see Section 1.2.4). Another important extension is on allowing plan exchange [4] (see Section 1.2.4).

Some of the features available in *Jason* are:

- speech-act based inter-agent communication (and annotation of beliefs with information sources);

- annotations on plan labels, which can be used by elaborate (e.g., decision theoretic) selection functions;

- the possibility to run a multi-agent system distributed over a network (using SACI, but other middleware can be used);

- fully customisable (in Java) selection functions, trust functions, and overall agent architecture (perception, belief-revision, inter-agent communication, and acting);

- straightforward extensibility (and use of) by means of user-defined "internal actions";

- clear notion of *multi-agent environments*, which can be implemented in Java (this can be a simulation of a real environment, e.g., for testing purposes before the system is actually deployed).

Interestingly, most of the advanced features are available as optional, customisable mechanisms. Thus, because the AgentSpeak core that is interpreted by *Jason* is very simple and elegant, yet having all the main elements for expressing reactive planning system with BDI notions, we think that *Jason* is also ideal for teaching AOP for under- and post-graduate studies.

An important strand of work related to AgentSpeak that adds to making *Jason* a promising platform is the work on formal verification of MAS systems implemented in AgentSpeak by means of model checking techniques (this is discussed in Section 1.2.2); that work in fact draws on there being precise definitions of the BDI notions in terms of states of AgentSpeak agents. Before we start describing *Jason* in more detail, we will introduce a scenario that will be used to give examples throughout this chapter. Although not all parts of the scenario are used in the examples given here, we introduce the whole scenario as we think it contains most of the important aspects of environments for which multi-agent systems are appropriate, and may therefore be useful more generally than its use in this chapter.

Scenario for a Running Example: The Airport Chronicle

The year is 2070 *ad*. Airports have changed a lot since the beginning of the century, but terrorist attacks are hardly a thing of the past. Anti-terror technology has improved substantially, arguably to compensate for the sheer irrationality of mankind when it comes to resolve issues such as economic greed, religious fanaticism, and group favouritism, all of which remain with us from evolutionary times when they may have been useful.

Airports are now completely staffed by robots, specially London Heathrow, where different robot models are employed for various specific tasks. In particular, security is now completely under the control of specialised robots: due to a legacy from XX and early XXI century, Heathrow is still number one... terrorist threat target, that is. The majority of the staff, however, is formed by CPH903 robots. These are cute, polite, handy robots who welcome people into the airport, give them a "hand" with pieces of luggage (e.g., lifting them to place on a trolley), and, of course, provide any information (in natural language, also using multi-media presentations whenever useful) that costumers may need.

Most of the security-related tasks are carried out by model MDS79 robots. The multi-device security robots are very expensive pieces of equipment, as they are endowed with all that technology can provide, in 2070, for bomb detection. They use advanced versions of the technology in use by the beginning of the century: x-ray, metal detectors, and computed tomography for detecting explosive devices, ion trap mobility spectrometry (ITMS) for detecting traces of explosives, as well as equipment for detecting radioactive materials (gamma ray and neutrons) used in "dirty bombs".

These days at Heathrow, check-in and security checks are no longer centralised, being carried out directly at the boarding gates. Thus, there are one or two replicas of robot model MDS79 at each departure gate. When unattended luggage is reported, all staff in the vicinity are informed of its location through a wireless local area network to which they all are connected. The robots then start a process of negotiation (with a very tight deadline for a final decision) in order to reach an agreement on which of them will be relocated to handle the unattended luggage report.

All staff robots know that, normally, one MDS79 and one CPH903 robot can cooperate to ensure that reported unattended luggage has been cleared away. The way they actually do it is as follow. The MDS79 robot replica uses all of its devices to check whether there is a bomb in the unattended luggage. If there is any chance of there being a bomb in the luggage, the MDS79 robot sends a high priority message to the bomb-disarming team of robots. (Obviously, robots communicate using speech-act based languages, such as those used for agent communication since the end of last century.) Only three of these very specialised robots are operational for all Heathrow terminals at the moment. Once these robots are called in, the MDS79 and CPH903 robots that had been relocated can go back to their normal duties. The bomb-disarming robots decide whether to set off a security alert to evacuate the airport, or alternatively they attempt to disarm the bomb or move it to a safe area, if they can ensure such courses of action would pose no threat to the population.

In case the MDS79 robot detects no signs of a bomb in the unattended luggage, the job is passed on to the accompanying CPH903 robot. Luggage these days usually come with a magnetic ID tag that records the details of the passenger who owns it. Replicas of robot CPH903 are endowed with a tag reader and, remember, they are heavily built so as to be able to carry pieces of luggage (unlike MDS79). Besides, MDS79 are expensive and much in demand, so they should not be relocated to carry the piece of luggage after it has been cleared. So, in case the luggage is cleared, it is the CPH903 robot's task to take the unattended luggage to the gate where the passenger is (details of flights and passengers are accessed through the wireless network) if the passenger is known to be already there, or to the lost luggage centre, in case the precise location of the passenger in the airport cannot be determined (which is rather unusual these days).

Thus, all staff robots have, as part of their knowledge representation, that normally an MDS79 robot and a CPH903 robot can cooperate to eventually bring about a state of affairs where the unattended luggage has been cleared away. When unattended luggage is reported, they negotiate (for a very limited period of time, after which a quick overriding decision based simply on distance to the unattended luggage is used) so as to determine the best group of robots to be relocated to sort out the incident. Ideally, the MDS79 robot to be relocated will be currently at a gate where two MDS79 robots are available, to avoid excessive delays in boarding at that gate. Robots of type CPH903 are easy to relocate as they exist in large numbers and do not normally execute critical tasks.

An important aspect to consider is that the whole negotiation process, under normal circumstances, is about the specific MDS79 robot to be relocated, and the choice of one CPH903 robot to help out. However, other more difficult situations may arise under unpredicted circumstances. For example, on the 9th of May 2070, at Heathrow, an unattended piece of luggage was reported near gate 54. It turned out that the robot with ID S39 (an MDS79 replica) was helping out another MDS79 in charge of gate 56 close by. After briefly considering the situation, S39 volunteered to check out the reported unattended luggage, and so did H124 (a CPH903 replica). However, while running a self check, S39 realised that its internal ITMS equipment had just been damaged, which it reported to other robots involved in the negotiation.

In the light of that recent information, negotiation was resumed among the involved robots, to try and define an alternative course of action. Another MDS79 robot could have been relocated, which would have led to delays at one of the nearby gates (gate 52), as that MDS79 robot was alone taking care of security at that gate. Based on an argument put forward by S39, the agreed course of action was that another (suitably positioned) CPH903 robot would be relocated to take (from a storage facility in that terminal) a handheld ITMS device, while S39 and H124 made their way to the location of the unattended luggage. Any of the three relocated robots can actually operate the portable ITMS device, so together they were able to bring about a state of affairs where the unattended luggage had been cleared away.

1.2 Language

The AgentSpeak(L) programming language was introduced in [180]. It is a natural extension of logic programming for the BDI agent architecture, and provides an elegant abstract framework for programming BDI agents. The BDI architecture is, in turn, the predominant approach to the implementation of *intelligent* or *rational* agents [237].

An AgentSpeak agent is defined by a set of *beliefs* giving the initial state of the agent's *belief base*, which is a set of ground (first-order) atomic formulæ, and a set of plans which form its *plan library*. Before explaining exactly how a plan is written, we need to introduce the notions of goals and triggering events. AgentSpeak distinguishes two types of *goals*: achievement goals and test goals. Achievement goals are formed by an atomic formulæ prefixed with the '!' operator, while test goals are prefixed with the '?' operator. An *achievement goal* states that the agent wants to achieve a state of the world where the associated atomic formulæ is true. A *test goal* states that the agent wants to test whether the associated atomic formulæ is (or can be unified with) one of its beliefs.

An AgentSpeak agent is a reactive planning system. The events it reacts to are related either to changes in beliefs due to perception of the environment, or to changes in the agent's goals that originate from the execution of plans triggered by previous events. A *triggering event* defines which events can initiate the execution of a particular plan. Plans are written by the programmer so that they are triggered by the *addition* ('+') or *deletion* ('-') of beliefs or goals (the "mental attitudes" of AgentSpeak agents).

An AgentSpeak plan has a *head* (the expression to the left of the arrow), which is formed from a triggering event (specifying the events for which that plan is *relevant*), and a conjunction of belief literals representing a *context*. The conjunction of literals in the context must be a logical consequence of that agent's current beliefs if the plan is to be considered *applicable* at that moment in time (only applicable plans can be chosen for execution). A plan also has a *body*, which is a sequence of basic actions or (sub)goals that the agent has to achieve (or test) when the plan is triggered. Plan bodies include *basic actions* — such actions represent atomic operations the agent can perform so as to change the environment. Such actions are also written

```
skill(plasticBomb).
skill(bioBomb).
~skill(nuclearBomb).

safetyArea(field1).

@p1
+bomb(Terminal, Gate, BombType) :  skill(BombType)
    <-   !go(Terminal, Gate);
         disarm(BombType).

@p2
+bomb(Terminal, Gate, BombType) :  ~skill(BombType)
    <-   !moveSafeArea(Terminal, Gate, BombType).

@p3
+bomb(Terminal, Gate, BombType) :  not skill(BombType) &
                                   not ~skill(BombType)
    <-   .broadcast(tell, alter).

@p4
+!moveSafeArea(T,G,Bomb) :   true
    <-   ?safeArea(Place);
         !discoverFreeCPH(FreeCPH);
         .send(FreeCPH, achieve,
               carryToSafePlace(T,G,Place,Bomb)).
  .
  .
  .
```

Figure 1.1.   Examples of AgentSpeak Plans for a Bomb-Disarming Robot.

as atomic formulæ, but using a set of *action symbols* rather than predicate symbols.

Figure 1.1 shows an example of AgentSpeak code for the initial beliefs and plans of a bomb-disarming agent described in Section 1.1. Initially, the agent believes it is skilled in disarming plastic and biological bombs, but not skilled in nuclear bombs; it knows that "field1" is a safe area to leave a bomb that it cannot disarm. When this agent receives a message from an MDS79 robot saying that a biological bomb is at terminal t1, gate g43, a new event for +bomb(t1, g43, bioBomb) is created. A bomb-disarming agent has three *relevant* plans for this event (identified by the labels p1, p2, and p3), given that the event matches the triggering event of those three plans. However, only the context of the first plan is satisfied (skill(bioBomb)), so that the plan is *applicable*. In plans p1–p3, the context is used to decide whether to attempt to disarm a bomb (in case the agent is skilled in disarming that type of bomb), to move it to a safe area (in case it is not skilled), or to set off a security alarm (if it is not sure it is sufficiently skilled). As only the first plan is applicable, an intention based on it is created and the plan starts to be executed. It adds a sub-goal `!go(t1, g43)` (the plans for achieving this goal are not included here) and performs a basic action `disarm(BombType)`. In plan `p4`, we have an example of a test goal whereby the agent consults its own beliefs about where to take the bomb (`?safeArea(Place)`), and an example of an internal action used to send a message (`.send(...)`). The details of the AgentSpeak code in Figure 1.1 will be explained in the next sections.

1.2.1   Specifications and Syntactical Aspects

The BNF grammar in Figure 1.2 gives the AgentSpeak syntax as accepted by *Jason* . Below, <ATOM> is an identifier beginning with a lowercase letter or '.', <VAR> (i.e., a variable) is an identifier beginning with an uppercase letter, <NUMBER> is any integer or floating-point number, and <STRING> is any string enclosed in double quote characters as usual.

The main differences to the original AgentSpeak(L) language are as follows. Wherever an atomic formulæ[2] was allowed in the original language, here a literal is used instead. This is either an atomic formulæ $p(t_1, \ldots, t_n)$, $n \geq 0$, or $\sim p(t_1, \ldots, t_n)$, where '~' denotes strong negation[3]. Default negation is used in the context of plans, and is denoted by 'not' preceding a literal. The context is therefore a conjunction of default literals. For more details on the concepts of strong and default negation, plenty of references can be found, e.g., in the introductory chapters of [135]. Terms now can be variables, lists (with Prolog syntax), as well as integer or floating point numbers, and strings (enclosed in double quotes as usual); further, any atomic formulæ can be treated as a term, and (bound) variables can be treated as literals (this became particularly important for introducing communication, but can be useful for various things). Infix relational operators, as in Prolog, are allowed in plan contexts.

Also, a major change is that atomic formulæ now can have "annotations". This is a list of terms enclosed in square brackets immediately following the formula. Within the belief base, annotations are used, e.g., to register the sources of information. A term `source(s)` is used in the annotations for

---

[2] Recall that actions are special atomic formulæ with an action symbol rather than a predicate symbol. What we say next only applies to usual predicates, not actions.

[3] Note that for an agent that uses Closed-World Assumption, all the user has to do is not to use literals with strong negation anywhere in the program, nor negated percepts in the environment (see "Creating Environments" under Section 1.3.1).

```
agent            → beliefs plans
beliefs          → ( literal "." )*
                   N.B.: a semantic error is generated if the
                   literal was not ground.
plans            → ( plan )+
plan             → [ "@" atomic_formula ]
                   triggering_event ":" context "<-" body "."
triggering_event → "+"      literal
                 | "-"      literal
                 | "+" "!" literal
                 | "-" "!" literal
                 | "+" "?" literal
                 | "-" "?" literal
literal          → atomic_formula
                 | "~" atomic_formula
                 | <VAR>
default_literal  → literal
                 | "not" literal
                 | "not" "(" literal ")"
                 | term ("<"|"<="|">"|">="|"=="|"\\=="|"=") term
                 | literal ("=="|"\\=="|"=") literal
context          → "true"
                 | default_literal ( "&" default_literal )*
body             → "true"
                 | body_formula ( ";" body_formula )*
body_formula     → literal
                 | "!" literal
                 | "?" literal
                 | "+" literal
                 | "-" literal
atomic_formula   → <ATOM>["("list_of_terms")"] ["["list_of_terms"]"]
list_of_terms    → term ( "," term )*
term             → atomic_formula
                 | list
                 | <VAR>
                 | <NUMBER>
                 | <STRING>
list             → "["
                   [ term ( ( "," term )*
                           | "|" ( list | <VAR> )
                           )
                   ] "]"
```

Figure 1.2. BNF of the AgentSpeak Extension Interpreted by *Jason*.

that purpose; *s* can be an agent's name (to denote the agent that communicated that information), or two special atoms, percept and self, that are used to denote that a belief arose from perception of the environment, or from the agent explicitly adding a belief to its own belief base from the execution of a plan body, respectively. The initial beliefs that are part of the source code of an AgentSpeak agent are assumed to be internal beliefs (i.e., as if they had a [source(self)] annotation), unless the belief has any explicit annotation given by the user (this could be useful if the programmer wants the agent to have an initial belief about the environment or as if it had been communicated by another agent). Fore more on the annotation of sources of information for beliefs, see [153].

Plans also have labels, as first proposed in [18]. However, a plan label can now be any atomic formula, including annotations, although we suggest that plan labels use annotations (if necessary) but have a predicate symbol of arity 0, as in `aLabel` or `anotherLabel[chanceSuccess(0.7)`, `expectedPayoff(0.9)]`. Annotations in formulæ used as plan labels can be used for the implementation of sophisticated applicable plan (i.e., option) selection functions. Although this is not yet provided with the current distribution of *Jason*, it is straightforward for the user to define, e.g., decision-theoretic selection functions; that is, functions which use something like expected utilities annotated in the plan labels to choose among alternative plans. The customisation of selection functions is done in Java (by choosing a plan from a list received as parameter by the selection functions), and is explained in Section 1.3.1. Also, as the label is part of an instance of a plan in the set of intentions, and the annotations can be changed dynamically, this provides all the means necessary for the implementation of efficient intention selection functions, as the one proposed in [18]. However, this also is not yet available as part of *Jason*'s distribution, but can be set up by users with some customisation.

Events for handling plan failure are already available in *Jason*, although they are not formalised in the semantics yet. If an action fails or there is no applicable plan for a subgoal in the plan being executed to handle an internal event with a goal addition `+!g`, then the whole failed plan is removed from the top of the intention and an internal event for `-!g` associated with that same intention is generated. If the programmer provided a plan that has a triggering event matching `-!g` and is applicable, such plan will be pushed on top of the intention, so the programmer can specify in the body of such plan how that particular failure is to be handled. If no such plan is available, the whole intention is discarded and a warning is printed out to the console. Effectively, this provides a means for programmers to "clean up" after a failed plan and before "backtracking" (that is, to make up for actions that had already been executed but left things in an inappropriate state for next attempts to achieve the goal). For example, for an agent that persist on a goal `!g` for as long as there are applicable plans for `+!g`, suffices it to include a plan `-!g : true <- !g.` in the plan library. Note that the body can be empty as a goal is only removed from the body of a plan when the intended means chosen for that goal finishes successfully. It is also simple to specify a plan which, under specific condition, chooses to drop the intention altogether (by means of a standard internal action mentioned below).

Finally, as also introduced in [18], *internal actions* can be used both in the context and body of plans. Any action symbol starting with '.', or having a '.' anywhere, denotes an internal action. These are user-defined actions which are run internally by the agent. We call them "internal" to make a clear distinction with actions that appear in the body of a plan and which denote the actions an agent can perform in order to change the shared environment (in the usual jargon of the area, by means of its "effectors"). In *Jason*, internal actions are coded in Java, or in indeed other programming languages through the use of JNI (Java Native Interface), and they can be organised in libraries of actions for specific purposes (the string to the left of '.' is the name of the library; standard internal actions have an empty library name).

There are several standard internal actions that are distributed with *Jason*, but we do not mention all them here (see [22] for a complete list). As an example (see Figure 1.1, plan p4), *Jason* has an internal action that implements KQML-like inter-agent communication. The usage is: `.send(+receiver, +illocutionary_force, +prop_content)` where each parameter is as follows. The `receiver` is simply referred to using the name given to agents in the multi-agent system (see Section 1.3.1). The `illocutionary_forces` available so far are: `tell`, `untell`, `achieve`, `unachieve`, `tellHow`, `untellHow`, `askIf`, `askOne`, `askAll`, and `askHow`. The effects of receiving messages with each of these types of illocutionary acts are explained in Section 1.2.4. Finally, the `prop_content` is a literal (see literal in the grammar above).

Another important class of standard internal actions are related to querying about the agent's current desires and intentions as well as forcing itself to drop desires or intentions. The notion of desire and intention used is exactly as formalised for AgentSpeak agents in [24]. The standard AgentSpeak language has provision for beliefs to be queried (in plan contexts and by test goals) and since our earlier extensions beliefs can be added or deleted from plan bodies. However, an equally important feature, as far as the generic BDI architecture is concerned, is for an agent to be able to check current desires/intentions and drop them under certain circumstances. In *Jason*, this can be done by the use of certain special standard internal actions.

1.2.2 Semantics and Verification

As we mentioned in the introduction, one of the important characteristics of *Jason* is that it implements the operational semantics of an extension of AgentSpeak. Having formal semantics also allowed us to give precise definitions for practical notions of beliefs, desires, and intentions in relation to running AgentSpeak agents, which in turn underlies the work on formal verification of AgentSpeak programs, as discussed later in this section. The formal semantics, using structural operational semantics [169] (a widely-used notation for giving semantics to programming languages) was given then improved and extended in a series of papers [152, 23, 24, 153, 229]. In particular, [229] presents a revised version of the semantics and include some of the extensions we have proposed to AgentSpeak, including rules for the interpretation of speech-act based communication.

However, due to space limitation, we are not able to include a complete formal account of the semantics of AgentSpeak here. In this section we will just provide the main intuitions behind the interpretation of AgentSpeak programs, and after that we will give examples of the rules that are part of the formal semantics.

Informal Semantics

Besides the belief base and the plan library, the AgentSpeak interpreter also manages a set of *events* and a set of *intentions*, and its functioning requires three *selection functions*. The event selection function ($S_{\mathcal{E}}$) selects a single event from the set of events; another selection function ($S_{\mathcal{O}}$) selects an "option" (i.e., an applicable plan) from a set of applicable plans; and a third selection function ($S_{\mathcal{I}}$) selects one particular intention from the set of intentions. The selection functions are supposed to be agent-specific, in the sense that they should make selections based on an agent's characteristics (though previous work on AgentSpeak did not elaborate on how designers specify such functions[4]). Therefore, we here leave the selection functions undefined, hence the choices made by them are supposed to be non-deterministic.

Intentions are particular courses of actions to which an agent has committed in order to handle certain events. Each intention is a stack of partially instantiated plans. Events, which may start off the execution of plans that have relevant triggering events, can be *external*, when originating from perception of the agent's environment (i.e., addition and deletion of beliefs based on perception are external events); or *internal*, when generated from the agent's own execution of a plan (i.e., a subgoal in a plan generates an event of type "addition of achievement goal"). In the latter case, the event is accompanied with the intention which generated it (as the plan chosen for that event will be pushed on top of that intention). External events create new intentions, representing separate focuses of attention for the agent's acting on the environment.

---

[4]Our extension of AgentSpeak in [18] deals precisely with the automatic generation of efficient intention selection functions. The extended language allows one to express relations between plans, as well as quantitative criteria for their execution. We then use decision-theoretic task scheduling to guide the choices made by the intention selection function.

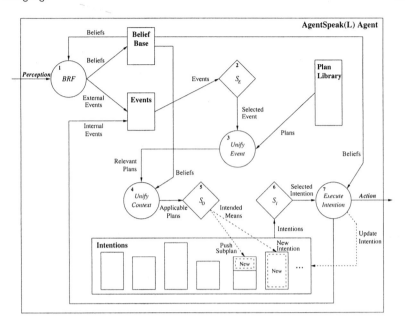

Figure 1.3. An Interpretation Cycle of an AgentSpeak Program [143].

We next give some more details on the functioning of an AgentSpeak interpreter, which is clearly depicted in Figure 1.3 (reproduced from [143]). Note, however, that this is a depiction of the essential aspects of the interpreter for the original (abstract) definition of AgentSpeak; it does *not* include the extensions implemented in *Jason*. In the figure, sets (of beliefs, events, plans, and intentions) are represented as rectangles. Diamonds represent selection (of one element from a set). Circles represent some of the processing involved in the interpretation of AgentSpeak programs.

At every interpretation cycle of an agent program, the interpreter updates a list of events, which may be generated from perception of the environment, or from the execution of intentions (when subgoals are specified in the body of plans). It is assumed that beliefs are updated from perception and whenever there are changes in the agent's beliefs, this implies the insertion of an event in the set of events. This belief revision function is not part of the AgentSpeak interpreter, but rather a necessary component of the agent architecture.

After $S_\mathcal{E}$ has selected an event, the interpreter has to unify that event with triggering events in the heads of plans. This generates the set of all *relevant plans* for that event. By checking whether the context part of the plans in that set follows from the agent's beliefs, the set of *applicable plans* is determined — these are the plans that can actually be used at that moment for handling the chosen event. Then $\mathcal{S}_O$ chooses a single applicable plan from that set, which becomes the *intended means* for handling that event, and either pushes that plan on the top of an existing intention (if the event was an internal one), or creates a new intention in the set of intentions (if the event was external, i.e., generated from perception of the environment).

All that remains to be done at this stage is to select a single intention to be executed in that cycle. The $\mathcal{S}_I$ function selects one of the agent's intentions (i.e., one of the independent stacks of partially instantiated plans within the set of intentions). On the top of that intention there is a plan, and the formula in the beginning of its body is taken for execution. This implies that either a basic action is performed by the agent on its environment, an internal event is generated (in case the selected formula is an achievement goal), or a test goal is performed (which means that the set of beliefs has to be checked).

If the intention is to perform a basic action or a test goal, the set of intentions needs to be updated. In the case of a test goal, the belief base will be searched for a belief atom that unifies with the atomic formula in the test goal. If that search succeeds, further variable instantiation will occur in the partially instantiated plan which contained that test goal (and the test goal itself is removed from the intention from which it was taken). In the case where a basic action is selected, the necessary updating of the set of intentions is simply to remove that action from the intention (the interpreter informs to the architecture component responsible for the agent effectors what action is required). When all formulæ in the body of a plan have been removed (i.e., have been executed), the whole plan is removed from the intention, and so is the achievement goal that generated it (if that was the case). This ends a cycle of execution, and everything is repeated all over again, initially checking the state of the environment after agents have acted upon it, then generating the relevant events, and so forth.

Formal Semantics

We emphasise again that the purpose of this section is to give a general idea of the style used for giving semantics to the language interpreted by *Jason*. For a complete account of the formal semantics, we refer the interested reader to [229].

We have defined the formal semantics of AgentSpeak using operational semantics, a widely used method for giving semantics to programming languages and studying their properties [169]. The operational semantics is given by a set of rules that define a transition relation between configurations $\langle ag, C, M, T, s \rangle$ where:

- An agent program ag is, as defined above, a set of beliefs and a set of plans.

- An agent's circumstance C is a tuple $\langle I, E, A \rangle$ where:

    - I is a set of *intentions* $\{i, i', \ldots\}$. Each intention i is a stack of partially instantiated plans.

    - E is a set of *events* $\{(te, i), (te', i'), \ldots\}$. Each event is a pair (te, i), where te is a triggering event and i is an intention (a stack of plans in case of an internal event or $\top$ representing an external event).

      When the belief revision function, which is not part of the AgentSpeak interpreter but rather of the general architecture of the agent, updates the belief base, the associated events (i.e., additions and deletions of beliefs) are included in this set. These are called *external* events; internal ones are generated by additions or deletions in the agent's goals.

    - A is a set of *actions* to be performed in the environment. An action expression included in this set tells other architecture components to actually perform the respective action on the environment, thus changing it.

- M is a tuple $\langle In, Out, SI \rangle$ whose components register the following aspects of communicating agents:

    - In is the mail inbox: the system includes all messages addressed to this agent in this set. Elements of this set have the form $\langle mid, id, ilf, cnt \rangle$, where mid is a message identifier, id identifies the sender of the message, ilf the illocutionary force of the message, and cnt its content (which can be an AgentSpeak atomic formula, a set of AgentSpeak atomic formulæ, or a set of AgentSpeak plans, depending on the illocutionary force of the message).

    - Out is where the agent posts all messages it wishes to send to other agents; the underlying multi-agent system mechanism makes sure that messages included in this set are sent to the agent addressed in the message. Messages here have exactly the same format as above, except that now id refers to the agent to which the message is to be sent.

    - SI is used to keep track of intentions that were suspended due to the processing of communication messages; this is explained in more detail in the next section, but the intuition is: intentions associated to illocutionary forces that require a reply from the interlocutor are suspended, and they are only resumed when such reply has been received.

- T is the tuple $\langle R, Ap, \iota, \varepsilon, \rho \rangle$, used to keep temporary information that is required in subsequent stages within a single reasoning cycle; its components are:

  - R for the set of *relevant plans* (for the event being handled).

  - Ap for the set of *applicable plans* (the relevant plans whose context are true).

  - ι, ε, and ρ keep record of a particular intention, event and applicable plan (respectively) being considered along the execution of an agent.

- The current step s within an agent's reasoning cycle is symbolically annotated by $s \in \{\text{ProcMsg, SelEv, RelPl, ApplPl, SelAppl, AddIM, SelInt, ExecInt, ClrInt}\}$, which stand for: processing a message from the agent's mail inbox, selecting an event from the set of events, retrieving all relevant plans, checking which of those are applicable, selecting one particular applicable plan (the intended means), adding the new intended means to the set of intentions, selecting an intention, executing the select intention, and clearing an intention or intended means that may have finished in the previous step.

Formally, all the selection functions an agent uses are also part of its configuration, (as is the social acceptance function that we mention below). However, as they are fixed, i.e., defined by the agent's designer when configuring the interpreter, we avoid including them in the configuration, for the sake of readability.

In order to keep the semantic rules clear, we adopt the following notations:

- If C is an AgentSpeak agent circumstance, we write C_E to make reference to the component E of C. Similarly for all the other components of a configuration.

- We write $T_\iota = \_$ (the underline symbol) to indicate that there is no intention being considered in the agent's execution. Similarly for T_ρ and T_ε.

- We write $i[p]$ to denote an intention i that has plan p on its top.

We now present a selection of the rules which define the operational semantics of the reasoning cycle of AgentSpeak. In the general case, an agent's initial configuration is $\langle ag, C, M, T, \mathsf{ProcMsg}\rangle$, where ag is as given by the agent program, and all components of C, M, and T are empty.

Updating the Set of Intentions: At the stage of the reasoning cycle where a relevant and applicable plan has been found for an event, the interpreter can then update the set of intentions. Events can be classified as external or internal (depending on whether they were generated from the agent's perception, or whether they were generated by the previous execution of other plans, respectively). Rule **ExtEv** says that if the event ε is external (which is indicated by T in the intention associated to ε) a new intention is created and its single plan is the plan p annotated in the ρ component. If the event is internal, rule **IntEv** says that the plan in ρ should be put on top of the intention associated with the event.

$$\frac{T_\varepsilon = \langle te, \mathsf{T}\rangle \qquad T_\rho = (p, \theta)}{\langle ag, C, M, T, \mathsf{AddIM}\rangle \longrightarrow \langle ag, C', M, T, \mathsf{SelInt}\rangle} \qquad \text{(ExtEv)}$$

$$\textit{where:} \quad C'_I \;=\; C_I \cup \{\, [p\theta]\,\}$$

$$\frac{T_\varepsilon = \langle te, i\rangle \qquad T_\rho = (p, \theta)}{\langle ag, C, M, T, \mathsf{AddIM}\rangle \longrightarrow \langle ag, C', M, T, \mathsf{SelInt}\rangle} \qquad \text{(IntEv)}$$

$$\textit{where:} \quad C'_I \;=\; C_I \cup \{\, (i[p])\theta \,\}$$

Note that, in rule **IntEv**, the whole intention i that generated the internal event needs to be inserted back in C_I, with p as its top. This issue is related to suspended intentions, see rule **Achieve**.

Intention Selection: Rule **IntSel$_1$** uses an agent-specific function ($\mathcal{S}_\mathcal{I}$) that selects an intention (i.e., a stack of plans) for processing, while rule **IntSel$_2$** takes care of the situation where the set of intentions is empty (in which case, the reasoning cycle is simply restarted).

$$\frac{C_I \neq \{\} \qquad \mathcal{S}_\mathcal{I}(C_I) = i}{\langle ag, C, M, T, \mathsf{SelInt}\rangle \longrightarrow \langle ag, C, M, T', \mathsf{ExecInt}\rangle} \qquad \text{(IntSel}_1\text{)}$$

$$\textit{where:} \quad T'_\iota \;=\; i$$

$$\frac{C_I = \{\}}{\langle ag, C, M, T, \mathsf{SelInt}\rangle \longrightarrow \langle ag, C, M, T, \mathsf{ProcMsg}\rangle} \qquad \text{(IntSel}_2\text{)}$$

Executing a Plan Body: Below we show part of the group of rules that define the effects of executing the body of a plan. The plan being executed is always the one on top of the intention that has been previously selected. Observe that all the rules in this group discard the intention ι; another intention can then be eventually selected.

Achievement Goals: this rule registers a new internal event in the set of events E. This event will, eventually, be selected and handled at another reasoning cycle.

$$\frac{T_\iota = i[head \leftarrow !at\,;h]}{\langle ag, C, M, T, \mathsf{ExecInt}\rangle \longrightarrow \langle ag, C', M, T, \mathsf{ProcMsg}\rangle} \quad \text{(Achieve)}$$

$$\textit{where:} \quad \begin{aligned} C'_E &= C_E \cup \{\langle +!at, i[head \leftarrow h]\rangle\} \\ C'_I &= C_I \setminus \{T_\iota\} \end{aligned}$$

Note how the intention that generated the internal event is removed from the set of intentions C_I. This denotes the idea of *suspended intentions* (see [23] for details).

Updating Beliefs: rule **AddBel** below simply adds a new event to the set of events E. The formula $+b$ is removed from the body of the plan and the set of intentions is updated properly. There is also a **DelBel** rule, for deleting beliefs, which works similarly. In both rules, the set of beliefs of the agent should be modified in a way that either the ground atomic formula b (with annotation "`source(self)`") is included in the new set of beliefs (rule **AddBel**) or it is removed from there (rule **DelBel**).

$$\frac{T_\iota = i[head \leftarrow +b\,;h]}{\langle ag, C, M, T, \mathsf{ExecInt}\rangle \longrightarrow \langle ag', C', M, T, s\rangle} \quad \text{(AddBel)}$$

$$\textit{where:} \quad \begin{aligned} ag'_{bs} &= ag_{bs} + b[\texttt{source(self)}] \\ C'_E &= C_E \cup \{\langle +b[\texttt{source(self)}], T\rangle\} \\ C'_I &= (C_I \setminus \{T_\iota\}) \cup \{i[head \leftarrow h]\} \\ s &= \begin{cases} \mathsf{ClrInt} & \text{if } h = \top \\ \mathsf{ProcMsg} & \text{otherwise} \end{cases} \end{aligned}$$

Verification

One of the reasons for the growing success of agent-based technology is that it has been shown to be quite useful for the development of various types of applications, including air-traffic control, autonomous spacecraft control, health care, and industrial systems control, to name just a few. Clearly, these are application areas for which *dependable systems* are in demand. Consequently, formal verification techniques tailored specifically for multi-agent systems is also an area that is attracting much research attention and is likely to have a major impact in the uptake of agent technology. One of the advantages of the approach to programming multi-agent systems resulting from the research reviewed in this chapter is precisely the fact that it is amenable to formal verification. In particular, model checking techniques (and state-space reduction techniques to be used in combination with model checking) for AgentSpeak have been developed [20, 21, 19, 26].

1.2.3 Software Engineering Issues

Although very little has been considered so far in regards to using agent-oriented software engineering methodologies for the development of designs for systems to be implemented with *Jason*, existing methodologies that specifically concern BDI agents, such as Prometheus [164], should be perfectly suitable for that purpose. In that book, the authors show an example of the use of JACK (see Chapter 7) for the implementation, but they explicitly say that any platform that provides the basic concepts of reactive planning systems (such as goals and plans) would be most useful in the sense of providing all the required constructs to support the implementation of designs developed in accordance to the Prometheus methodology. Because AgentSpeak code is considerably more readable than other languages such as JACK and Jadex (see Chapter 6), it is arguable that *Jason* will provide at least a much more clear way of implementing such designs. However, being an industrial platform, JACK has, currently, far better supporting tools and documentation, but on the other hand, *Jason* is *open source*, whereas JACK is not.

A construct that has an important impact in maintaining the right level of abstraction in AgentSpeak code even for sophisticated systems is that of internal actions (described earlier in Section 1.2.1). Internal actions necessarily have a boolean value returned, so they are declaratively represented within a logic program in AgentSpeak — in effect, we can keep the agent program as a high-level representation of the agent's reasoning, yet allowing it to be arbitrarily sophisticated by the use of existing software implemented in Java, or indeed any programming language through the use of JNI. Thus, the way in which integration with traditional object-oriented programming and use of legacy code is accomplished in *Jason* is far more elegant than with other agent programming languages (again, such as JACK and Jadex).

1.2.4 Other Features of the Language

Communication in AgentSpeak

The performatives that are currently available for communication in AgentSpeak are largely inspired by KQML performatives. We also include some new performatives, related to plan exchange rather than communication about propositions. The available performatives are briefly described below, where s denotes the agent that sends the message, and r denotes the agent that receives the message. Note that `tell` and `untell` can be used either for an agent to pro-actively send information to another agent, or as replies to previous `ask` messages.

`tell`: s intends r to believe (that s believes) the sentence in the message's content to be true;

`untell`: s intends r not to believe (that s believes) the sentence in the message's content to be true;

`achieve`: s requests that r try to achieve a state of the world where the message content is true;

`unachieve`: s requests that r try to drop the intention of achieving a state of the world where the message content is true;

`tellHow`: s informs r of a plan;

`untellHow`: s requests that r disregard a certain plan (i.e., delete that plan from its plan library);

`askIf`: s wants to know if the content of the message is true for r;

`askAll`: s wants all of r's answers to a question;

`askHow`: s wants all of r's plans for a triggering event;

A mechanism for receiving and sending messages asynchronously is used. Messages are stored in a mail box and one of them is processed by the agent at the beginning of a reasoning cycle. The particular message to be handled at the beginning of the reasoning cycle is determined by a selection function, which can be customised by the programmer, as three selection functions that are originally part of the AgentSpeak interpreter.

Further, in processing messages we consider a "given" function, in the same way that the selection functions are assumed as given in an agent's specification. This function defines a set of *socially acceptable* messages. For example, the receiving agent may want to consider whether the sending agent is even allowed to communicated with it (e.g., to avoid agents being attacked by malicious communicating agents). For a message with illocutionary force `achieve`, the agent will have to check, for example, whether the sending agent has sufficient social power over itself, or whether it wishes to act altruistically towards that agent and then do whatever it is being asked.

Note that notions of trust can also be programmed into the agent by considering the annotation of the sources of information during the agent's practical reasoning. When applied to `tell` messages, the function only determines if the message is to be processed at all. When the source is "trusted" (in this limited sense used here), the information source for a belief acquired from communication is annotated with that belief in the belief base, enabling further consideration on degrees of trust during the agent's reasoning.

When the function for checking message acceptance is applied to an `achieve` message, it should be programmed to return true if, e.g., the agent has a subordination relation towards the sending agent. However this "power/subordination" relation should not be interpreted with particular social or psychological nuances: the programmer defines this function so as to account for all possible reasons for an agent to do something for another agent (from actual subordination to true altruism). Similar interpretations for the result of this function when applied to other types of messages (e.g., `askIf`) can be derived easily. For more elaborate conceptions of trust and power, see [42].

As a simple example of how the user can customise this power relation in *Jason*, we may consider that a CPH903 robot only does what an MDS79 robot asks. The following agent customisation class implements that:

```
package cph;
import jason.asSemantics.Agent;

public class CPHAgent extends Agent {

  public boolean socAcc(Message m) {
    if (m.getSender().startsWith("mds") &&
        m.getIlForce().equals("achieve")) {
      return true;
    } else {
      return false;
    }
  }
}
```

In order to endow AgentSpeak agents with the capability of processing communication messages, we annotate, for each belief, what is its source. This annotation mechanism provides a very elegant notation for making explicit the sources of an agent's belief. It has advantages in terms of expressive power and readability, besides allowing the use of such explicit information in an agent's reasoning (i.e., in selecting plans for achieving goals). For example, the triggering event of MDS79's plan pb1, seen later in Figure 1.8, uses this annotation to identify the sender of the bid.

Belief sources can be annotated so as to identify which was the agent in the society that previously sent the information in a message, as well as to denote internal beliefs or percepts (i.e., in case the belief was acquired through perception of the environment). By using this information source annotation mechanism, we also clarify some practical problems in the implementation of AgentSpeak interpreters relating to internal beliefs (the ones added during the execution of a plan). In the interpreter reported in [18], we dealt with the problem by creating a separate belief base where the internal beliefs were included or removed.

Due to space restriction, we do not discuss the interpretation of received messages with each of the available illocutionary forces. This is presented both formally and informally in [229].

Cooperation in AgentSpeak

Coo-BDI (Cooperative BDI, [4]) extends traditional BDI agent-oriented programming languages in many respects: the introduction of *cooperation* among agents for the retrieval of external plans for a given triggering event; the extension of plans with *access specifiers*; the extension of *intentions* to take into account the external plan retrieval mechanism; and the modification of the the interpreter to cope with all these issues.

The *cooperation strategy* of an agent *Ag* includes the set of agents with which it is expected to cooperate, the plan retrieval policy, and the plan acquisition policy. The cooperation strategy may evolve during time, allowing greater flexibility and autonomy to the agents, and is modelled by three functions:

- trusted(*Te,TrustedAgentSet*), where *Te* is a (not necessarily ground) triggering event and *TrustedAgentSet* is the set of agents that *Ag* will contact in order to obtain plans relevant for *Te*.

- retrievalPolicy(*Te,Retrieval*), where *Retrieval* may assume the values always and noLocal, meaning that relevant plans for the trigger *Te* must be retrieved from other agents in any case, or only when no local relevant plans are available, respectively.

- acquisitionPolicy(*Te,Acquisition*), where *Acquisition* may assume the values discard, add and replace meaning that, when a relevant plan for *Te* is retrieved from a trusted agent, it must be used and discarded, or added to the plan library, or used to update the plan library by replacing all the plans triggered by *Te*.

Plans. Besides the standard components which constitute BDI plans, in this extension plans also have a *source* which determines the first owner of the plan, and an *access specifier* which determines the set of agents with which the plan can be shared. The source may assume two values: self (the agent possesses the plan) and *Ag* (the agent was originally from *Ag*). The access specifier may assume three values: `private` (the plan cannot be shared), `public` (the plan can be shared with any agent) and `only`*(TrustedAgentSet)* (the plan can be shared only with the agents contained in *TrustedAgentSet*).

The Coo-AgentSpeak mechanism to be available in *Jason* soon will allow users to define cooperation strategies in the Coo-BDI style, and takes care of all other issues such as sending the appropriate requests for plans, suspending intentions that are waiting for plans to be retrieved from other agents, etc. The Coo-AgentSpeak mechanism is described in detail in [4].

One final characteristic of *Jason* that is relevant here is the configuration option on what to do in case there is no applicable plan for a relevant event. If an event is relevant, it means that there are plans in the agent's plan library for handling that particular event (representing that handling that event is normally a desire of that agent). If it happens that none of those plans are applicable at a certain time, this can be a problem as the agent does not know how to handle the situation at that time. Ancona and Mascardi [4] discussed how this problem is handled in various agent-oriented programming languages. In *Jason*, a configuration option is given to users, which can be set in the file where the various agents and the environment composing a multi-agent system are specified. The option allows the user to state, for events which have relevant but not applicable plans, whether the interpreter should discard that event altogether (`events=discard`) or insert the event back at the end of the event queue (`events=requeue`). Because of *Jason*'s customisation mechanisms, the only modification that were required for *Jason* to cope with Coo-AgentSpeak was a third configuration option that is available to the users — no changes to the interpreter itself was required. When Coo-AgentSpeak is to be used, the option `events=retrieve` must be used in the configuration file. This makes *Jason* call the user-defined `selectOption` function *even when no applicable plans exist for an event*. This way, part of the Coo-BDI approach can be implemented by providing a special `selectOption` function which takes care of retrieving plans externally, whenever appropriate.

1.3   Platform

1.3.1   Main Features of the *Jason* Platform

Configuring Multi-Agent Systems

The configuration of a complete multi-agent system is given by a very simple text file. Figure 1.4 shows an example of this configuration file for the Heathrow scenario. Briefly, the environment is implemented in a class named **HeathrowEnv**; the system has three types of agents: five instances of MDS79, ten CPH903, and three bomb-disarmers; MDS79 agents have a

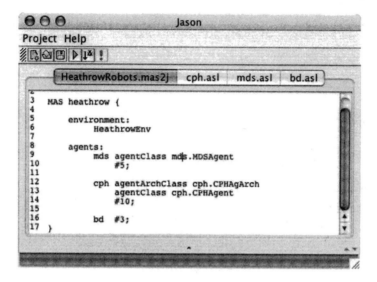

Figure 1.4. Jason IDE.

customised agent class and CPH903 have customised agent and agent architecture classes.

The BNF grammar in Figure 1.5 gives the syntax that can be used in the configuration file. In this grammar, <NUMBER> is used for integer numbers, <ASID> are AgentSpeak identifiers, which must start with a lowercase letter, <ID> is any identifier (as usual), and <PATH> is as required for defining file pathnames as usual in ordinary operating systems.

The <ID> used after the keyword MAS is the name of the society. The keyword architecture is used to specify which of the two overall agent architectures available with *Jason*'s distribution will be used. The options currently available are either "Centralised" or "Saci"; the latter option allows agents to run on different machines over a network. It is important to note that the user's environment and customisation classes remain the same with both (system) architectures.

Next an environment needs to be referenced. This is simply the name of Java class that was used for programming the environment. Note that an optional host name where the environment will run can be specified. This only works if the SACI option is used for the underlying system architecture.

The keyword agents is used for defining the set of agents that will take part in the multi-agent system. An agent is specified first by its symbolic name given as an AgentSpeak term (i.e., an identifier starting with a lowercase letter); this is the name that agents will use to refer to other agents in

```
mas            →  "MAS" <ID> "{"
                     [ "architecture" ":" <ID> ]
                     environment
                     agents
                  "}"
environment    →  "environment" ":" <ID> [ "at" <ID> ]
agents         →  "agents" ":" ( agent )+
agent          →  <ASID>
                     [ filename ]
                     [ options ]
                     [ "agentArchClass" <ID> ]
                     [ "agentClass" <ID> ]
                     [ "#" <NUMBER> ]
                     [ "at" <ID> ]
                     ";"
filename       →  [ <PATH> ] <ID>
options        →  "[" option ( "," option )* "]"
option         →  "events" "=" ("discard" | "requeue" | "retrieve")
               |  "intBels" "=" ( "sameFocus" | "newFocus" )
               |  "verbose" "=" <NUMBER>
```

Figure 1.5.   BNF of the Language for Configuring Multi-Agent Systems.

the society (e.g., for inter-agent communication). Then, an optional filename can be given where the AgentSpeak source code for that agent is given; by default *Jason* assumes that the AgentSpeak source code is in file <name>.asl, where <name> is the agent's symbolic name. There is also an optional list of settings for the AgentSpeak interpreter available with *Jason* (these are explained below). An optional number of instances of agents using that same source code can be specified by a number preceded by #; if this is present, that specified number of "clones" will be created in the multi-agent system. In case more than one instance of that agent is requested, the actual name of the agent will be the symbolic name concatenated with an index indicating the instance number (starting from 1). As for the environment keyword, an agent definition may end with the name of a host where the agent(s) will run (preceded by "at"). As before, this only works if the SACI-based architecture was chosen.

The following settings are available for the AgentSpeak interpreter available in *Jason* (they are followed by '=' and then one of the associated keywords, where an underline denotes the option used by default):

events: options are either discard, requeue, or retrieve; the discard option means that external events for which there are no applicable plans are discarded, whereas the requeue option is used when such events should be inserted back at the end of the list of events that the agent needs to handle. When option `retrieve` is selected, the user-defined `selectOption` function is called even if the set of relevant/applicable plans is empty. This can be used, for example, for allowing agents to request plan from other agents who may have the necessary know-how that the agent currently lacks, as mentioned in Section 1.2.4 and described in detail in [4].

`intBels`: options are either <u>sameFocus</u> or newFocus. When internal beliefs are added or removed explicitly within the body of a plan, the associated event is a triggering event for a plan, the intended means resulting from the applicable plan chosen for that event is pushed on top of the intention (i.e., the focus of attention) which generated the event, if the sameFocus option is used). If the newFocus option is used, the event is treated as external (i.e., as the addition or deletion of belief from perception of the environment), creating a new focus of attention.

`verbose`: a number between 0 and 6 should be specified. The higher the number, the more information about that agent (or agents if the number of instances is greater than 1) is printed out in the console where the system was run. The default is in fact 1, not 0; verbose 1 prints out only the actions that agents perform in the environment and the messages exchanged between them.

Finally, user-defined overall agent architectures and other user-defined functions to be used by the AgentSpeak interpreter for each particular agent can be specified with the keywords `agentArchClass` and `agentClass`.

Creating Environments

Jason agents can be situated in real or simulated environments. In the former case, the user would have to customise the "overall agent architecture", as described in the next part of this section; in the latter case, the user must provide an implementation of the simulated environment. This is done directly in a Java class that extends the *Jason* base **Environment** class. A very simple simulated version of the environment for the Heathrow airport scenario is shown in Figure 1.6 as an example.

All percepts (i.e., everything that is perceptible in the environment) should be added to the list returned by **getPercepts**; this is a list of literals, so strong negation can be used in applications where there is open-world assumption. It is possible to send individualised perception; that is, in programming the environment the developer can determine what subset of the environment properties will be perceptible to individual agents. Recall that within an agent's overall architecture you can further customise what beliefs

```
public class HeathrowEnv extends Environment {

   Map agsLocation = new HashMap();

   public List getPercepts(String agName) {
      if ( ... unattended luggage has been found ... ) {
         // all agents will perceive the fact that
         // there is unattendedLuggage
         getPercepts().add(Term.parse("unattendedLuggage"));
      }

      if (agName.startsWith("mds")) {
         // mds robots will also perceive their location
         List customPerception = new ArrayList();
         customPerception.addAll(getPercepts());
         customPerception.add(agsLocation.get(agName));
         return customPerception;
      } else {
         return getPercepts();
      }
   }

   public boolean executeAction(String ag, Term action) {
      if (action.hasFunctor("disarm")) {
         ... the code that implements the disarm action
         ... on the environment goes here
      } else if (action.hasFunctor("move")) {
         ... the code for changing the agents' location and
         ... updating the agsLocation map goes here
      }
      return true;
   }
}
```

Figure 1.6. Simulated Environment of the Airport Scenario.

the agent will actually aquire from what it perceives. Intuitively, the environment properties available to an agent from the environment definition itself are associated to what is actually perceptible at all in the environment (for example, if something is behind my office's walls, I cannot see it). The customisation at the agent overall architecture level should be used for simulating faulty perception (i.e., even though something is perceptible for that agent in that environment, it may still not include some of those properties in its belief revision process, because it failed to perceive it). Customisation of agent's individual perception within the environment is done by overriding the "getPercepts(agName)" method; the default methods simply provide all current environment properties as percepts to all agents. In the example above, only MDS79 robots will perceive their location at the airport.

Most of the code for building environments should be (referenced) in the body of the method **executeAction** which must be declared as described above. Whenever an agent tries to execute a basic action (those which are supposed to change the state of the environment), the name of the agent and a **Term** representing the chosen action are sent as parameter to this method. So the code for this method needs to check the **Term** (which has the form of a Prolog structure) representing the action (and any parameters) being executed, and check which is the agent attempting to execute the action, then do whatever is necessary in that particular model of an environment — normally, this means changing the percepts, i.e., what is true or false of the environment is changed according to the actions being performed. Note that the execution of an action needs to return a **boolean** value, stating whether the agent's attempt at performing that action on the environment was executed or not. A plan fails if any basic action attempted by the agent fails.

Customising Agents

Certain aspects of the cognitive functioning of an agent can be customised by the user overriding methods of the **Agent** class (see Figure 1.7). The three first selection functions are discussed extensively in the AgentSpeak literature (see Section 1.2.2 and Figure 1.3). The social acceptance function (socAcc, which is related to pragmatics, e.g., trust and power social relations) and the message selection function are discussed in [229] and Section 1.2.4. By changing the message selection function, the user can determine that the agent will give preference to messages from certain agents, or certain types of messages, when various messages have been received during one reasoning cycle. While basic actions are being executed by the environment, before the (boolean) feedback from the environment is available the intention to which that action belongs must be suspended; the last internal function allows customisation of priorities to be given when more than one intention can be resumed because feedback from the environment became available during the last reasoning cycle.

As an example of customising an agent class, consider again the Heathrow scenario. The MDS79 robots must give priority to events related to unattended luggage over any other type of event. A customised MDS79 agent class which overrides the **selectEvent** method can implement this priority as follows:

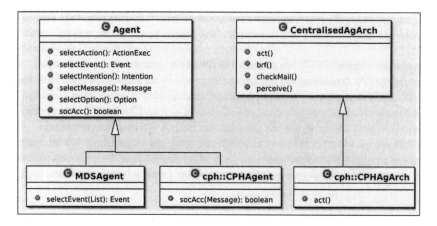

Figure 1.7. Customising Agents for the Airport Scenario.

```
public class MDSAgent extends Agent {

  public Event selectEvent(List evList) {
    Iterator i = evList.iterator();
    while (i.hasNext()) {
      Event e = (Event)i.next();
      if (e.getTrigger().getFunctor().equals(
                                "unattendedLuggage")) {
        i.remove();
        return e;
      }
    }
    return super.selectEvent(evList);
  }
}
```

Similarly, the user can customise the functions defining the overall agent architecture (see Figure 1.7, **AgArch** class). These functions handle: (i) the way the agent will perceive the environment; (ii) the way it will update its belief base given the current perception of the environment, i.e., the so called belief revision function (BRF) in the AgentSpeak literature; (iii) how the agent gets messages sent from other agents (for speech-act based inter-agent communication); and (iv) how the agent acts on the environment (for the basic actions that appear in the body of plans) — normally this is provided by the environment implementation, so this function only has to pass the action selected by the agent on to the environment, but clearly for multi-agent systems situated in a real-world environment this might be more complicated, having to interface with, e.g., available process control hardware.

For the perception function, it may be interesting to use the function defined in *Jason*'s distribution and, after it has received the current percepts, then process further the list of percepts, in order to simulate faulty perception, for example. This is on top of the environment being modelled so as to send different percepts to different agents, according to their perception abilities (so to speak) within the given multi-agent system (as with ELMS environments, see [25]).

It is important to emphasise that the belief revision function provided with *Jason* simply updates the belief base and generates the external events (i.e., additions and deletion of beliefs from the belief base) in accordance with current percepts. In particular, it does not guarantee belief consistency. As percepts are actually sent from the environment, and they should be lists of terms stating everything that is true (and explicitly false too, if closed-world assumption is dropped), it is up to the programmer of the environment to make sure that contradictions do not appear in the percepts. Also, if AgentSpeak programmers use addition of internal beliefs in the body of plans, it is their responsibility to ensure consistency. In fact, the user might be interested in modelling a "paraconsistent" agent, which can be done easily.

Suppose, for example, that under no circumstances a CPH903 robot is allowed to disarm a bomb. To prevent them from performing this action, even if they have decided to do so (e.g., they could be infected by a software virus), the developer could override the **act** method in the CPH903's customised **AgArch** class and ensure that the selected action is not disarm before allowing it to be executed in the environment:

```
public class CPHAgArch extends CentralisedAgArch {
  public void act() {
    // get the current action to be performed
    Term action = fTS.getC().getAction().getActionTerm();

    if ( !action.getFunctor().equals("disarm") ) {
      // ask the environment to execute the action
      fEnv.executeAction(getName(), action));
      ...
    }
  }
}
```

Defining New Internal Actions

An important construct for allowing AgentSpeak agents to remain at the right level of abstraction is that of internal actions, which allows for straightforward extensibility and use of legacy code. As suggested in [18], internal actions that start with '.' are part of a standard library of internal actions that are distributed with *Jason*. Internal actions defined by users should be organised in specific libraries, which provides an interesting way of organising such code, which is normally useful for a range of different systems. In the AgentSpeak program, the action is accessed by the name of the library, followed by '.', followed by the name of the action. Libraries are defined as Java packages and each action in the user library should be a Java class, the name of the package and class are the names of the library and action as it will be used in the AgentSpeak programs.

When unattended luggage is perceived by the MDS79 robots, they send bids to each other that represent how suitable they are for coping with the new situation (see Figure 1.8, plan pn2). The robot with the highest bid will be relocated to handle the unattended luggage. Now, suppose a complex formula is used to calculate the initial bid and further checks and calculations are requested to adjust the bid; clearly imperative languages are normally more suitable for implementing this kind of algorithms. The user can thus use the following Java class to implement this algorithm, and refer to it from within the AgentSpeak code as `mds.calculateMyBid(Bid)`:

```
package mds;
import ...

public class calculateMyBid implements InternalAction {

  public boolean execute(TransitionSystem ts, Unifier un,
                                Term[] args) throws Exception {
     int bid = ... a complex formula ...;
     ... plus complex algorithm and calculations
         for adjusting the agent's bid ...

     un.unifies(args[0], Term.parse(""+bid));
     return true;
  }
}
```

It is important that the class has an **execute** method declared *exactly* as above, since *Jason* uses class introspection to call it. The internal action's arguments are passed as an array of **Terms**. Note that this is the third argument of the **execute** method. The first argument is the transition system (as defined by the operational semantics of AgentSpeak), which contains all information about the current state of the agent being interpreted. The second is the unifying function currently determined by the execution of the plan, or the checking of whether the plan is applicable[5]; the unifying functions is important in case the value bound to AgentSpeak variables need to be used in the implementation of the action.

---

[5]This depends on whether the internal action being run appears in the body or the context of a plan.

```
free.  // I'm not currently handling unattended luggage

+unattendedLuggage(Terminal,Gate) :  true
   <-  !negotiate.

@pn1
+!negotiate :  not free
   <-  .broadcast(tell, bid(0)).

@pn2
+!negotiate :  free
   <-  .myName(I); // Jason internal action
       +winner(I); // belief I am the negotiation winner
       +bidsCount(1);
       mds.calculateMyBid(Bid); // user internal action
       +myBid(Bid);
       .broadcast(tell, bid(Bid)).

@pb1 // for a bid better than mine
+bid(B)[source(Sender)] :
                  myBid(MyBid) & MyBid < B &
                  .myName(I) & winner(I)
   <-  -winner(I);
       +winner(Sender).

@pb2 // for other bids (and I'm still the winner)
+bid(B) : .myName(I) & winner(I)
   <-  !addBidCounter;
       !endNegotiation.

@pend1 // all bids was received
+!endNegotiation :  bidsCount(N) & numberOfMDS(M) & N >= M
   <-  -free; // I'm no longer free
       !checkUnattendedLuggage.

@pend2 // void plan for endNegotiation not to fail
+!endNegotiation :  true <- true.
  ⋮
```

Figure 1.8. Example of AgentSpeak Plans for an Airport Security Robot.

1.3.2   Available Tools and Documentation

Jason is distributed with an Integrated Development Environment (IDE) which provides a GUI for editing a MAS configuration file as well as AgentSpeak code for the individual agents. Through the IDE, it is also possible to control the execution of a MAS, and to distribute agents over a network in a very simple way. There are three execution modes:

Asynchronous: in which all agents run asynchronously. An agent goes to its next reasoning cycle as soon as it has finished its current cycle. This is the default execution mode.

Synchronous: in which each agent performs a single reasoning cycle in every "global execution step". That is, when an agent finishes a reasoning cycle, it informs *Jason*'s execution controller, and waits for a "carry on" signal. The *Jason* controller waits until all agents have finished their current reasoning cycle and then sends the "carry on" signal to them.

Debugging: this execution mode is similar to the synchronous mode; however, the *Jason* controller also waits until the user clicks on a "Step" button in the GUI before sending the "carry on" signal to the agents.

There is another tool provided as part of the IDE which allows the user to inspect agents' internal states when the system is running in debugging mode. This is very useful for debugging MAS, as it allows "inspection of agents' minds" across a distributed system. The tool is called "mind inspector", and is shown in Figure 1.9.

Jason's distribution comes with documentation which is also available online at `http://jason.sourceforge.net/Jason.pdf`. The documentation has something of the form of a tutorial on AgentSpeak, followed by a description of the features and usage of the platform. Although it covers all of the currently available features of *Jason*, we still plan to improve substantially the documentation, in particular because the language is at times still quite academic. Another planned improvement in the available documentation, in the relatively short term, is to include material (such as slides and practical exercises) for teaching Agent-Oriented Programming with *Jason*. Because of the elegance and simplicity of the core agent language interpreted by *Jason*, at the same time having all the important elements for the implementation of BDI-based reactive planning systems, we think *Jason* can become an important tool for teaching multi-agent systems.

1.3.3 Standards Compliance, Interoperability, and Portability

As *Jason* is implemented in Java, there is no issue with portability, but very little consideration has been given so far to standards compliance and interoperability. However, components of the platform can be easily changed by the user. For example, at the moment there are two "system architectures"

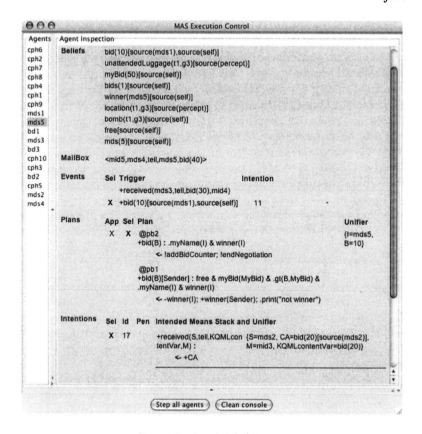

Figure 1.9. Jason's Mind Inspector.

available with *Jason's* distribution: a centralised one (which means that the whole system runs in a single machine) and another which uses SACI for distribution. It should be reasonably simple to produce another system architecture which uses, e.g., JADE (see Chapter 5) for FIPA-compliant distribution and management of agents in a multi-agent system.

1.3.4   Applications Supported by the Language and the Platform

As yet, *Jason* has been used only for a couple of application described below, and also for simple student projects in academia. However, due to its AgentSpeak basis, it is clearly suited to a large range of applications for which it is known that BDI systems are appropriate; various applications of

PRS [98] and dMARS [126] for example have appeared in the literature [238, Chapter 11].

Although we aim to use it for a wide range of applications in the future, in particular Semantic Web and Grid-based applications, one particular area of application in which we have great interest is Social Simulation [74]. In fact, *Jason* is being used as part of a large project to produce a platform tailored particularly to Social Simulation. The platform is called MAS-SOC and is described in [25]; it includes a high-level language called ELMS [162] for defining multi-agent environments. This approach was used to develop a simple social simulation on social aspects of urban growth is also mentioned (the simulation was briefly presented in [131]). Another area of application that has been initially explored is the use of AgentSpeak for defining the behaviour of animated characters for computer animation (or virtual reality) [223].

1.4   Final Remarks

Jason is constantly being improved and extended. The long term objective is to have a platform which makes available important technologies resulting from research in the area of Multi-Agent Systems, but doing this in a sensible way so as to avoid the language becoming cumbersome and, most importantly, having formal semantics for most, if not all, of the essential features available in *Jason*. We have ongoing projects to extend *Jason* with organisations, given that social structure is an essential aspect of developing complex multi-agent systems, and with ontological descriptions underlying the belief base, thus facilitating the use of *Jason* for Semantic Web and Grid-based applications. We aim to contribute, for example, to the area of e-Social Science, developing large-scale Grid-based social simulations using *Jason*.

Acknowledgments

As seen from the various references throughout this document, the research on AgentSpeak has been carried out with the help of many colleagues. We are grateful for the many contributions received over the last few years from: Davide Ancona, Marcelo G. de Azambuja, Deniel M. Basso, Ana L.C. Bazzan, Antônio Carlos da Rocha Costa, Guilherme Drehmer, Michael Fisher, Rafael de O. Jannone, Romulo Krafta, Viviana Mascardi, Victor Lesser, Rodrigo Machado, Álvaro F. Moreira, Fabio Y. Okuyama, Denise de Oliveira, Carmen Pardavila, Marios Richards, Maíra R. Rodrigues, Rosa M. Vicari, Willem Visser, Michael Wooldridge.

Chapter 2

PROGRAMMING MULTI-AGENT SYSTEMS IN 3APL

Mehdi Dastani, M. Birna van Riemsdijk, and John-Jules Ch. Meyer

Institute of Information and Computing Sciences
Utrecht University
The Netherlands
{ mehdi,birna,jj } @cs.uu.nl

Abstract   This chapter presents 3APL, which is a multi-agent programming language, and its corresponding development platform. The 3APL language is motivated by cognitive agent architectures and provides programming constructs to implement individual agents directly in terms of beliefs, goals, plans, actions, and practical reasoning rules. The syntax and semantics of the 3APL programming language is explained. Various features of the language and platform and some software engineering issues are discussed.

Keywords: Multi-Agent Programming Language, Cognitive Agents, Multi-Agent Systems

2.1   Motivation

In research on agents, besides architectures, the areas of agent theories and agent programming languages are distinguished. Theories concern descriptions of (the behavior of) agents. Agents are often described using logic [181, 224]. Concepts that are commonly incorporated in such logics are for instance knowledge, beliefs, desires, intentions, commitments, goals and plans.

It has been argued in the literature that it can be useful to analyze and specify a system in terms of these concepts [58, 182]. However, if the system would then be implemented using an arbitrary programming language, it will be difficult to verify whether it satisfies its specification: if we cannot identify what for instance the beliefs, desires and intentions of the system are, it will be hard to check the system against its specification expressed in these terms. This is referred to by Wooldridge as the problem of ungrounded semantics for agent specification languages [238][1]. It will moreover be more difficult to go from specification to implementation if there is no clear correspondence between the concepts used for specification and those used for implementation.

To support the practical development of intelligent agents, several programming languages have thus been introduced that incorporate some of the concepts from agent logics. 3APL ("triple-a-p-l") is one such language. The first version of 3APL was designed by Hindriks et al. [107]. In this version, beliefs, plans[2], and rules for revising plans are the basic building blocks of 3APL agents. An extension to this first version was the addition of declarative goals [54, 228]. Declarative goals[3] describe the state an agent wants to reach and can be used to program pro-active behavior. Plans form the procedural part of an agent and can be executed by the agent in order to achieve its goals. The notion of a goal is important in agent logics and the extension of 3APL with goals is thus important if we are to deal with the issue of ungrounded semantics. Together with the addition of goals, rules were introduced to generate plans on the basis of these goals (and beliefs). Another extension to 3APL was the addition of communication to allow describing multi-agent 3APL systems [53], in the vein of work on ACPL [225].

A 3APL agent thus consists of beliefs, plans, goals and reasoning rules. Given these mental attitudes, issues arise with respect to the operation of the agent; these are issues such as which plan should be executed at a certain point, which goal(s) should be pursued, which (type of) rule should be applied, etc. The choices made affect the operation of the agent and it is thus an important point to consider. To be able to make these kinds of choices explicit, Hindriks et al. introduced a meta-language on top of basic 3APL [107]. This deliberation language was extended by Dastani et al. [52] and includes constructs for tests, planning, and different types of selection functions by means of which plans and rules can be selected.

In this paper, we present the concrete syntax and semantics of the 3APL programming language and give examples to illustrate how cognitive agents can be implemented. The presented version of 3APL is extended with a shared environment in which 3APL agents can perform actions. We then discuss the use of the 3APL programming language from a software engi-

---

[1]Note that the way the problem is named suggests the problem resides in the specification language, which uses terms that do not relate to computational notions, and should therefore be changed). Although we agree that there is a problem here, we believe that it might also be solved by introducing the notions used in the specification language into the implementation (viz. the programming language), thus in effect *grounding* the specification language.

[2]What we refer to as plans are called "goals" in [107].

[3]From now on, we will use the term "goal" to refer to the notion of declarative goal.

neering point of view and describe the 3APL platform that supports the development of 3APL multi-agent systems.

2.2 Language

In general, the implementation of a multi-agent system requires two programming languages: one single-agent programming language to implement individual agents, and one multi-agent programming language to implement multi-agent aspects, such as which and how individual agents should be executed. The multi-agent programming language can be used to implement organization and coordination of multi-agent systems directly and explicitly. Using the multi-agent programming language one can, for example, implement sequential or parallel execution of individual agents or block the execution of individual agents when their actions are not permitted.

A 3APL multi-agent system consists of a set of concurrently executed 3APL agents that can interact with each other either directly through communication or indirectly through the shared environment. In order to implement a 3APL multi-agent system, the 3APL platform has been built to support the design, implementation, and execution of a set of 3APL agents that share an external environment. The 3APL platform thus allows the implementation and parallel execution of a set of 3APL agents and therefore it fulfills the function of a 3APL multi-agent programming language. This choice implies that all organization and coordination issues should be implemented implicitly through the implementations of individual 3APL agents.

The individual 3APL agents can be implemented by the 3APL programming language that facilitates direct implementation of various aspects of cognitive agents, and the shared environment can be implemented in the Java [99] programming language. In particular, the shared environment is implemented as a Java class such that its methods correspond with the actions that agents can perform in the environment. Besides the interaction with the environment, the agents can interact with each other through direct communication. Using 3APL, one can implement agents that observe the shared environment, communicate with each other, reason about and update their states, and execute actions in the shared environment.

In designing the 3APL programming language, a separation was created between mental attitudes (data structures) and the deliberation process (programming instructions) that manipulate the mental attitudes. Therefore, the 3APL programming language consists of programming constructs to implement the agent's mental attitudes, represented as data structures, as well as the agent's deliberation process, represented as instructions, to manipulate the mental attitudes. In particular, 3APL allows direct specification of mental attitudes such as beliefs, goals, plans, actions and reasoning rules. Actions form the basic building blocks of plans and can be internal mental actions, external actions, or communication actions. The deliberation constructs allow the implementation of selection and execution of actions and plans through which an agent's belief base can be updated and through which the shared environment can be modified. It also allows the selection and application of reasoning rules through which the goal and plan bases can be modified.

The basic deliberation constructs can be composed by means of sequential composition and by using if-then-else and while constructs, forming the deliberation language (see [52] for the formal specification). This enables the programmer to implement, for example, a deliberation program that consists of (the iteration of the sequential composition of) two conditional iterations (while-loops) such that the condition of the first holds as long as there is no emergency situation while the condition of the second holds as long as there is an emergency situation. The body of the first iteration could then be used to plan new goals, while the body of the second could generate emergency plans and execute them. This example illustrates that the language is expressive enough to implement important aspects of subsumption architectures [36], in which emergency behavior can be realized at the reactive layer while complex behavior can be realized at higher deliberative layers. Note that also the usual 'standard' sense-reason-act cycle can be implemented in this deliberation language.

This view on programming multi-agent systems has resulted in the 3APL multi-agent platform architecture and the 3APL agent architecture, as illustrated in figure 2.1. The 3APL platform consists of a number of agents, a directory facilitator called agent management system (AMS), a message transport system which delivers messages between agents, a shared environment, and a plugin interface that allows agents to execute actions in the shared environment. The function of the agent management system is to register agents that are loaded and executed on the platform and it answers a set of questions from agents about other agents that are present on the platform. These questions can be, for example, about the names of agents, their functions, and the services they provide. Each individual 3APL agent consists of a belief base, a goal base, a plan base, an action base for the specification of internal mental actions, a base for goal planning rules (which can be applied to plan a goal), and a base for plan revision rules (which can be used to revise, adopt, and drop plans).

2.2.1   Specifications and Syntactical Aspects

In the following subsections, we explain how various ingredients of the individual 3APL agent architecture and the 3APL platform can be imple-

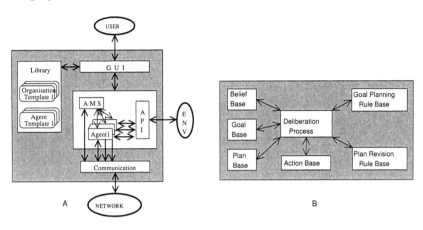

Figure 2.1. The architectures of 3APL platform (A) and individual 3APL agents (B)

mented. In particular, we describe the programming constructs to implement individual agents, explain how the deliberation cycle of individual
agents can be implemented, and discuss the implementation of the shared
environment. Before starting to describe the programming constructs for
implementing individual agents, we present the EBNF grammar of the language.

The EBNF specification of the 3APL programming language for individual agents is illustrated in Figure 2.2.1. In this specifications, we use ⟨*atom*⟩
to denote an atomic formula[4] the terms of which can include Prolog-like list
representations of the form [a,b,[3,f]], [X|T], and [a,[4,d]|T],
etc. Moreover, we use ⟨*ground_atom*⟩ to denote a ground atomic formula, which is an atomic formula that contains no variables. The terms
of ground atomic formulae can include Prolog-like list representations such
as [a,b,c], [e,[9,d,g],3]. Finally, we use ⟨*Atom*⟩ to denote atomic
formulae where the predicate letter starts with a capital letter, ⟨*ident*⟩ to
denote a string, and ⟨*var*⟩ to denote a variable.

Beliefs and goals

The *beliefs* of a 3APL agent describe the situation the agent is in. Beliefs
are implemented by the belief base, which contains information the agent
believes about the world. The *goals* of the agent on the other hand denote

---

[4]A predicate name parameterized with a number of terms, e.g. on(a,b).

$\langle Program \rangle ::=$ `"Program"` $\langle ident \rangle$
         `(` `"Load"` $\langle ident \rangle$ `)?`
         `"Capabilities :"` `(` $\langle capabilities \rangle$ `)?`
         `"BeliefBase :"` `(` $\langle beliefs \rangle$ `)?`
         `"GoalBase :"` `(` $\langle goals \rangle$ `)?`
         `"PlanBase :"` `(` $\langle plans \rangle$ `)?`
         `"PG − rules :"` `(` $\langle p\_rules \rangle$ `)?`
         `"PR − rules :"` `(` $\langle r\_rules \rangle$ `)?`

$\langle capabilities \rangle ::=$ $\langle capability \rangle$ `( "," ` $\langle capability \rangle$ ` )*`
$\langle capability \rangle ::=$ `"{"` $\langle query \rangle$ `"}"` $\langle Atom \rangle$ `"{"` $\langle literals \rangle$ `"}"`
$\langle beliefs \rangle ::=$ `(` $\langle belief \rangle$ ` )*`
$\langle belief \rangle ::=$ $\langle ground\_atom \rangle$ `"."` `|` $\langle atom \rangle$ `": −"` $\langle literals \rangle$ `"."`
$\langle goals \rangle ::=$ $\langle goal \rangle$ `( "," ` $\langle goal \rangle$ ` )*`
$\langle goal \rangle ::=$ $\langle ground\_atom \rangle$ `( "and"` $\langle ground\_atom \rangle$ ` )*`
$\langle plans \rangle ::=$ $\langle plan \rangle$ `( "," ` $\langle plan \rangle$ ` )*`
$\langle plan \rangle ::=$ $\langle basicaction \rangle$ `|` $\langle composedplan \rangle$
$\langle basicaction \rangle ::=$ `"ϵ"` `|` $\langle Atom \rangle$ `|` `"Send("` $\langle iv \rangle$ `,` $\langle iv \rangle$ `,` $\langle atom \rangle$ `")"` `|`
         `"Java("` $\langle ident \rangle$ `,` $\langle atom \rangle$ `,` $\langle var \rangle$ `")"` `|` $\langle wff \rangle$ `"?"` `|` $\langle atom \rangle$
$\langle composedplan \rangle ::=$ `"if"` $\langle wff \rangle$ `"then"` $\langle plan \rangle$ `( "else"` $\langle plan \rangle$ `)?` `|`
         `"while"` $\langle query \rangle$ `"do"` $\langle plan \rangle$ `|`
         $\langle plan \rangle$ `";"` $\langle plan \rangle$
$\langle p\_rules \rangle ::=$ $\langle p\_rule \rangle$ `( "," ` $\langle p\_rule \rangle$ ` )*`
$\langle p\_rule \rangle ::=$ $\langle atom \rangle$ `"<−"` $\langle query \rangle$ `"|"` $\langle plan \rangle$
$\langle p\_rule \rangle ::=$ `"<−"` $\langle query \rangle$ `"|"` $\langle plan \rangle$
$\langle r\_rules \rangle ::=$ $\langle r\_rule \rangle$ `( "," ` $\langle r\_rule \rangle$ ` )*`
$\langle r\_rule \rangle ::=$ $\langle plan \rangle$ `"<−"` $\langle query \rangle$ `"|"` $\langle plan \rangle$
$\langle literals \rangle ::=$ $\langle literal \rangle$ `( "," ` $\langle literal \rangle$ ` )*`
$\langle literal \rangle ::=$ $\langle atom \rangle$ `|` `"not("` $\langle atom \rangle$ `")"`
$\langle wff \rangle ::=$ $\langle literal \rangle$ `|` $\langle wff \rangle$ `"and"` $\langle wff \rangle$ `|` $\langle wff \rangle$ `"or"` $\langle wff \rangle$
$\langle query \rangle ::=$ $\langle wff \rangle$ `|` `"true"`
$\langle iv \rangle ::=$ $\langle ident \rangle$ `|` $\langle var \rangle$

Figure 2.2. The EBNF specification of the 3APL language for programming individual agents.

the situation the agent wants to realize, which is implemented by an agent's goal base.

The belief base is implemented by a Prolog program consisting of Prolog facts and rules. The initial belief base of a 3APL agent is preceded by the keyword `"BeliefBase :"`. Note that the syntax of Prolog is in accordance with the specification of $\langle beliefs \rangle$ as given above. The following is an example of the initial belief base of a 3APL agent which indicates that blocks a and b are on the floor, block c is on block a, and that a block is clear if there is no block placed on top of it.

```
BeliefBase:
on(a,fl).
on(b,fl).
on(c,a).
clear(Y) :- not(on(X,Y)).
```

Note that, like in Prolog, the specification of beliefs allows the use of negation in the body of the rules. The `not` in these rules stands for negation-as-failure.

We allow individual agents to load a separate file containing the background knowledge. The syntax of the background knowledge is the same as the syntax of beliefs and is implemented by a Prolog program that can be loaded into the initial belief base of an agent through the optional `"Load"` construct. The argument of the load construct is the name of a file that contains a Prolog program. Such a file can be loaded by different agents. In this way, one can implement the background knowledge once and allow different agents to load it as part of their initial beliefs.

The goal base of a 3APL agent is a set of goals, each of which is implemented by a conjunction of ground Prolog atoms. The initial goal base of a 3APL agent is preceded by the keyword `"GoalBase:"`. The following is an example of the initial goal base of a 3APL agent which indicates that the agent has two goals. The first goal is to have block a on block b and block b on block c, and the second goal is to have block d on the floor.

```
GoalBase:
on(a,b) and on(b,c) , on(d,fl)
```

The difference between the two goals in this goal base and the single goal `on(a,b) and on(b,c) and on(d,fl)` is that the two separate goals in the goal base may be fulfilled at different times, whereas the three conjuncts of the single goal have to be satisfied at the same time.

As we will see below, it is useful to be able to check whether a formula follows from the belief base or the goal base, for example for test actions, for the application of reasoning rules, or for performing mental actions. For these purposes, we use the so-called belief and goal query expressions (i.e. ⟨*query*⟩) which are either the special atomic formulae `true` or a well-formed formula (i.e. ⟨*wff*⟩) constructed from atoms and logical connectors. In the implementation of 3APL, the keywords `and`, `or`, and `not` are used as logical connectives. For example, `(on(X,b) and on(b,Y)) or not(on(b,fl))` can be a belief query expression which is derivable from the belief base if either `on(X,b)` and `on(b,Y)` is derivable from the belief base or `on(b,f1)` is not derivable[5].

Basic Actions

In order to reach its goals, a 3APL agent adopts plans. A plan is built from basic actions that can be composed through co-called program operators. We first discuss the various kinds of basic actions and then explain how they can be composed to form plans. In 3APL, beside the neutral action (denoted by ϵ) that does not change the current state of affairs, five other types of actions are distinguished: mental actions, communication actions, external actions, test actions, and so-called abstract plans.

The *mental actions* can update the belief base of agents, if successfully executed. A mental action has the form of an atomic formula and thus consists of a predicate name and a list of terms with the exception that the first letter of the predicate name is a capital letter (i.e. $\langle Atom \rangle$). The effect of the execution of a mental action is a change in the agent's belief base. The conditions under which a mental action can be successfully executed (also called the pre-condition of the mental action), and its effects on the belief base (also called the post-condition of the mental action) should be specified in the 3APL program.

The pre- and post-conditions of mental actions are specified through so-called capabilities which consist of three parts: the mental action itself (i.e. $\langle Atom \rangle$), a pre-condition which is a belief query expression (i.e. a $\langle query \rangle$), and a post-condition which is a list of literals (i.e. $\langle literals \rangle$). An agent can execute a mental action if the pre-condition of the corresponding capability holds. The effect of the execution of a mental action is then a change in the agent's belief base such that the post-condition of the corresponding capability holds. In order to realize this effect, a function is defined in the interpreter that adds the positive literals to the belief base and retracts the atoms of the negative literals from the belief base, if present. In the implementation of 3APL, the specification of capabilities is preceded by the keyword `"Capabilities:"`. The following is an example of a capability that defines the effect of the mental `Move` action.

```
Capabilities:
{on(X,Y)} Move(X,Y,Z) {not(on(X,Y)) , on(X,Z)}
```

The idea is, that the action `Move(X,Y,Z)` moves a block `X` from

---

[5]Note that as we use the Prolog reasoning engine to implement the evaluation of the query expressions, the `or` and `and` operators are not commutative.

block Y to block Z. If this Move(X,Y,Z) action is executed, the variables X, Y and Z will be instantiated with a value. Assume for example that X = a, Y = b and Z = c. The action can then be executed in case on(a,b) is derivable from the belief base, i.e., if block a is on b. The result should be that not(on(a,b)) and on(a,c) are derivable from the belief base. This is implemented by removing fact on(a,b) and adding on(a,c).

A *send action* can be used to pass a message to another agent. A message contains the name of the receiver of the message, the speech act or performative (e.g. inform, request, etc.) of the message, and the content. The send action is like an atomic formula which has Send as the predicate name and has three arguments. The first argument is either an identifier or a variable (i.e. $\langle iv \rangle$) denoting the name of the receiving agent, the second argument is also either an identifier or a variable (i.e. $\langle iv \rangle$) denoting the performative of the message, and the third argument is an atomic formula (i.e. $\langle atom \rangle$), which specifies the content of the message. If the receiver or the performative is a variable, they should be instantiated with constants denoting the name of the receiver and the performative, respectively, before the send action is executed. An example of a send action is Send(ag$_2$, inform, on(a,b)), which specifies that agent ag$_1$ informs agent ag$_2$ that block a is on block b.

If an agent sends a message Send(Receiver, Performative, Content) to another agent, the belief base of the sender is updated with the formula sent(Receiver, Performative, Content) and the belief base of the receiver is updated with the formula received(Sender, Performative, Content). Agents can receive a message in their belief base at each moment in time. Note that unlike the mental actions, the send actions can always be executed.

The *external actions* are means to change the external environment in which the agents operate. The effects of external actions are assumed to be determined by the environment and might not be known to the agents. The agent thus decides to perform an external action and the external environment determines the effect of this action. The agent can come to know the effects of an external action by performing a sense action. This sense action can be defined as an external action in an agent's plan, or it could be a pre-defined operation that is part of the sense-reason-act loop of the agent's deliberation cycle.

External actions are performed by 3APL agents with respect to an environment which is assumed to be implemented as a Java class. In particular, the actions that can be performed in this environment are determined by the methods of the Java class (i.e., the methods specify the effect of those actions in that environment), and the state of the environment is represented by the instance variables of the class.

The external actions that can be performed by 3APL agents have the form `Java(Classname, Method, List)` where `Classname` is the name of the Java class that implements the environment, `Method` is the action to be performed in the environment, and `List` is a list of returned values. The parameter `Method` corresponds with a parameterized method of the Java class `Classname` and `List` is a list of values returned by `Method`. The method can be implemented to return the result of the action in the list, or the list could for example be empty. In that case, an explicit sense action would have to be executed to obtain the result of the action.

An example of an external action is `Java(BlockWorld, east()`, `L)` where the external action `east()` is performed in the environment `BlockWorld`.[6] The effect of this action is that the position of the agent in the block world environment is shifted one slot to the east.

A *test action* checks whether a well-formed formula (i.e. ⟨*wff*⟩) is derivable from the belief base. Such an action, which consists of a well-formed formula followed by a question mark, will be blocked if the formula is not derivable from the belief base. Note that the derivation relation is implemented by the Prolog reasoning engine. If the arguments of a test action are variables and the well-formed formula is derivable from the belief base, then the effect of the test action is a substitution that assigns terms to the variables. The assignment is useful for retrieving information from the belief base and passing it to other actions for further manipulation.

An example of a test action is `(on(a,X) and on(X,c))?` which will be successfully executed if the agent believes that there is a block `X` placed on top of block `c` such that block `a` is placed on top of it. The result of a successful execution is a substitution such as `{X/b}` which indicates that the relevant block is block `b`.

An *abstract plan*, which is represented as an atomic formula (i.e. ⟨*atom*⟩), is an abstract representation of a plan which can be instantiated with a (more concrete) plan during execution. An abstract plan cannot be executed directly and should be rewritten into another plan, possibly (and even probably) containing executable basic actions, through application of reasoning rules (see below for a detail description of these rules). The application of rules to abstract plans involves a unification of abstract plans with the head of rules through which values can be passed to the instantiated plan.

---

[6]`BlockWorld` is in this case a two-dimensional grid with obstacles in which the agents may move in any direction that is not blocked by obstacles (or walls).

Plans

Basic actions, as discussed above, can be composed to build plans through so-called program operators. There are three 3APL program operators: the sequential operator (denoted by ;), the iteration operator (denoted by a while-do construct), and the conditional choice operator (denoted by an if-then-else construct). In particular, if β is a well-formed formula, β' is a query expression (i.e. a well-formed formula or true), and *Actions* is the set of basic actions as defined above, then the set of plans, denoted by *Plans* is defined as follows:

- *Actions* $\subseteq$ *Plans*

- if $\pi, \pi' \in$ *Plans*, then if β then π else $\pi' \in$ *Plans*

- if $\pi \in$ *Plans*, then while β' do $\pi \in$ *Plans*

- if $\pi, \pi' \in$ *Plans*, then $\pi; \pi' \in$ *Plans*

We use ϵ to denote the empty plan and we identify $\epsilon; \pi$ with π.

The plan base of a 3APL agent consists of a set of plans. In the implementation of 3APL, the specification of the initial plan base of an agent is preceded by the keyword "PlanBase :" and consists of a number of plans separated by a comma. The following is an example of the initial plan base of a 3APL agent.

```
PlanBase:
while (on(X,fl) and not(on(V,X))) do {
        (on(Y,Z) and not(Z==fl))?;
        Move(X,fl,Y)
}
```

This plan base consists of one plan which will find all free blocks (blocks with no block on top) that are placed on the floor and move them to an existing block which itself is not placed on the floor.

Reasoning Rules

In order to reason with goals and plans, 3APL has two types of rules: goal planning rules and plan revision rules. These rules are conditionalized by beliefs. Let β be a query expression, κ be an atomic formula, and π, π_h, π_b be plans. The set of goal planning rules (*PG*) and the set of plan revision rules (*PR*) are then defined as follows:

$$\kappa \leftarrow \beta \mid \pi, \; \leftarrow \beta \mid \pi \in PG$$
$$\pi_h \leftarrow \beta \mid \pi_b \in PR.$$

The *goal planning rules* are used to generate plans to achieve goals. In the first goal planning rule, the belief condition β indicates when the plan π could be generated to achieve the specified goal κ. The second goal planning rules can be used to model reactive behavior by omitting the head of the rule. This special kind of goal planning rule states that under the belief condition β, a plan can be adopted. The specification of the set of goal planning rules is preceded by the keyword "PG − rules :". The following is an example of the specification of a goal planning rule of a 3APL agent.

```
PG-rules:
on(X,Z) ← on(X,Y)    |    Move(X,Y,Z)
```

This rule states that if the agent wants to have block X on block Z, but it believes that X is on block Y, then it plans to move X from Y onto Z.

The *plan revision rules* are used to revise plans from the plan base. The specification of the set of plan revision rules is preceded by the keyword "PR − rules :". The following is an example of the specification of a plan revision rule of a 3APL agent.

```
PR-rules:
Move(X,Y,Z) ← not(clear(X))    |
                on(U,X)?;Move(U,X,fl);Move(X,Y,Z)
```

This plan revision rule informally means that if the agent plans to move block X from block Y onto block Z, but it cannot move X because (it believes that) there is a block on X, then the agent should revise its plan by finding out which block (U) is on X, moving U onto the floor, and finally moving X from Y onto Z.

A plan revision rule $\pi_h \leftarrow \beta \mid \pi_b$ can be applied to a plan π, if π_h can be matched to a prefix of π, i.e., if π is of the form $\pi_h; \pi'$. For example, a plan $Move(a, b, c); Move(b, fl, a)$ can be revised into a plan $Move(a, b, fl); Move(b, fl, a)$ by applying the plan revision rule $Move(a, b, c) \leftarrow \text{true} \mid Move(a, b, fl)$. Note that a plan revision rule could be used to drop (part of) a plan if its body π_b is the empty plan ϵ.

Deliberation Cycle

The beliefs, goals, plans and reasoning rules form the mental attitudes or data structures of 3APL agents. These data structures can be modified by deliberation operations such as applying a rule or executing a plan. These deliberation operations constitute the deliberation process of individual agents. The deliberation process or program can be viewed as the interpreter, as it determines which deliberation operations should be performed in which order. For example, it can be programmed to determine whether a goal should be dropped if it is not reachable using any possible plan and plan revision rule. A deliberation process programmed in this way could be viewed as an implementation of "single minded" agents [182]. Some more moderate alternatives are also possible. Moreover, the interpreter can determine if and when to check the relation between plans and goals. For example, the interpreter can check whether a goal still exists during plan execution to avoid continuing with a plan of which the goal is reached (or dropped) already. The interpreter can also perform a kind of "garbage collection" and remove a left-over plan for a goal that no longer exists. If this would not be done, the left-over plan could become active again at a later time and this might not be desired behavior.

Another issue that the interpreter can determine is related to multiple (parallel) goals and/or plans. For example, it can decide whether only one or more plans can be adopted for the same goal at any time. It seems not unreasonable to allow only one plan at a time for each goal, which coincides with the idea that we try different plans consecutively and not in parallel, because this might lead to a lot of unnecessary interactions between plans and also a waste of resources. If we allow only one current plan for each goal, the plans in the plan base will all be for different goals. Also in this case one has to determine whether the plans will be executed interleaved or consecutively. Interleaving might be beneficial, but can also lead to resource contention between plans in a way that no plan executes successfully anymore (see also [222, 221, 220]). E.g., a robot needs to go to two different rooms that are in opposite directions. If it has a plan to arrive in each room and interleaves those two plans, it will keep oscillating around its starting position. Many of the existing work on concurrent planning can however be applied in this setting to avoid most problems in this area.

For 3APL, a set of deliberation operations is proposed [52], including `SelectPlanningGoalrule`, `SelectPlanRevisionrule`, `SelectPlan`, `ExecutePlan`, `ApplyPlanningGoalrule`, and `ApplyPlanRevisionrule`. These operations can be composed to form a deliberation program by using operators such as sequential composition, test (on both belief, goal and plan bases), conditional choice (if-then-else construct), and conditional iteration (while loop).

In order to facilitate the implementation of a deliberation process and since the 3APL interpreter is implemented in Java, we have implemented each mental attitude as a Java class, i.e., a Java class for the belief base, one for the capabilities, one for the goal base, one for the plan base, one for the goal planning rule base, and one for the plan revision rule base. Each of these classes has an internal representation for its specific mental attitude, which will initially be set by parsing the input 3APL program. The parser is part of the Java implementation of the 3APL interpreter.

Each class implementing a mental attitude has a set of methods. These methods implement the deliberation operations that are relevant for that mental attitude. For example, the class that implements the belief base has a method for updating the belief with new facts, and the class that implements the goal planning rule base has a method for selecting a goal planning rule and another method for applying that rule. In order to implement a deliberation process for 3APL agents, a programmer should thus have the source code of the interpreter and implement a Java class that calls the methods of the classes that correspond to the mental attitudes.

Although the idea is that the agent programmer implements the deliberation process, an interpreter is provided that implements a cyclic order of deliberation operations as illustrated in figure 2.3. According to this deliberation program, an agent starts with searching for an applicable planning rule (in their order of occurrence) to generate a plan for one of its goals and applies the first applicable planning rule that it finds. The agent then continues with searching for an applicable plan revision rule (in their order of occurrence) to revise one of its plans. A plan needs to be revised when, for example, it starts with an abstract plan which is not executable. The agent applies the first applicable plan revision rule that it finds. Then, the agent continues with searching for the executable plans (in their order of occurrence) and executes the first plan it finds. Note that a plan that starts, for example, with a mental action of which the pre-condition does not hold, cannot be executed. Finally, the agent continues with either the same cycle of operations or it suspends its activities until a message is arrived. The agent suspends its activities if no sensible operation could be performed during the previous cycle, i.e. if no rules could be applied and no plan could be executed. Note that the arrival of a message may make either a rule applicable or a plan executable.

This order of operations is by no means universal, since it does not guarantee the proper agent behavior for all kinds of situations. For example, in an emergency situation it may be more plausible that an agent does not continue executing its current plans, but starts adopting and executing emergency plans. As we have argued in [52], we believe that an agent's interpreter should be programmable to allow the implementation of different types of behavior. The proposed interpreter for 3APL is an example which can in principle be modified by the agent programmers to generate different types of behavior. At this moment, the source code of 3APL is under development and is not available for modifying and implementing the deliberation cycle. However, we hope to make this possible in the near future.

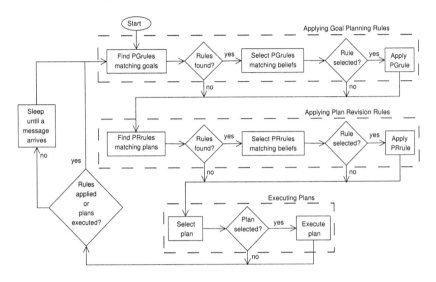

Figure 2.3. A cyclic interpreter (deliberation cycle) for the 3APL agents.

3APL Platform

The 3APL platform provides a user interface that allows 3APL agents to be programmed, loaded, and executed. During execution there are various facilities in the interface such as the sniffer, which allows monitoring the exchanges of messages between agents, and specific windows, which allow monitoring the changes of all mental attitudes of individual agents. Also, there are various icons in the interface that allow monitoring the execution of agents, either step by step or continuously. The graphical user interface of the 3APL platform is illustrated in Figure 2.4 and described in section 2.3. A detailed description of the platform interface can be found in the 3APL user guide [51].

The only part of the platform architecture that is programmable to this date is the shared environment. As noted, the environment of 3APL agents is assumed to be implemented as a Java class, the actions that can be performed in this environment are determined by the methods of the Java class (i.e., the methods specify the effect of those actions in that environment), and the state of the environment is represented by the instance variables of the class. In particular, the environment is modelled as plugin to the platform. This is a systematic way to interface between the 3APL platform and Java classes. The plugin facilitates the interaction between individual agents running on the platform and the instantiation of the Java classes. These interactions include method calls from agents to Java classes and event notification from the platform interface. To create a plugin you need to implement three interfaces.

1. `ics.TripleApl.Plugin`: factory class

2. `ics.TripleApl.Instance`: product class

3. `ics.TripleApl.Method`: plugin method (function).

At startup, the platform loads all Plugin-implementing classes from the `plugins/` directory (this directory is created when the 3APL platform is downloaded and unpacked). It then queries the found plugin classes for their external functionalities (Java methods) they provide to individual agents. This is done by the platform through invocation of the method `getMethods` of the Plugin interface. The idea behind the plugin is to systematize the relation between agent platform and environment that can be used by the agents. In particular, the environment should be linked to the *individual* agents running on the platform such that the effect of any change on individual agents (create, reset or remove) on the platform can be realized and passed on to the environment.

For example, consider a two-dimensional grid such as the block world environment in which the agents running on the platform can be present and move around. In such a case, if the user creates, resets or removes an agent on or from the platform, the agent should be added to, reset (moved to initial position), or removed from the block world environment, respectively. The effects of the mentioned events (on the platform) are realized by the platform through invocation of one of the following methods from the Plugin interface: createInstance, resetInstance, and removeInstance. The downloadable version of the 3APL platform comes with an implementation of a block world environment. The details of this environment and its Java implementation are described in the 3APL user guide [51]. Note that this environment is just an example and that the programmer can implement its own environment.

2.2.2 Semantics and Verification

To program a 3APL multi-agent system is to program individual 3APL agents and to specify the initial state of their shared environment. To program an agent means to specify its initial beliefs, goals, plans and capabilities, and to specify sets of goal planning rules and plan revision rules. The initial state of the shared environment is specified by a set of facts.

DEFINITION 2.1 (3APL AGENT) *An individual 3APL agent is a tuple* $\langle \iota, \sigma_0, \gamma_0, Cap, \Pi_0, PG, PR, \xi \rangle$ *where ι is the agent identifier, σ_0 is the initial belief base, γ_0 is the initial goal base, Cap is the capability base, $\Pi_0 \subseteq Plans \times \{\texttt{true}\}$ is the initial plan base, PG is a set of goal planning rules, PR is a set of plan revision rules, and ξ is the environment the agent shares with other agents, which is represented by a set of ground atoms.*

The plan base of a 3APL agent consists of a set of plan-goal pairs. The goal for which a plan is selected is recorded with the plan, because this for instance provides for the possibility to drop a plan of which the goal is reached. The initial plan base of a 3APL agent consists of a set of plans, rather than a set of plan-goal pairs. We take these initial plans as having the associated goal $\texttt{true}$[7]. Furthermore, goals may be revised or dropped and one might want to remove a plan associated with a goal which has been dropped, from the plan base (see also the discussion on the deliberation cycle of section 2.2.1).

The beliefs, goals and plans of individual agents and their shared environment are the elements that change during the execution of the agent, while the capabilities and the reasoning rules remain unchanged. Together with a *substitution* component, these changing components of the agent constitute a *3APL agent configuration*. The substitution part of the configuration is used to store values or bindings associated with variables.

DEFINITION 2.2 ((GROUND) SUBSTITUTION, BINDING, DOMAIN, FREE VARIABLES) *A substitution θ is a finite set of the form $\{x_1/t_1, \ldots, x_n/t_n\}$, where $x_i \in Var$ and $t_i \in Term$ and $\forall i \neq j : x_i \neq x_j$. θ is called a ground substitution if all t_i are ground terms. Each element x_i/t_i is then called a binding for x_i. The set of variables $\{x_1, \ldots, x_n\}$ is the domain of θ and will be denoted by $dom(\theta)$. The application of a substitution θ to a syntactic expression e is denoted as $e\theta$. It refers to the expression resulting from simultaneously replacing all occurrences of variable x in e for which $x/t \in \theta$ by t.*

Below, we first define the configuration of an individual 3APL agent in terms of the elements that change during the execution of the agent. Then, we define the configuration of a 3APL multi-agent system in terms of the configurations of the involved agents and their shared environment.

DEFINITION 2.3 (CONFIGURATION) *A configuration of an individual 3APL agent is a tuple $\langle \iota, \sigma, \gamma, \Pi, \theta, \xi \rangle$, where ι is an agent identifier, σ is the belief base of the agent, γ is the goal base of the agent, Π is the plan base of the agent, θ is a ground substitution that binds domain variables to domain terms,*

---

[7]Although $\texttt{true}$ as a logical formula cannot be an agent's goal according to the 3APL semantics, we use it only to indicate that there is no specific goal associated to a plan.

and ξ is the environment it interacts with, where ξ is a set of ground atoms. The goal base in a configuration is such that for any goal φ ∈ γ it holds that φ is not entailed by the agent's beliefs.

A configuration of a 3APL multi-agent system is a tuple $\langle A_1, \ldots, A_n, \xi \rangle$ *where A_i for $1 \leq i \leq n$ is the configuration of individual agent i and ξ is the shared environment. This shared environment is the same as the environment of each individual agent.*

The rationale behind the condition on the goal base is the following. The beliefs of an agent describe the state the agent is in and the goals describe the state the agent wants to realize. If an agent believes φ is the case, it cannot have the goal to achieve φ, because the state of affairs φ is already realized. This is thus an implementation of achievement goals, as opposed to maintenance goals.

Transition system

In the following, we present the general idea of the type of semantics that is given to the 3APL programming language. It is an operational semantics which is defined in terms of a transition system [169]. A transition system is a set of derivation rules for deriving transitions. A transition is a transformation of one configuration into another and it corresponds to a single computation step. For the purpose of this paper, we present only a subset of derivation rules. A complete set of derivation rules is presented in [54].

We define first a derivation rule for transitions between multi-agent configurations. This derivation rule, which captures the parallel execution of the set of individual agents, forms the only transition at the multi-agent level.

DEFINITION 2.4 (MULTI-AGENT EXECUTION) *Let* $A_1, \ldots, A_i, \ldots, A_n, A_i'$ *be agent configurations and let ξ and ξ′ be specifications of the environment. Further, let* $A_i = \langle \sigma, \gamma, \Pi, \theta, \xi \rangle$ *and let* $A_i' = \langle \sigma', \gamma', \Pi', \theta', \xi' \rangle$. *Then the derivation rule for multi-agent configurations is defined as follows.*

$$\frac{A_i \rightarrow A_i'}{\langle \{A_1, \ldots, A_i, \ldots, A_n\}, \xi \rangle \rightarrow \langle \{A_1, \ldots, A_i', \ldots, A_n\}, \xi' \rangle}$$

This derivation rule states that a transition between multi-agent configurations can be defined in terms of a transition between single-agent configurations. This amounts to an *interleaved* execution of the agents in the system. Note that the environment of the multi-agent configuration is shared among all individual agents.

We now define transition rules that can derive transitions transforming single-agent configurations. These derivation rules specify the semantics of the execution of plans and the application of reasoning rules.

The first derivation rule specifies the execution of the plan base of a 3APL agent. The plan base of the agent is a set of plan-goal pairs. This set can be executed by executing one of the constituent plans. The execution of a plan can change the agent's configuration.

DEFINITION 2.5 *(plan base execution) Let*
$\Pi = \{(\pi_1, \kappa_1), \ldots, (\pi_i, \kappa_i), \ldots, (\pi_n, \kappa_n)\}$ *and*
$\Pi' = \{(\pi_1, \kappa_1), \ldots, (\pi_i', \kappa_i), \ldots, (\pi_n, \kappa_n)\}$ *be plan bases, θ, θ' be ground substitutions, and ξ, ξ' be environment specifications. Then, the derivation rule for the execution of a set of plans is specified in terms of the execution of individual plans as follows.*

$$\frac{\langle \iota, \sigma, \gamma, \{(\pi_i, \kappa_i)\}, \theta, \xi \rangle \rightarrow \langle \iota, \sigma', \gamma', \{(\pi_i', \kappa_i)\}, \theta', \xi' \rangle}{\langle \iota, \sigma, \gamma, \Pi, \theta, \xi \rangle \rightarrow \langle \iota, \sigma', \gamma', \Pi', \theta', \xi' \rangle}$$

Now we will introduce some of the derivation rules for the execution of individual plans. We introduce derivation rules for external actions, communication actions and tests.

An external action `Java(Classname,` $\alpha(t_1, \ldots, t_n)$`,` x`)` has two functionalities. First, based on the input terms and the state of the environment, it generates a term and assigns it to variable x. The term assigned to x is the output of the action which is returned to the agent from the environment. For sense actions, this output can be programmed to be the sensed information. For other actions, the output could for example be information such as whether the action has been performed, or the result of the action. Note that this term can be a list of terms. Second, actions are assumed to have effects on the environment.

In order to capture these two functionalities, i.e., calculating a value for x and updating the current environment, we assume for each external action with a method name α a function F_α which maps terms $t_1, \ldots, t_n$ and the environment ξ to a term which will be assigned to variable x. Further, we assume a function G_α which maps terms $t_1, \ldots, t_n$ and the environment ξ to a new environment ξ'. An agent can execute an external action only if the goal associated to the action is still a goal of the agent.

DEFINITION 2.6 *(external action execution) Let $t, t_1, \ldots, t_n$ be terms, x be a variable, let ξ, ξ' be agent environments, α be the method name of an external action, and assume functions F_α and G_α as explained above. The execution of an external action is then defined as follows:*

$$\frac{\gamma \models \kappa}{\langle \iota, \sigma, \gamma, (\text{Java}(\text{Classname}, \alpha(t_1, \ldots, t_n), x), \kappa), \theta, \xi \rangle \rightarrow \langle \iota, \sigma, \gamma, (\epsilon, \kappa), \theta', \xi' \rangle}$$

where $\theta' = \theta \cup \{x/t\}$ with $t = F_\alpha(t_1, \ldots, t_n, \xi)$, and $\xi' = G_\alpha(t_1, \ldots, t_n, \xi)$.

Note that the execution of an external action thus influences only the substitution and the environment component of the configuration.

The next type of basic action is the communication action $Send(r, p, \phi)$. We assume that each agent can receive a message at any moment in time. We use then a synchronization mechanism for sending and receiving messages. This synchronization mechanism takes care of simultaneously taking a message from the sending agent and putting it in the belief base of the receiving agent. How these messages are then handled by the receiving agent is done in a completely asynchronous fashion.

The semantics of a $Send(r, p, \phi)$ action affects both sending and receiving agents. The communication action $Send(r, p, \phi)$ is removed from the plan base of the sending agent and the formula $sent(r, p, \phi)$ is added to its belief base. Moreover, the formula $received(s, p, \phi)$ is added to the belief base of the receiving agent, where s is the name of the sending agent. This information about incoming and outgoing messages can respectively be used by the receiving and sending agents for their future deliberations. In order to be able to identify the sending agent when defining the addition of a fact of the form $received(s, p, \phi)$ to the belief base of the receiver, we add the name of the sending agent to messages.

DEFINITION 2.7 (COMMUNICATION ACTION EXECUTION) *Let*
$\langle s, r, p, \varphi \rangle$ *be the format of the message that is sent and received by the agents, where s is the name of the sending agent, r is the name of the receiving agent, p is the communication performative, and ϕ is the message content. The following three transition rules specify the semantics for sending and receiving messages between agents, and their synchronization, respectively.*

- *The transition rule for the sending agent:*

$$\frac{\gamma \models \kappa}{\langle s, \sigma, \gamma, (Send(r, p, \phi), \kappa), \theta, \xi \rangle \xrightarrow{<s,r,p,\phi>!} \langle s, \sigma', \gamma, (\epsilon, \kappa), \theta, \xi \rangle}$$

where $\sigma' = \sigma \cup \{sent(r, p, \phi)\}$.

- *The transition rule for the receiving agent:*

$$\frac{}{\langle r, \sigma, \gamma, \Pi, \theta, \xi \rangle \xrightarrow{<s,r,p,\phi>?} \langle r, \sigma', \gamma, \Pi, \theta, \xi \rangle}$$

where $\sigma' = \sigma \cup \{received(s, p, \phi)\}$.

- *The transition rule for synchronization:*

$$\frac{\langle \mathcal{A}_i, \xi \rangle \xrightarrow{\varphi?} \langle \mathcal{A}'_i, \xi \rangle \, , \, \langle \mathcal{A}_j, \xi \rangle \xrightarrow{\varphi!} \langle \mathcal{A}'_j, \xi \rangle}{\langle \{\mathcal{A}_1, \ldots, \mathcal{A}_i, \ldots, \mathcal{A}_j, \ldots, \mathcal{A}_n\}, \xi \rangle \rightarrow \langle \{\mathcal{A}_1, \ldots, \mathcal{A}'_i, \ldots, \mathcal{A}'_j, \ldots, \mathcal{A}_n\}, \xi \rangle}$$

Note that the second transition rule guarantees that each agent can receive the messages that are directed to the agent at any moment in time. More discussion on communication between 3APL agents can be found in [53].

Next, we specify the derivation rule for the execution of the test action. A test action can bind the free variables that occur in the test formula for which no bindings have been computed yet.

DEFINITION 2.8 (TEST EXECUTION) *Let β be a well-formed formula and let τ be a ground substitution.*

$$\frac{\sigma \models \beta\theta\tau \;\&\; \gamma \models \kappa}{\langle \iota, \sigma, \gamma, \{(\beta?, \kappa)\}, \theta, \xi \rangle \rightarrow \langle \iota, \sigma, \gamma, \{(\epsilon, \kappa)\}, \theta\tau, \xi \rangle}$$

The entailment relation $\models$ in the condition $\sigma \models \beta\theta\tau$ is implemented by the Prolog inference engine. When posing a query β, the substitution θ is first applied to β. The substitution τ is the substitution returned by Prolog and should bind the variables of $\beta\theta$. The entailment relation $\models$ in $\gamma \models \kappa$ is implemented in a similar fashion.

The derivation rules for the execution of composite plans are defined in a standard way.

Next, we define the transition rule for the goal planning rule. A goal planning rule $\kappa \leftarrow \beta \mid \pi$ specifies that the goal κ can be achieved by plan π if β is derivable from the agent's beliefs. A goal planning rule only affects the plan base of the agent.

DEFINITION 2.9 (GOAL PLANNING RULE APPLICATION) *Let $\kappa \leftarrow \beta \mid \pi$ be a goal planning rule. Let also τ_1, τ_2 be ground substitutions.*

$$\frac{\gamma \models \kappa\tau_1 \;\&\; \sigma \models \beta\tau_1\tau_2}{\langle \iota, \sigma, \gamma, \Pi, \theta, \xi \rangle \rightarrow \langle \iota, \sigma, \gamma, \Pi \cup \{(\pi\tau_1\tau_2, \kappa\tau_1)\}, \theta, \xi \rangle}$$

Note that the goal $\kappa\tau_1$ that should be achieved by the plan $\pi\tau_1\tau_2$ is associated with it. It is only this rule that associates goals with plans. The goal base of the agent does not change because the plan $\pi\tau_1\tau_2$ is not executed yet; the goals of agents may change only after execution of plans: goals are removed if believed to be achieved. We do not add substitutions τ_1, τ_2 to θ since these substitutions should only influence the new plan π.

Finally, the transition rule for the goal planning rule that defines reactive behavior, i.e. the goal planning rule in which the head is omitted, is a modification of the above transition rule.

DEFINITION 2.10 (REACTIVE GOAL PLANNING RULE APPLICATION) *Let $\leftarrow \beta \mid \pi$ be a reactive goal planning rule and let also τ be a ground substitution.*

$$\frac{\sigma \models \beta\tau}{\langle \iota, \sigma, \gamma, \Pi, \theta, \xi \rangle \rightarrow \langle \iota, \sigma, \gamma, \Pi \cup \{(\pi\tau, \texttt{true})\}, \theta, \xi \rangle}$$

Note that the goal associated to the generated plan is set to true, which means that the plan is not generated to achieve a specific goal.

Semantics of a 3APL agent

The semantics of an individual 3APL agent as well as the semantics of a 3APL multi-agent system is derived directly from the transition relation $\rightarrow$. The meaning of individual agents and multi-agent systems consists of a set of so called computation runs.

DEFINITION 2.11 (COMPUTATION RUN) *Given a transition system, a computation run* $CR(s_0)$ *is a finite or infinite sequence* $s_0, \ldots, s_n$ *or* $s_0, \ldots$ *where* s_i *are configurations, and* $\forall_{i>0} : s_{i-1} \rightarrow s_i$ *is a transition in the transition system.*

We can now use the concept of a computation run to define the semantics of individual 3APL agents and the semantics of 3APL multi-agent systems.

DEFINITION 2.12 (SEMANTICS OF 3APL MULTI-AGENT SYSTEMS) *The semantics of a 3APL multi-agent system* $\langle \mathcal{A}_1, \ldots, \mathcal{A}_n, \xi \rangle$ *is the set of computation runs* $CR(\langle \mathcal{A}_1, \ldots, \mathcal{A}_n, \xi \rangle)$ *of the transition system for 3APL multi-agent systems.*

Note that the computation runs of a 3APL multi-agent system consist of multi-agent transitions which can be derived by means of two multi-agent transition rules. The first is defined in definition 2.4 and the second is the synchronization rule specified in definition 2.7.

3APL Verification

We deem the verification of multi-agent systems very important (cf. [150]). At the moment we do not yet have verification tools for 3APL agents. We have done some theoretical work on agent verification in general [116, 108], and some work more focused on the language 3APL in particular [226]. However, this work is still too theoretical to be the basis of a practical tool. Following related work on the verification of AgentSpeak programs [19] we plan to employ model-checking techniques. At the moment we are investigating if we can check (LTL) temporal properties of agents programmed in a light version of 3APL, using PROMELA, the finite state model specification language for the SPIN LTL model checker [110].

2.2.3 Software Engineering Issues

The 3APL platform and 3APL programming language are designed to respect a number of software engineering and programming principles. Below we give an overview of these principles and how they can be used.

Separation of concerns

Development methodologies for multi-agent systems [234] differ from each other in many respects. Some of them focus on inter-agent aspects, while others also provide support for the design of internal components of an agent, such as mental attitudes and the deliberation process. Finally, some methodologies explicitly deal with the environment, while others do not. The tools to develop and implement multi-agent systems should therefore support each of these issues separately.

The 3APL programming language supports the implementation of inter-agent issues by providing the communication action *Send*, and the 3APL platform manages the transportation of the communicated messages. Moreover, the platform provides information about existing agents to other agents through the Agent Management System (AMS). The information provided by the AMS to agents is required for agents' interactions. The environment of 3APL multi-agent systems can be implemented directly and· explicitly through external programs accessible to the agents through API's (application program interfaces).

Finally, the 3APL programming language respects the separation of concerns related to the distinction between an agent's data structures and an agent's operations. In particular, the data structures are mental attitudes such as beliefs, goals, and plans while operations concern manipulation of the mental attitudes such as updating of beliefs, plans and goals, and execution of plans. This distinction is made explicit by introducing two levels of programming: at the data level one can specify the mental attitudes of the agents and at the operation level one can implement the deliberation process of the agent.

Modularity

The implementation of an agent is modular in the sense that an agent can be implemented in terms of seven different modules. The first module is the capability base of the agent which implements the mental actions that an agent can perform to update its beliefs. The second module is the belief base of the agent which contains information the agent believes about the world as well as information that is internal to the agent. The initial beliefs of the agents can be distinguished in two kinds. The first kind of initial beliefs constitutes the background knowledge which can be used by different agents. The second kind of initial beliefs is specific to agents and cannot be used by other agents. Since the background knowledge can be used by different agents, we allow individual agents to load a separate file containing the background knowledge. In this way, one can implement the background knowledge once and allow different agents to load it as part of their initial beliefs. The third module is the goal base that denotes the situation the agent wants to realize. The fourth module is the plan base of the agent which contains the plans that the agent intends to perform. The fifth module is the goal planning rule base that contains the rules that can be used to generate a plan for the possible goals of an agent. The sixth module is the plan revision rule base that contains rules to revise existing agent's plans. Finally, the seventh module is the deliberation module that allows the implementation of an agent's deliberation process.

Abstraction

The abstraction mechanisms that can be exploited in the 3APL programming language are related to external actions and abstract plans. In particular, the external actions allow the 3APL programmers to use external programs through their corresponding API's without having any access to the internal data and operations of the programs. The second abstraction mechanism is related to abstract plans which allow users to abstract over certain parts of plans. The abstract plans can be instantiated with a plan through the application of plan revision rules. It is very important to note that an abstract plan should be introduced, not only because it occurs in different plans, but also because its specific instantiation depends on the conditions known only at run time. For example, going to work can be considered an abstract plan since its specific instantiations such as going to work by bus, by taxi, by train, or by own car depend on the conditions that hold when the plan is to be executed. For example, if the agent does not have enough money, then it may consider going by bus or train, otherwise it may consider using a taxi.

The introduction of abstract plans in 3APL implies the introduction of plan revision rules. In implementing 3APL agents, the programmers tend to conceive abstract plans as a kind of procedure calls and the plan revision rules as the corresponding procedure. It is important to note that this is not the optimal and principal use of abstract plans and their corresponding plan revision rules.

Reusability

Finally, the 3APL platform allows reusing multi-agent systems by providing a library of templates for individual agents and templates for multi-agent systems. Using the templates for individual agents, the 3APL programmer can use generic agents that have certain initial mental attitudes. The templates for multi-agent systems, also known as projects, allow the 3APL programmers to use a set of generic agents that, in addition to their initial mental attitudes, follow a specified interaction protocol. Such a template can include an environment with which the agents are supposed to interact. An example of a multi-agent template is a template for an auction. In order to implement such an auction, a 3APL programmer can load such a multi-agent template and implement both the details of the agents, such as their specific initial mental attitudes, as well as the details of their environment.

2.2.4 Language integration

The 3APL programming language together with its platform allows the integration of Prolog and Java. The Prolog programs can be integrated since they can be loaded in 3APL and used as background knowledge. Given a loaded Prolog program, the agent can pose queries in three different contexts: as the pre-condition of mental actions, as test actions in plans, and as the guard of the reasoning rules. The Prolog programs can thus be used to control the execution of mental actions, the execution of plans, and the application of reasoning rules. Note that the queries may yield substitutions that can bind other variables used in the post-conditions of the mental actions, in the rest of plans that follow a test action, and in the bodies of reasoning rules.

Moreover, the 3APL programming language allows Java programs to be used through external actions. The external actions can be used to call methods of Java classes. Using the arguments of these methods, it is possible to pass data from 3APL to Java and vice versa. In this way, data can be passed from Java to the plans of the agent to the Prolog part (belief base) of the agent and vice versa. Note that the integration of Java is also used to implement the multi-agent environment with which the agents interact.

2.3 Platform

2.3.1 Available tools and documentation

The 3APL platform is an experimental tool, designed to support the development, implementation, and execution of 3APL agents [54]. The detailed information about installation and deployment of the 3APL platform can be found in the 3APL user guide which is available online at the following URL:

`http://www.cs.uu.nl/3apl/download/java/userguide.pdf`

or in [217]. Moreover, we are developing a tutorial and training material which will be available soon from the 3APL web page:

`http://www.cs.uu.nl/3apl`

Also, various papers on 3APL can help to understand how to deploy the 3APL platform [107, 228, 54, 52, 227]. Finally, the implementation documentation of the platform can be found at:

`http://www.cs.uu.nl/3apl/docs/aplp-refman/index.html`

The 3APL platform provides a graphical interface, as shown in Figure 2.4, through which a user can develop and execute 3APL agents using several facilities, such as a syntax-colored editor and several debugging tools. The platform allows communication among agents and provides the Agent Management System (AMS) that is responsible for registration of the hosted agents. Multiple 3APL platforms can run on different machines connected in a network at the same time, such that agents hosted on these platforms can communicate with each other. When the 3APL platform is started, the user should select whether the multi-agent application is intended to act as a server or as a client. The server option must be selected the first time the 3APL platform is run. The client option can be selected only if the 3APL platform is running as a server already. When the user selects the client option, the IP of the server with which the (client) platform should connect, must be filled in.

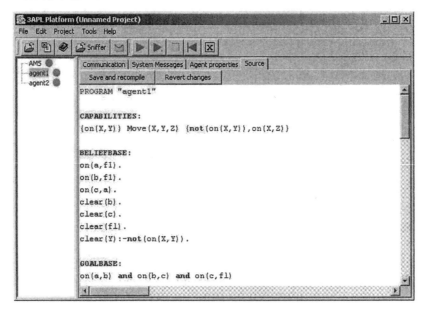

Figure 2.4. An illustration of the graphical user interface of the 3APL platform.

The graphical interface shows in the left side window the names of the agents that are hosted and running on the platform in a tree-like structure. The tree includes also the AMS (Agent Management System) which is modelled as a non-programmable agent that provides information about hosted agents to each of the running agent. The information will be provided only on request. The same window of the graphical interface presents also the status of the hosted agents such as initial, running, stopped, final, and erroneous. Moreover, the Communication tab of the graphical interface provides a message window that displays the messages that are exchanged between agents. The System Messages tab is a window that shows the system messages such as parse errors or the errors that are generated during the execution. The Agent properties tab is a window that can be used to monitor the (mental) states of the agents during their execution. The Source tab provides an editor that allows programmers to modify the initial mental state of agents. In addition, the interface provides a sniffer button that displays the graphical representation of the message exchange.

2.3.2 Standards compliance, interoperability and portability

The 3APL platform has been tested on Windows 98, Windows NT and Windows XP, as well as on Linux, Unix (Solaris) and Mac OS X. 3APL is written in Java 2 SDK 1.4, and makes use of the Prolog engine of JIProlog, which is also implemented in Java. We have tested it for Java 2 SDK 1.4.0_02 and upwards. The downloadable 3APL package consists of a .jar file that contains all the .class files needed, as well as examples of 3APL programs. The package needs approximately 800 KB.

The 3APL platform adheres to the FIPA standard to the extent that it provides a simplified version of an Agent Management System which provides a combination of name service and yellow-page services. Moreover, the format of the messages that are communicated between 3APL agents are based on FIPA standards, consisting of the identifiers of the sender and receiver of the message, the performative or speech act, and the content of the message. The 3APL platform supports only the development, implementation, and execution of multi-agent systems that consist of 3APL agents. At this moment, the platform does not support open multi-agent systems, mobile agents, or heterogeneous agents.

The 3APL platform is still in a prototyping stage and can execute only a small number of agents. The performance of the platform decreases if the number of agents, which are loaded and executed concurrently on the platform, grows. One reason for the low performance is the complex and cognitive nature of agents and the fact that agents have the capability to reason with their mental attitudes. The platform can handle the messages that are exchanged by the agents, although the number of agents that can be run efficiently on the 3APL platform is small.

The platform provides distributed control such that the agents can be executed concurrently. This enables loading, executing, and stopping agents while other agents are running. The platform also provides the possibility to build a library of agents, multi-agent systems and agent templates. The templates can be loaded and extended to build multi-agent systems. Finally, based on the templates it is possible to have interaction protocols in the platform's library, since the protocols can be defined in terms of a set of agent templates in which only the actions prescribed by the protocols are specified.

2.4   Applications supported by the language and/or the platform

The applications that can be developed using the 3APL platform and the 3APL programming language are those that are best understood in terms of cognitive and social concepts like beliefs, goals, plans, actions, norms, organizational structures, resources and services that are part of the multi-agent environment. We have already implemented a number of toy problem applications such as block world logistics, Axelrod's tournament, English Auction, and Contract Net protocols. Also, 3APL is already applied to implement the high-level control of mobile robots. In this project, external actions of 3APL were defined and connected to some simple sensory and motor actions of the mobile robot. In this way, a programmer can implement a 3APL program that senses the position of the robot it is controlling and determine how to reach a goal position in a rectangular environment, a model of which is accessible to the 3APL program. Currently, 3APL is also being applied to control the behavior of SONY AIBO robots and to implement small device mobile applications.

2.5   Final Remarks

The 3APL platform can be employed to implement multi-agent systems where each individual agent is implemented through the 3APL programming language. Using the 3APL programming language, individual agents can directly be implemented in terms of cognitive concepts such as beliefs, goals, plans, actions, and reasoning rules. Experience from deploying the 3APL platform for educational purposes have proved it to provide appropriate programming constructs for direct and easy implementation of applications that are analyzed and designed by existing multi-agent system development methodologies such as Prometheus [163] and Gaia [242].

The programming language 3APL is subject to constant theoretical and practical improvements. For example, the definition of the 3APL language is extended with specific programming constructs to implement the agent's deliberation process, declarative goals, other types of reasoning rules such as goal planning rules, and external and communication actions. Also, the specification of belief is distinguished from the belief query expressions. The practical development consists of the implementation of the 3APL platform that allows the design, implementation, and testing of multi-agent applications. Facilities provided by the platform ease the task of developing multi-agent systems.

Currently, we are working to extend and refine the implementation of the 3APL platform by adding additional features needed to facilitate the development of multi-agent systems. One of the extensions is to provide programming constructs for adopting different types of goals such as achievement goals, perform goals and maintenance goals at run time. The extension will add basic actions dedicated for adopting different types of goals such that executing plans that include these types of basic actions generates goals. Another extensions is to provide programming constructs to allow explicit implementation of the organizational structures and the multi-agent environment. In particular, we are building on the existing coordination mechanisms designed for concurrent component-based systems and extend them with social and organizational concepts needed to specify multi-agent organizations. Moreover, we aim at using the existing web technologies such as XML and web services to define the environment of multi-agent systems. Our aim is that any introduced extension and refinement should have a theoretical foundation, being defined in terms of formal syntax and semantics.

Acknowledgments

Thanks to Frank de Boer and Frank Dignum for discussion on the issues raised in this paper.

Chapter 3

IMPACT: A MULTI-AGENT FRAMEWORK WITH DECLARATIVE SEMANTICS

Jürgen Dix[1] and Yingqian Zhang[2]

[1] *Clausthal University of Technology*
Department of Computer Science
Chair for Computational Intelligence
Julius-Albert-Str. 5, 38678 Clausthal
Germany
dix@tu-clausthal.de

[2] *University of Manchester*
School of Computer Science
Oxford Road, Manchester M13 9PL
United Kingdom
zhangy@cs.man.ac.uk

Abstract   The *IMPACT* project (http://www.cs.umd.edu/projects/impact) aims at developing a powerful multi-agent system platform, which (1) is able to deal with heterogenous and distributed data, (2) can be realised on top of arbitrary legacy code, (3) is built on a clear foundational basis, and (4) scales up for realistic applications. We will describe its main features and several extensions of the language that have been investigated (and partially implemented).

Keywords: formal methods, heterogeneity, legacy code, annotated logic programming, reasoning with time, uncertainty and beliefs

3.1   Motivation

One of the main features of *IMPACT* is the idea of *agentisation*: *IMPACT* agents are usually built around given legacy code (see [209]). Another important feature is to provide a clear semantics for agents (based on the notion of an *agent program*) that can be easily extended (incorporating time, uncertainty, beliefs etc). The third feature is to identify classes of programs that can be efficiently implemented (polynomial modulo the underlying code).

In this chapter we are trying to illustrate these features through two examples. While Example 3.2 serves to illustrate the syntax and semantics of (temporal) agent programs, Example 3.3 shows the *agentisation* idea by turning a dedicated planning system into an agent collaborating with other agents in a wider environment. This example is also used to demonstrate some aspects of the third feature.

Before turning to the examples in Section 3.2, we need to make some general remarks. In order to turn legacy codeinto an agent a, we need to abstract from the given code and describe its main features. Such an abstraction is given by the set of all datatypes and functions the software is managing. We call this a *body of software code* and denote it by $\mathcal{S}^a =_{def} (\mathcal{T}_S{}^a, \mathcal{F}_S{}^a, \mathcal{C}_S{}^a)$. $\mathcal{F}_S{}^a$ is a set of predefined functions which makes access to the data objects $(\mathcal{T}_S{}^a)$ managed by the agent available to external processes. $\mathcal{C}_S{}^a$ are composition operators to build new datatypes from the given ones.

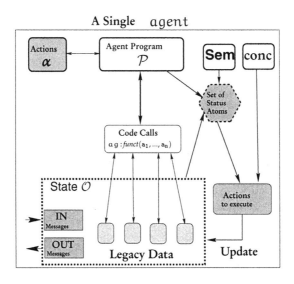

Figure 3.1.   An Agent in *IMPACT*.

To get a bird's eye view of *IMPACT*, here are the most important features (see Figure 3.1):

- Each *IMPACT* agent has certain *actions* α available. Agents act in their environment according to their *agent program* $\mathcal{P}$ and a well defined *semantics* **Sem** determining which of the actions the agent should execute.

- Each agent continually undergoes the following cycle:

  1. Get messages sent by other agents. This changes the state $\mathcal{O}$ of the agent.

  2. Determine (based on its program $\mathcal{P}$, its semantics **Sem** and its state $\mathcal{O}$) for each action α its *status* (permitted, obliged, forbidden, ...). The agent ends up with a *set of status atoms*.

  3. Based on a notion of concurrency **conc**, determine the actions that can be executed and update the state accordingly.

- *IMPACT* agents are built on top of arbitrary software code $\mathcal{S}^a =_{def} (\mathcal{T}_S{}^a, \mathcal{F}_S{}^a, \mathcal{C}_S{}^a)$ (*Legacy Data*).

- A methodology for transforming arbitrary software (legacy code) into an *agent* has been developed.

A complete description of all these notions is out of scope of this paper and we refer to [209] for a detailed presentation.

Before explaining an agent in more detail, we start with some remarks about the general architecture. In *IMPACT* agents communicate with other agents through the network. Not only can they send out (and receive) messages from other agents, they can also ask the server to find out about services that other agents offer. For example a planning agent (let us call it **A-SHOP**), confronted with a particular planning problem, can find out if there are agents out there with the data needed to solve the planning problem; or agents can provide **A-SHOP** with information about relevant legacy data.

In many applications a statistics agent is needed. This agent keeps track of distances between two given points and the authorised range or capacity of certain vehicles. This information can be stored in several databases. Another example is the supplier agent. It determines through its databases which vehicles are accessible at a given location.

DEFINITION 3.1 (STATE OF AN AGENT, $\mathcal{O}_{S(t)}$) *At any given point t in time, the state of an agent, denoted $\mathcal{O}_{S(t)}$, is the set of all data objects that are currently stored in the relations the agent handles—the types of these objects must be in the base set of types in $\mathcal{T}_S$.*

The state of the statistics agent consists of all tuples stored in the databases it handles. The state of the supplier agent is the set of all tuples describing which vehicles are accessible at a given location.

IMPACT Architecture

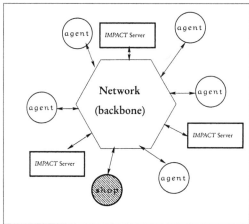

Figure 3.2.   SHOP as a planning agent in *IMPACT*.

We noted that agents can send and receive messages. There is therefore a special datastructure, the *message box*, part of each agent. This message box is just one of those types. Thus a state change already occurs when a message is received.

3.2   Language

Agents are specified in *IMPACT* through *agent programs*. The basic language of *IMPACT* does not allow to formalise *mental attitudes*, or *temporal* or *probabilistic reasoning*. However all these features have been investigated (see [65, 64, 63, 70, 72]) and the approach using both temporal as well as probabilistic reasoning is currently implemented.

In order to illustrate the language and semantics of *IMPACT* with an example, that is not too technical nor too trivial, we have chosen one involving temporal reasoning alone. This example serves to show the salient features of *IMPACT*.

EXAMPLE 3.2 (RESCUE SCENARIO I, TEMPORAL REASONING)
Consider a simplistic rescue operation where a natural calamity (e.g., a flood) has stranded many people. Rescuing these people requires close coordination between helicopters and ground vehicles. For the sake of this example, we assume the existence of:

1. A helicopter agent that conducts aerial reconnaissance and supports aerial rescues;

2. A set gv1, gv2, gv3 of ground vehicles that move along the ground to appropriate locations—such vehicles may include ambulances as well as earth moving vehicles.

3. An immobile command centre agent comc that coordinates between the helicopter and the ground vehicles.

Here is a typical statement that should be expressible in an agent language.

> "If the maximal time previously taken to ship some equipment E from location A to location B is T_1, and if equipment E is required to be at location B at time T, then ship E sometime between time $T - T_1 - 10$ and $T - T_1$."

This is a very reasonable statement to make not only in our rescue example, but in any logistics application. The time T might depend on the production schedule of the company at location B (which may be determined at run-time from a database), and T_1 likewise might depend on the identities of locations A, B (which may be instantiated at run time and whose locations might therefore need to be inferred at run-time from a database).

The second example, similar in spirit, is used to illustrate the *agentisation procedure*.

EXAMPLE 3.3 (RESCUE SCENARIO II, AGENTISING A PLANNER) *The planner SHOP [155] is a stand-alone system which did very well in planning competitions. It uses a particular framework to encode planning problems:* hierachical task networks. *While SHOP is a very efficient planner, it requires that all data is stored locally and given in a particular format (atomic facts in Lisp notation). Such planning systems usually support only one kind of reasoning:* symbolic or numeric, *but not both.*

How can such a planning system be agentised in *IMPACT* as a planning agent A-SHOP?

The typical test domain for a planner where data is heterogenous and stored at different places is a simple transportation planning problem for a rescue mission (NEO [154]). Computing plans involves performing a rescue mission where a task force is grouped and transported between an initial location *(the assembly point) and the NEO site (where the evacuees are located). After the troops arrived at the NEO site, evacuees are re-located to a safe haven.*

The planning task involves:

1. *selecting possible pre-defined routes, consisting of four or more segments each;*

2. *choosing a transportation mode for each segment;*

3. determining conditions such as whether communication exists with State Department personnel and the type of evacuee registration process.

Here we have four different IMPACT information sources available:

- **Transport Authority:** *Maintains information about the transportation assets available at different locations.*

- **Weather Authority:** *Maintains information about the weather conditions at the different locations.*

- **Airport Authority:** *Maintains information about availability and conditions of airports at different locations.*

- **Math Agent:** math *evaluates arithmetic expressions. Typical evaluations include to subtract a certain number of assets use for an operation and update time delays.*

Agentising given legacy code cannot be done automatically: the agent designer has to determine the abstraction level. In particular she has to decide which of the data structures find their way into the state of the agent (to be built) and which are considered mere "implementation details".

3.2.1   Specifications and Syntactical Aspects

In *IMPACT*, each agent a is built on top of a body of software code (built in any programming language) that supports a well defined application programmer interface (either part of the code itself, or developed to augment the code).

DEFINITION 3.4 (SOFTWARE CODE) *We may characterise the code on top of which an agent a is built as a triple $S^a =_{def} (T_S{}^a, F_S{}^a, C_S{}^a)$ where:*

1. *$T_S{}^a$ is the set of all data types managed by S,*

2. *$F_S{}^a$ is the set of predefined (API) functions over $T_S{}^a$ through which external processes may access a's data, and*

3. *$C_S{}^a$ is a set of type composition operations. A type composition operator is a partial n-ary function c which takes as input types $\tau_1, \ldots, \tau_n$ and yields as output a type $c(\tau_1, \ldots, \tau_n)$.*

This characterisation of a piece of software code is widely used (cf. the *Object Data Management Group*'s *ODMG* standard [43] and the *CORBA* framework [207]).

Each agent also has a message box having a well defined set of associated code calls that can be invoked by external programs.

EXAMPLE 3.5 (RESCUE SCENARIO I) *Consider the rescue mission described earlier. The* heli *agent may have the following data types and code calls.*

- *Data Types: speed, bearing of type* int, location *of type* point *(record containing x, y, z fields), nextdest of type* string, *and inventory—a relation having schema* (Item, Qty, Unit).

- *Functions:*
    - heli : *location*()*: which returns the* (x, y, z) *coordinates of the current position of the helicopter.*
    - heli : *inventory*(Item)*: returns a pair of the form* $\langle Qty, Unit \rangle$. *For example,* heli : *inventory*(blood) *may return* $\langle 25, litres \rangle$ *specifying that the helicopter currently has* 25 *units of blood available.*

An agent's state may change because it took an action, or because it received a message. We assume that except for appending messages to an agent a's mailbox, another agent b cannot directly change a's state. However, it might do so indirectly by sending the other agent a message requesting a change.

EXAMPLE 3.6 (RESCUE SCENARIO I: STATE) *For instance, at a given instant of time, the state of the* heli *agent may consist of location* $=$ $\langle 45, 50, 9000 \rangle$, *and inventory containing the tuples:* $\langle fuel, 125, gallons \rangle$, $\langle blood, 25, litres \rangle$, $\langle bandages, 50, - \rangle$, $\langle cotton, 20, lbs \rangle$.

Queries and/or conditions may be evaluated w.r.t. an agent state using the notion of a code call atom and a code call condition (CC) defined below.

DEFINITION 3.7 (CODE CALL (**CC**)/CODE CALL ATOM) *If* S *is the name of a software package,* f *is a function defined in this package, and* $(d_1, \ldots, d_n)$ *is a tuple of arguments of the input type of* f, *then the term* $S : f(d_1, \ldots, d_n)$ *is called a* code call *(denoted by* **CC***).*
If cc *is a code call, and* X *is either a variable symbol, or an object of the output type of* cc, *then* in(X, cc) *is called a* code call atom.

If X is a variable over type τ and τ is a record structure with field f, then X.f is a variable ranging over objects of the type of field f.

DEFINITION 3.8 (CODE CALL CONDITION (**CC**))

1. *Every code call atom is a code call condition.*

2. *If* s, t *are either variables or objects, then* s $=$ t *is a code call condition.*

3. *If* s, t *are either integers/real valued objects, or are variables over the integers/reals, then* s $<$ t, s $>$ t, s $\geq$ t, s $\leq$ t *are code call conditions.*

4. If χ_1, χ_2 are code call conditions, then χ_1 & χ_2 is a code call condition.

For example, $in(\texttt{X}, \texttt{heli}: inventory(\texttt{fuel}))$ & $\texttt{X.Qty} < 50$ is a code call condition that is satisfied whenever the helicopter has less than 50 gallons of fuel left.

The code call condition

$in(\texttt{FinanceRec}, \texttt{rel}: select(finRel, date, " = ", "\text{Nov. 99}"))$ &
$\texttt{FinanceRec.sales} \geq 10K$ &
$in(\texttt{C}, \texttt{excel}: chart(excFile, \texttt{FinanceRec}, day))$ &
$in(\texttt{Slide}, \texttt{ppt}: include(\texttt{C}, "\texttt{presnt.ppt}"))$

is a complex condition that accesses and merges data across a relational database, an Excel file, and a PowerPoint file. It first selects all financial records associated with "Nov. 99": this is done with the variable FinanceRec in the first line. It then filters out those records having sales more than $10K$ (second line). Using the remaining records, an Excel chart is created with day of sale on the x-axis and the resulting chart is included in the PowerPoint file "presentation.ppt" (fourth line).

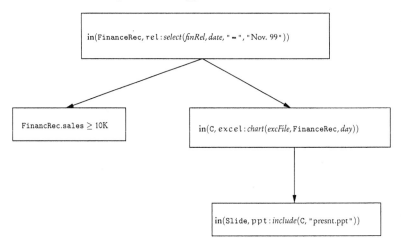

Figure 3.3. A code call evaluation graph

In the above example, it is very important that the first code call be evaluable. If, for example, the constant $finRel$ were a variable, then

$$\texttt{rel}: select(\texttt{finRel}, date, " = ", "\text{Nov. 99}")$$

would not be evaluable, unless there were another condition instantiating this variable.

We have introduced syntactic conditions, similar to *safety* in classical databases, to ensure *evaluability* of CCC's. It is also quite easy to store CCC's as evaluation graphs (see Figure 3.3), thereby making explicit the dependency relation between its constituents (see [71]).

Code call conditions provide a simple, yet powerful language syntax to access heterogeneous data structures and legacy software code. However, in general their use in agent programs is not constrained: it is perfectly possible that a CCC cannot be evaluated (and thus the status of actions cannot be determined). A reason for this could be uninstantiated variables (so that the underlying functions cannot be executed).

Actions in *IMPACT*

Each agent has an associated action-base describing various actions that the agent is capable of executing. An action (whose behaviour is that of a partial function from states to states) is implemented by a body of code in any suitable imperative (or declarative) programming language. The agent reasons about actions via a set of preconditions and effects defining the conditions an agent state must satisfy for the action to be considered executable, and the new state that results from such an execution. We assume that the preconditions and effects associated with an action correctly specify the behaviour of the code implementing the action. Note, that in addition to changing the state of the agent, an action may change the state of other agents' msgboxes.

Here is an example of a timed action *drive*() of the truck agent which may be described via the following components:

Name: *drive*(From, To, Highway)

Schema: (String,String,String)

Pre: in(From, truck : *location*())

Dur: $\{T \mid in(X, math : distance(From, To)) \,\&\, in(T, math : compute(\frac{60X}{70}))\}$

Tet:

       1st arg   : rel: $\{20\}$
       2nd arg : $\{in(\text{NewPosition}, truck : location(X_{now}))\}$
       3rd arg : $\{in(\text{OldPosition}, truck : location(X_{now} - 20))\}$

The **Tet** part says that the truck agent updates its location every 20 minutes (assuming a time period is equal to 1 minute) during the expected time it takes it to drive the distance between From to To at 70km per hour.

3.2.2   Semantics and Verification

One of the main features of *IMPACT* is that it has a precise, formal semantics based on the notion of *agent programs*. These programs are, from an abstract point of view, logic programs (*if-then-else* rules). The semantics of such programs has been investigated extensively in the last three decades. Consequently there is a vast amount of techniques we can build on.

Our language is not purpose-specific: it is a general framework to design arbitrary agents collaborating together. While the original framework did not support *temporal* or *probabilistic* reasoning, these features are currently implemented.

While we have not yet developed the formal machinery for *verifying* agents, the path for doing so is certainly laid.

Each agent has (i) a set of **integrity constraints** $\mathcal{IC}$—only states that satisfy these constraints are considered to be *valid* or *legal* states, (ii) a notion of **concurrency** specifying how to combine a set of actions into a single action, (iii) a set of **action constraints** that define the circumstances under which certain actions may be concurrently executed, and (iv) an **agent program** that determines what actions the agent can take, what actions the agent cannot take, and what actions the agent must take. Agent programs are defined in terms of status atoms defined below.

DEFINITION 3.9 (STATUS ATOM/STATUS SET) *If $\alpha(\vec{t})$ is an action, and $Op \in \{\mathbf{P}, \mathbf{F}, \mathbf{W}, \mathbf{Do}, \mathbf{O}\}$, then $Op\alpha(\vec{t})$ is called a* status atom. *If A is a status atom, then $A, \neg A$ are called* status literals. *A* status set *is a finite set of ground status atoms.*

Intuitively, $\mathbf{P}\alpha$ means α is permitted, $\mathbf{F}\alpha$ means α is forbidden, $\mathbf{O}\alpha$ means α is obligatory, $\mathbf{Do}\,\alpha$ means α is to be done, and $\mathbf{W}\alpha$ means that the obligation to perform α is waived. Note that these operators are not independent from each other. For example, an action α cannot have the status $\mathbf{F}$ and $\mathbf{O}$ at the same time. And $\mathbf{O}\alpha$ should always imply $\mathbf{Do}\,\alpha$. These interrelations are taken into account by the semantics.

DEFINITION 3.10 (AGENT PROGRAM) *An agent program $\mathcal{P}$ is a finite set of rules of the form $A \leftarrow \chi \,\&\, L_1 \,\&\, \ldots \,\&\, L_n$, where χ is a code call condition, L_i are status literals and A is a status atom.*

Several alternative semantics for agent programs are presented in [78, 77].

For example, the heli agent in our Rescue Example may execute the action $fly(\texttt{"BigRag"}, \texttt{"StonyPoint"})$. This action lasts for a period of time during which the location of heli is changing continuously. More importantly, if we know the location of the plane *now* and we know the plane's velocity and climb angle, we can precisely compute its location in the future (assuming no change in these parameters). Thus, in order to specify a *timed action*, we must:

1. Specify an estimate of the total amount of time it takes for the action to be "completed".

2. Specify exactly how the state of the agent changes *while* the action is being executed.

It is worth noting that the duration of an action can be precisely specified in some cases, but not in others. For instance, saying that *the action drive(i95, south, 60) should be executed for 2 hours* is a precise specification saying that the action "Drive south on Interstate I-95 at 60 mph" is to be executed for 2 hours. However, it is hard to specify durations of actions such as *drive(washington, baltimore)*. In this case, the above definition requires an *estimate* to be provided.

DEFINITION 3.11 (TEMPORAL AGENT RULE/PROGRAM $\mathcal{TP}$) *A temporal agent rule is an expression of the form* $Op\,\alpha \,:\, [tah_1, tah_2] \,\leftarrow\, \rho_1 : ta_1 \,\&\, \cdots \,\&\, \rho_n : ta_n$, *where* $Op \in \{\mathbf{P}, \mathbf{Do}, \mathbf{F}, \mathbf{O}, \mathbf{W}\}$, *and* $\rho_1 : ta_1, \ldots, \rho_n : ta_n$ *are* **tascs**[1]. *A temporal agent program* (tap) *is a finite set of temporal agent rules.*

> **Intuitive Reading of Temporal Agent Rule**
> *"If for all* $1 \leq i \leq n$, *there exists a time point* t_i *such that* ρ_i *is true at time* t_i *such that* $t_i \in ta_i$ *then* $Op\,\alpha$ *is true at some point* $t \geq t_{now}$ *(i.e., now or in the future) such that* $tah_1 \leq t \leq tah_2$".

How can **taps** be used to express the statement in Example 3.2? We use two relational databases—one called `shipdata` containing at least the attributes `shiptime, orig, dest` (and perhaps other ones as well) which specifies data (such as shipping time) associated with past shipments. The other relational table is called `sched` which has at least the attributes `reqtime, place, item` specifying which items are required at what time by what places.

> $\mathbf{Do}\ ship(\mathrm{P, A, B}) : [\mathrm{T} - \mathrm{T}_1 - 10, \mathrm{T} - \mathrm{T}_1] \leftarrow$
> $\quad (\mathbf{in}(\mathrm{T}_1, \mathrm{db} : sql(\text{'SELECT time FROM data WHERE orig} = \mathrm{A}\,\&\,\text{dest} = \mathrm{B}))) \,\&$
> $\mathbf{in}(\mathrm{T}, \mathrm{db} : sql(\text{'SELECT reqtime FROM place WHERE item} = \mathrm{P}'))) : [\mathrm{X}_{now}, \mathrm{X}_{now}].$

Here is another example. *"If a prediction package expects a stock to rise K% after T_K units of time and $K \geq 25$ then buy the stock at time $(X_{now} + T_K - 2)$."* We assume a prediction package that given a stock uses some stock expertise to predict the change in the value of the stock at future time points. This

---

[1] A **tasc** (temporal action status conjunct) is, intuitively, a conjunction of temporal status actions. We refer to [63] for further detail.

function returns a set of pairs of the form (T, C). Intuitively, this says that T time units from now, the stock price will change by C percent (positive or negative).

$$\textbf{Do } buy(\textsc{s}) : [X_{now} + X.T - 2, X_{now} + X.T - 2] \leftarrow$$
$$(\text{in}(X, \text{pred}: dest(\textsc{s})) \ \& \ X.C \geq 25) : [X_{now}, X_{now}].$$

Finally, here is a **tap** using several rules and different status atoms.

1. $\textbf{F}drive(\text{was}, \text{bal}, \text{hw295}) : [t_{now}, t_{now} + 2] \leftarrow$
   $\quad \text{in}(\text{hw295}, \text{msgbox}: gatherWarning(\text{comc})) : [t_{now} - 3, t_{now}]$

2. $\textbf{Do } fill\_fuel() : [t_{now}, t_{now}] \leftarrow$
   $\quad \text{in}(\textbf{true}, \text{truck}: tank\_empty()) : [t_{now} - 2, t_{now}]$

3. $\textbf{O} order\_item(\text{fa\_bag}) : [t_{now}, t_{now} + 4] \leftarrow$
   $\quad \text{in}(1, \text{truck}: inventory(\text{fa\_bag}))[t_{now} - 3, t_{now}]$

4. $\textbf{P} drive(\text{was}, \text{bal}, \text{hw95}) : [t_{now}, t_{now}] \leftarrow$
   $\quad \text{in}(\textbf{false}, \text{truck}: tank\_empty()) : [t_{now}, t_{now}] \ \&$
   $\quad \textbf{F} drive(\text{was}, \text{bal}, \text{hw295}) : [t_{now} + 1, t_{now} + 2]$

Figure 3.4 shows two rules (with **Do**'s in the head) of the monitoring agent in **A-SHOP**.

Our approach is to base the semantics of agent programs on *consistent* and *closed* status sets. Consistent means that there are no inconsistencies (such as $\textbf{F}\alpha$ and $\textbf{P}\alpha$ in the same set) and closed means that when $\textbf{Do } \alpha$ is in the set, then so is $\textbf{P}\alpha$.

However, we also have to take into account not only the rules of the program but also the integrity constraints $\mathcal{IC}$. This leads us to the notion of a feasible status set. The operator $\textbf{App}_{\mathcal{P}, \mathcal{O}_S}(S)$ is similar to the immediate consequence operator in logic programming: it computes all the consequences obtainable from applying all agent rules once.

DEFINITION 3.12 (FEASIBLE STATUS SET) *Let $\mathcal{P}$ be an agent program, and let $\mathcal{O}_S$ be an agent state. Then, a status set S is a* feasible status set *for $\mathcal{P}$ on $\mathcal{O}_S$, if the following conditions hold:*

(S1) *(closure under the program rules)* $\quad \textbf{App}_{\mathcal{P}, \mathcal{O}_S}(S) \subseteq S$;

(S2) *(deontic/action consistency)* $\quad S$ *is deontically and action consistent;*

(S3) *(deontic/action closure)* $\quad S$ *is action closed and deontically closed;*

(S4) *(state consistency)* $\quad \mathcal{O}'_S \models \mathcal{IC}$, *where $\mathcal{O}'_S = apply(\textbf{Do}(S), \mathcal{O}_S)$ is the state which results after taking all actions in $\textbf{Do}(S)$ on the state $\mathcal{O}_S$.*

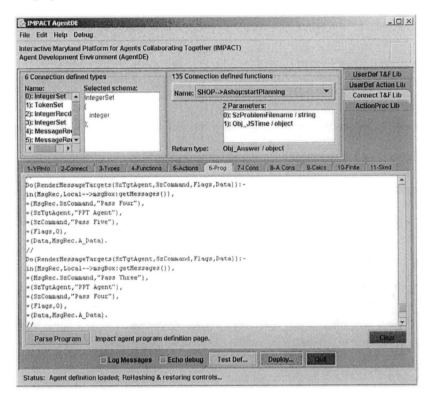

Figure 3.4. AgentDE Program

The last condition ensures that the successor state (when all doable actions are executed) still satisfies the integrity constraints $\mathcal{IC}$.

The semantics of agent programs is then defined by *rational status sets*.

DEFINITION 3.13 (GROUNDEDNESS; RATIONAL STATUS SET) *A status set S is* grounded, *if there exists no status set $S' \subsetneq S$ such that S' satisfies conditions* (S1)–(S3) *of a feasible status set.*

A status set S is a rational status set *if S is a feasible status set and S is grounded.*

Thus given an agent program, our semantics computes all rational status sets of this program. In the case of positive agent programs (all examples in this chapter have this property) it can be shown that there always exists exactly one rational status set. Rational status sets are natural generalisations of stable models (or answer sets) in logic programming.

Figure 3.5 shows the successful compilation of an agent program (the monitoring agent in A-SHOP). In the first phase the rules are organised in several layers, then the program is unfolded (sometimes producing more rules but obtaining an optimised version), the data connection is checked, and the status set is generated.

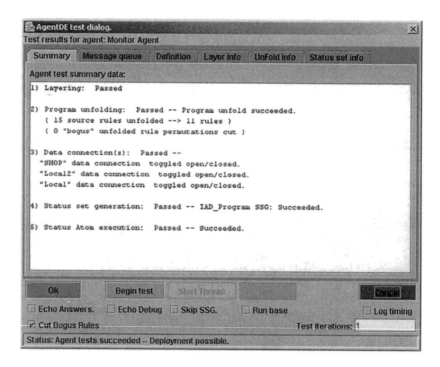

Figure 3.5.   AgentDE Summary Table

3.2.3   Software Engineering Issues

We have finished the *IMPACT* implementation based on our main theory (extensions are underway for temporal programs, temporal probabilistic programs, etc.). Several nontrivial multiagent applications have been developed with *IMPACT*. The *IMPACT* implementation has a simple Java-based, web accessible interface which allows the user to specify an agent's different component definitions (type, function, action, agent program, etc.) and communication between agents. It provides an easy way to maintain and test the different components within a multiagent system. We will introduce it further later in this chapter.

As we showed in the previous section, *IMPACT* is able to *agentise* any software program and plug it into the provided solution. *IMPACT* supports this both in its theory and in its implementation. *Code call condition* mechanism supports queries to arbitrary legacy code or specialised data structures. Moreover, the implementation of *IMPACT* supports execution of code call conditions over a wide variety of software packages.

We also consider the reliability issue in our method. The reliability of *IMPACT* is provided by replication and by minimising the dependency of individual agents in *IMPACT*. We refer to [209] for further detail.

3.2.4 Other features of the language

As already mentioned in the beginning, *IMPACT* is based on two important features.

Complexity: special emphasis is put on identifying classes of programs that can be efficiently implemented. The class of *regular* agents (based on a special class of agent programs) ensures that its complexity modulo the underlying legacy code is only polynomial [79].

Legacy code: existing legacy code can be turned into an *IMPACT* agent (*agentisation*). This is illustrated with **A-SHOP**, which is an agentised version of **SHOP**, a well-known planning system ([66, 68, 69, 67]).

Our framework supports the design of mobile agents because mobility can be considered as an action that any agent can execute. In addition, we show in [209] that Java applets can be viewed as IMPACT agents.

Our language is modular and can be easily extended by new constructs. Not only syntactic sugar, but also non trivial features such as temporal or probabilistic reasoning can be incorporated (through annotated logic programs). These extensions are not always trivial, but the overall system is designed so as to allow them. We consider this to be a salient feature of our framework.

Complexity Issues

We mentioned in Subsection 3.2.1 the condition of safeness to ensure evaluability of a code call. We also mentioned that an evaluable **CC** does not need to terminate. Consider the code call

$$\text{in}(X, \text{math}: geq(25)) \ \&$$
$$\text{in}(Y, \text{math}: square(X)) \ \& \ Y \leq 2000,$$

which constitutes all numbers that are less than 2000 and that are squares of an integer greater than or equal to 25.

Clearly, over the integers there are only finitely many ground substitutions that cause this code call condition to be true. Furthermore, this code call condition is safe. However, its evaluation may never terminate. The reason for this is that safety requires that we first compute the set of all integers that are greater than 25, leading to an infinite computation.

Thus, in general, we must impose some restrictions on code call conditions to ensure that they are finitely evaluable. This is precisely what the condition of *strong safeness* ([79, 209]) does for the code-call conditions. Intuitively, by requiring that the code call condition is safe, we are ensuring that it is executable and by requiring that it is strongly safe, we are ensuring that it will only return finitely many answers.

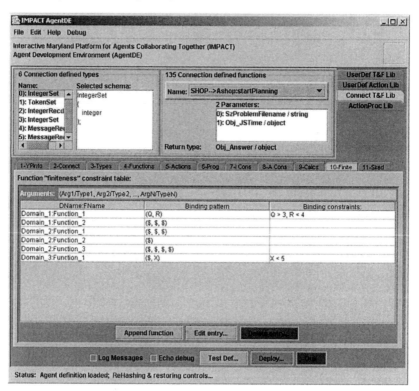

Figure 3.6. AgentDE Finiteness Table

Note that the problem of deciding whether an arbitrary code call execution terminates is undecidable (and so is the problem of deciding whether a code call condition χ holds in $\mathcal{O}$). Therefore we need some input of the agent designer (or of the person who is responsible for the legacy code the agent is built upon). The information needed is stored in a *finiteness table* (see [79, 209] and Figure 3.6). This information is used in the *purely syntactic* notion of strong safeness. It is a *compile-time check*, an extension of the well-known (syntactic) safety condition in databases.

Agentisation

Our Example 3.3 serves to illustrate how to turn a planner into an planning agent within a multi-agent environment.

SHOP, as an *HTN* planner, is based on the concepts of *tasks*, *operators* and *methods*. Methods are used to decompose a nonprimitive task and form the heart of *HTN* planning.

A comparison between *IMPACT*'s actions and SHOP's methods shows that *IMPACT* actions correspond to fully instantiated methods. While SHOP's methods and operators are based on STRIPS, the first step is to modify the atoms in SHOP's preconditions and effects, so that SHOP's preconditions will be evaluated by *IMPACT*'s code call mechanism and the effects will change the state of the *IMPACT* agents. This is a fundamental change in the representation of SHOP. In particular, it requires replacing SHOP's methods and operators with *agentised* methods and operators. These are defined as follows.

DEFINITION 3.14 (RESCUE II, **Agentised Operator**) *An* agentised operator *is an expression of the form* (**AgentOp** $h\ \chi_{add}\ \chi_{del}$), *where h (the* head*) is a primitive task and* χ_{add} *and* χ_{del} *are lists of code calls (called the* add- *and* delete-lists*). The set of variables in the tasks in* χ_{add} *and* χ_{del} *is a subset of the set of variables in h.*

LEMMA 3.15 (RESCUE II, **Evaluating Agentised Operators**) *Let* (**AgentOp** $h\ \chi_{add}\ \chi_{del}$) *be an agentised operator. If the add and delete-lists* χ_{add} *and* χ_{del} *are strongly safe wrt. the variables in h, the problem of applying the agentised operator to* $\mathcal{O}$ *can be algorithmically solved.*

In SHOP, preconditions were logical atoms, and SHOP would infer these preconditions from its current state of the world using Horn-clause inference. In contrast, the preconditions in an agentised method are *IMPACT*'s code call conditions rather than logical atoms. Also A-SHOP (the agentised version of SHOP) does not use Horn-clause inference to establish these preconditions but instead simply invokes those code calls, which are calls to other agents (which may be Horn-clause theorem provers or may instead be something entirely different). This opens the way to use arbitrary reasoning mechanisms and data distributed over the net.

THEOREM 3.16 (RESCUE SCENARIO II, **Sound- and Completeness**) *Let* $\mathcal{O}$ *be a state and* $\mathcal{D}$ *be a collection of agentised methods and operators. If* *all the preconditions in the agentised methods and add- and delete-lists in the agentised operators are strongly safe wrt. the respective variables in the heads, then A-SHOP is sound and complete.*

Figure 3.7 shows a method for our application to logistics planning. The method indicates how to transport a cargo that has a certain weight between two locations. The method calls the statistics agent three times, in order to evaluate the *distance* between two geographic locations: (1) the *authorised range* of a certain aircraft type (the authorised range is lower than the real distance that the aircraft can fly), and (2) the *authorised capability* (in metric tones) of an aircraft. The method calls the *supplier* agent to evaluate the cargo planes that are available at a location.

Head:
   AirTransport(LocFrom, LocTo, Cargo, CargoWeight)

Preconditions:
   in(CargoPL, supplier : *cargoPlane*(LocFrom))&
   in(Dist, statistics : *distance*(LocFrom, locTo))&
   in(DCargoPL, statistics : *authorRange*(CargoPL))&
   Dist $\leq$ DCargoPL&
   in(CCargoPL, statistics : *authorCapacity*(CargoPL))&
   CargoWeight $\leq$ CCargoPL&

Subtasks:
   load(Cargo, LocFrom)
   fly(Cargo, LocFrom, LocTo)
   unload(Cargo, LocTo)

Figure 3.7. Agentised method for a logistics problem.

This top level task is decomposed into several subtasks, one for each segment in the route that the task force must cover (these segments are predetermined as part of the problem description). Within each segment, A-SHOP must plan for the means of transportation (planes, helicopters, vehicles, etc.) to be used and select a route for that segment. The selection of the means of transportation depends on their availability for that segment, the weather conditions, and, in the case of airplanes, the availability and conditions of airports. The selection of the route depends on the transportation vehicle used and may lead to backtracking. For example, the choice of ground transportation assets needs to be revised if no roads are available, or they are blocked, or too risky to take.

Our test domain was a simplification of the actual conditions that occur in practice. Primarily because many more information sources are available in practice, and as such the resulting plans will be more complicated.

A-SHOP's knowledge base included six agentised operators and 22 agentised methods. We ran our experiments on 30 problems of increasing size and refer to [244, 69, 67] for detailed results.

3.3 Platform

3.3.1 Features of the platform

The *IMPACT* system consists of five major software components to support the development and deployment of *IMPACT* agents.

Agent Development Environment. Agent developers can easily build and test agents within the *IMPACT* Agent Development Environment (*AgentDE* for short). As described earlier, the core parts of an *IMPACT* agent are:

1. a set of data type definitions and *API* function calls manipulated by the agent;

2. a set of actions that the agent may take;

3. a set of integrity constraints $\mathcal{IC}$ on the agent state and action constraints $\mathcal{AC}$;

4. an agent program $\mathcal{P}$ specifying the behaviour of the agent;

5. a notion of concurrency **conc**.

The *AgentDE* provides a network accessible, easy-to-use graphical user interface through which an agent developer can specify all the above parameters of an agent, compile and then test if they work properly.

AgentDE contains libraries of data types, *API* functions, actions and notions of concurrency. When the agent developer builds a new agent, each data type must be explicitly defined via the *AgentDE*. The agent manipulates its data types via *API* function calls, which can be defined within the *AgentDE*. Similarly, the developer needs to specify a set of actions that the agent can execute via *AgentDE*. Figure 3.8 shows how the developer can reuse actions in the library and assign them to the monitoring agent.

Figure 3.9 shows the interface of the *AgentDE* when the developer has finished specifying the data types, *API* functions and actions. The tab marked "Calcs" allows the user to specify the notion of concurrency[2] he wants to

---

[2]For example a very simple **conc** would be to just take the union of all add-lists and the union of all delete-lists. A more sophisticated **conc** would check whether all actions can be ordered in a way such that there are no conflicting actions, and then execute them one after the other. The latter is of course more complex than the first.

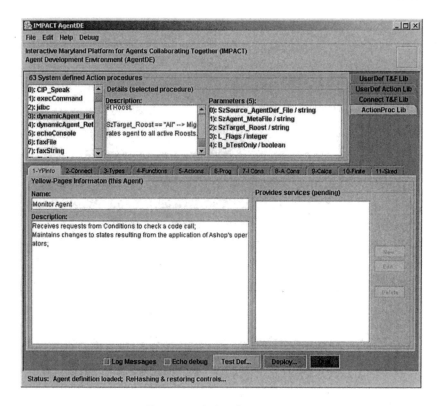

Figure 3.8. Actions for monitor

use. All these new items are added to the appropriate library so that during the development process, whenever the developer accesses the *AgentDE*, the definitions will be directly imported from the libraries for use.

After defining these parameters, the agent developer may start testing the agent. The *AgentDE* performs compile-time checks such as strong safety check, deontic satisfaction, and boundedness check. Pressing "Test Program" in Figure 3.9 triggers the test. When the test is started, unfolding is done first, then the data connections requested by the program are tested and established. After the test phase is completed, status sets are generated and executed. Figure 3.10 shows the status set computations.

IMPACT Connection. The *IMPACT* connection library allows *IM-PACT* agents to access third party platforms. The developer can define a connection alias and specific parameters for the target connection in the *AgentDE* Connection specification dialog. Figure 3.11 shows the *AgentDE*

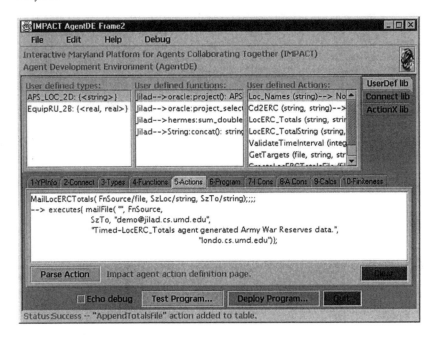

Figure 3.9. Actions in *AgentDE*

interface with the accepted Jilad connection definition, which taps a Hermes data mediator, through the remote Hermes interface accessed through the jilad.cs.umd.edu:8222 port. When a connection is established, *IMPACT* can execute code call over the data source and process the returned requests. Some currently implemented examples also include IBM Aglet, Oracle servers, ODBC (Open Database Connectivity), JDBC (Java Database Connectivity) and *CORBA* (Common Object Request Broker Architecture).

IMPACT Server. The *IMPACT* Server provides various services that are required by a group of agents as a whole. It supports the following services:

Registration Services: When the agent developer deploys an agent within the *IMPACT AgentDE*, it automatically provides her with the option of registering this agent with the registration server. The developer can register the services provided by the agent and also specify who can use those services.

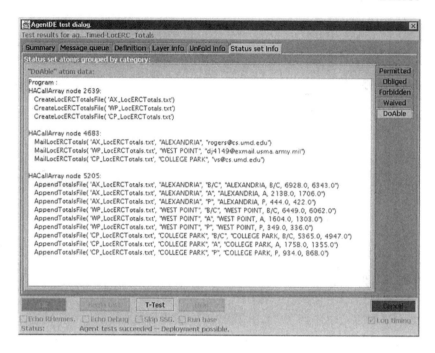

Figure 3.10. AgentDE Status Set Screen

Yellow Pages Services: the Yellow Pages Server can access the data structures created by the Registration Server. *IMPACT* agents can find the desired services by other agents via the Yellow Pages Server.

Type Services: Agent developers can specify the datatypes they use as well as the relationship between the newly created datatypes and other existing types within the *IMPACT* Type Server.

Thesaurus Server: This server receives requests when new agent services are being registered and when the *IMPACT* Yellow Pages Server is looking for agents providing a service.

Ontology Services: The *IMPACT* server is able to provide ontology services. An agent can reformulate its query in terms the other agent can understand.

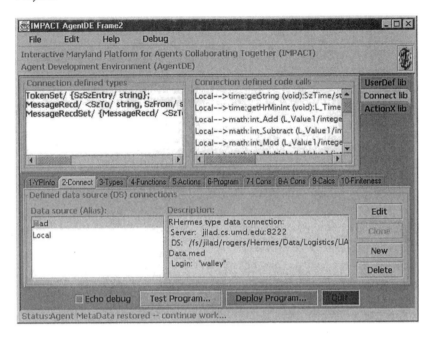

Figure 3.11. AgentDE Connect Library Screen

Agent Roost. An agent roost is a location where a set of deployed agents resides (Figure 3.12 shows the five agents in **A-SHOP**: the screen depicts the moment when the codecallconditions agent is active and sends a message to the monitoring agent). An agent roost serves as a duty officer since it manages all messages for this set of agents. Initially, all agents are inactive. When one of these agents receives a message, the agent roost includes it in this agent's message box and lets it run. If an agent sends out a message to another internal agent (i.e., an agent who is managed by the same roost), this message can be delivered by the roost in the same way. If the message is addressed to an external agent, the roost first contacts the *IMPACT* server to determine the location of the target agent. It then routes the message to the appropriate roost, which will pass it to the specified agent.

Agent Log. The agent log allows an agent developer to maintain a record of agent communication and agent actions. The log supports log queries by content or time, and action browse, playback of video, text and image message objects. It can be used for many purposes such as record keeping, usage statistics, and it is essential for monitoring system performance and debugging.

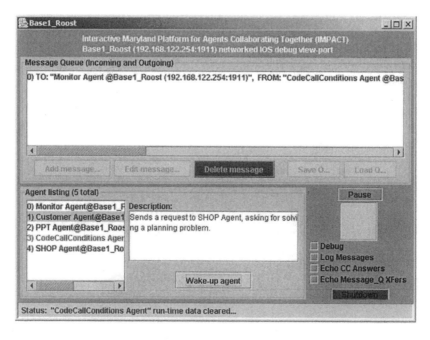

Figure 3.12. Agent Roost

3.3.2   Available tools and documentation

A tutorial about *IMPACT* can be found at `http://www.cs.umd.edu/projects/impact`. In particular, there is an *IMPACT* software library user documentation, which is available at `http://www.cs.umd.edu/projects/impact/Docs`, and includes: *(1)* implementation overview, *(2)* introduction of agent instantiation life cycle, *(3)* agent definition syntax, *(4)* sample agent development, and *(5)* selected user and developer code *API* JavaDocs.

3.3.3   Standards compliance, interoperability and portability

The implementation code consists of three main components: the *IMPACT AgentDE* (containing a series of compilers, written in Java, which render an agent instantiation from a given agent definition (text)); the *IMPACT* Yellow-pages server, written in Java and C, provides agent directory lookup services necessary for agent construction and run-time communication; the *IMPACT* Roost, written in Java, provides a run-time environment for *IMPACT* agents to work, sleep, or travel the network. Most of the implementation code is written currently compliant to the Java 1.2 specification. This provides maximal code portability across operating systems and platforms. It does, however, require loading Java 1.2 runtime library on the target platform. The existing implementation code libraries appear fairly generic. The code should prove readily adaptable to most micro-device environments through cross-compilation techniques. Some applications have been created to show the interoperability between *IMPACT* agents and IBM Aglets.

Future enhancements include an enhanced Roost network viewport for debugging global agent communities distributed across multiple roosts, and Java Jini enabled server front-ends to facilitate network configuration.

3.4 Applications supported by the language and the platform

The *IMPACT* project has built applications in the following areas:

1. US Army Logistics Integration Agency's "Virtual Operations Centre" involves the integration of a wide variety of distributed, heterogeneous databases, together with diverse alert, analysis and visualisation requirements.

2. US Army Research Laboratory's "Combat Information Processor" project where *IMPACT* is used to provide yellow pages matchmaking services, and is also providing alert mechanisms for multiple users with diverse battlefield monitoring requirements.

3. Aerospace applications where *IMPACT* technology has led to the development of a multi-agent solution to the "Controlled Flight into Terrain" problem which is the single largest cause of human fatalities in aircraft crashes (Washington Post, Feb. 7, 1998).

4. US Army STRICOM's JANUS project where *IMPACT* technology is used to analyse massive amounts of simulation data.

5. Coordinated route and flight planning applications over free terrain.

New applications in the banking and finance sector are under consideration. In addition, *IMPACT* has been used for student projects in academia, including University of Maryland, Technical University of Vienna, The University of Manchester, and Clausthal Institute of Technology.

3.5 Final Remarks

IMPACT has been started by VS Subrahmanian in 1997 and its core has been developed in a series of papers [6, 78, 77, 79] and also in a book [209].

Chapter 4

CLAIM AND SYMPA:
A PROGRAMMING ENVIRONMENT FOR
INTELLIGENT AND MOBILE AGENTS

Amal El Fallah Seghrouchni and Alexandru Suna

LIP6 · CNRS UMR 7606 University of Paris 6
8, Rue du Capitaine Scott
75015, Paris
{ Amal.Elfallah,Alexandru.Suna } @lip6.fr

Abstract   The multi-agent systems (MAS) paradigm is one of the most important and promising approaches to occur in computer science during the 90s. However, for an effective use of the agent technology in real life applications, specific programming languages are required. CLAIM is a high-level agent-oriented programming language that combines cognitive aspects such as knowledge, goals and capabilities and computational elements such as communication, mobility and concurrency in order to reduce the gap between the design and the implementation phase. CLAIM has an operational semantics that is a first step towards the verification of the built MAS. The language is supported by a distributed platform called SyMPA, implemented in Java, compliant with the specifications of the MASIF standard from the OMG, that offers all the necessary mechanisms for a secure execution of a distributed MAS. CLAIM and SyMPA have been used for developing several applications that proved the expressiveness of the language and the robustness of the platform.

Keywords: Agent-oriented programming, mobile agents, ambient calculus.

4.1   Motivation

The emergence of autonomous agents and multi-agent technology is one of the most exciting and important events to occur in computer science during the 1990s. The main focus of the multi-agent systems (MAS) community has been on the development of informal and formal tools (*e.g.* consortiums such as FIPA[1] or OMG[2] have attempted to propose a wide range of standards to cover the main aspects of MAS engineering), concepts (*e.g.* concerning mental or social attitudes, communication, co-operation, organization), techniques (*e.g.* AUML[3]) and modal languages (*e.g.* BDI[182]) in order to be able to analyze and specify MAS. Unfortunately, the design of declarative languages and tools which can effectively support MAS programming and allow implementing the key concepts of MAS remained at an embryonic stage. In addition, the potential of MAS technology for large-scale, cross-functional deployment of general purpose in industrial setting has been hampered by insufficient progress on infrastructure, architecture, security and scalability issues.

Recently, the mobile agents technology (the mobility is seen as a transversal property for agents) tries to improve the systems' performances since it provides powerful programming constructs for designing distributed and mobile applications. Thanks to the mobile agents paradigm, it becomes easy to design *active entities* that move over the network and perform tasks on hosts (*target sites* or *computers*), thus reducing the network traffic and increasing the scalability and the flexibility of such applications.

Despite the plethora of approaches and platforms that have been proposed for mobile agents, the main focus remains on the development of mobile objects and processes. Mainly implemented using object-oriented frameworks, the mobile agents provide a collection of extensible classes modelling simple concepts of agent that are specified rather at the implementation level.

For an effective use of the MAS paradigm, we claim that specific high-level programming languages are required. The programming environment presented in this chapter is motivated by three main objectives:

1. Propose an agent oriented programming language that:

   - helps the designer to reduce the gap between the design and the implementation phases; *i.e.* the designer should think and implement using the same paradigm, namely through agents;

   - allows the representation of cognitive skills such as knowledge, beliefs, goals and more complex mechanisms such as planning, decision making and reasoning;

   - meets the requirements of mobile computation in order to support the geographic distribution of complex systems and of their computation over the net;

---

[1] FIPA on-line : http://www.fipa.org
[2] OMG : http://www.omg.org
[3] AUML : http://www.auml.org/

- allows the dynamic adaptability and reconfiguring of the MAS. Thanks to mobility, to the hierarchical representation of agents and to the language' features, our agents (and consequently the MAS) are able to reconfigure themselves autonomously, to acquire new knowledge and capabilities and to dynamically adapt their structure in accordance with the changes in the environment and the demands of target applications.

2. Make possible the verification of MAS. Indeed, at a short term we would like an agent-oriented programming language that allows the verification of the built systems. A first and necessary step towards developing methods for verifying formally agent-oriented programs is the design of a suitable operational semantics. It opens the way to the application of standard techniques like type systems or model-checking to the setting of agent-oriented programming.

3. Provide a distributed platform that supports the proposed language and the deployment and secure execution of mobile MAS.

To reach our objectives, we proposed a high-level declarative language called CLAIM (Computational Language for Autonomous, Intelligent and Mobile agents) [81] that combines the main advantages of the intelligent agents paradigm (*e.g.* intelligence, autonomy, communication primitives and cognitive skills) with those of the concurrent languages such as the ambient calculus [41] (*e.g.* concurrence, hierarchical representation of agents and mobility primitives). CLAIM has an operational semantics [83] that is a first step towards the verification of the built MAS. The language is supported by a distributed platform, called SyMPA (SYstem Multi-Platform of Agents) [211] that offers all the necessary mechanisms for the deployment of distributed MAS designed in CLAIM and for its secure execution.

4.2 Language

CLAIM is a high-level declarative language allowing to design intelligent and mobile agents.

4.2.1 Specifications and Syntactical Aspects

A MAS in CLAIM is a set of hierarchies of agents distributed over a network. The notion of hierarchy in our approach can be also seen as a membership relation. Thus, "an agent is sub-agent of another agent" means that he is contained in the higher-level agent. A CLAIM agent is a node in a hierarchy; he is an autonomous, intelligent and mobile entity that can be seen as a bounded place where the computation happens and has a parent, a list of local processes and a list of sub-agents. In addition, an agent has intelligent components such as knowledge, capabilities, goals, that allow a reactive or proactive behavior.

In CLAIM, agents and classes of agent can be defined using:

> *defineAgent agentName {*
>   *authority = null; | agentName ;*
>   *parent = null; | agentName ;*
>   *knowledge = null; | { (knowledge;)+ }*
>   *goals = null; | { (goal;)+ }*
>   *messages = null; | { (queueMessage;)+ }*
>   *capabilities = null; | { (capability;)+ }*
>   *processes = null; | { (process |)* process }*
>   *agents = null; | { (agentName;)+ }*
> *}*
> *defineAgentClass className ((arg,)*) {...}*

An new agent can be instantiated from an already defined class using the primitive:

> *newAgent name:className ((arg,)*)*

In CLAIM, variables (denoted by *?x*) can be used to replace agents' names, messages, goals, etc. There are global (for a class) or local (to a capability) variables. The agents' components we propose allow representing the agents' mental state, communication and mobility and will be presented below. Most of the components are *null* in the definition (*e.g.* parent, messages, etc.) but will evolve during the agent's execution.

An agent is uniquely identified in the MAS by his name and he belongs to an authority. Thus, the **authority** component is instantiated at the agent's creation and is composed of the authority and the name of the agent that has created the current agent. This component is necessary for security reasons (*e.g.* for authentication).

The agents in CLAIM are hierarchically represented, like the *ambients* [41]. So an agent's **parent** is represented by the name of the agent that currently contains him. When an agent is created, his parent and his authority indicate the same agent; after the migration, his parent will change, but his authority will always be the same.

The **knowledge** component contains pieces of information about other agents (*i.e.* about theirs capabilities or their classes) or about the world (divers propositions). This knowledge base is a set of elements of *knowledge* type, defined as follows:

> *knowledge ::=   agentName(capabilityName,message,effect)*
>   *| agentName:className*
>   *| proposition*

We can notice that the knowledge about other agents has a standard format, containing the name of the known agent and his class or capability. In addition, the user can define his own ontology of information about the world, represented as propositions containing a name and a list of arguments.

$$proposition = name(arg_1, arg_2, ..., arg_n)$$

Propositions can also be used for denoting goals or messages.

The current **goals** of an agent are represented as user-defined propositions, in accordance with the current application. The agent will try to achieve his goals using his capabilities or services offered by other agents.

The CLAIM agents communicate asynchronously using messages. Every agent has a queue for storing the received **messages**. The messages are processed using a FIFO policy and are used to activate capabilities. A message from the queue contains the sender of the message and the arrived message:

queueMessage ::= *agentName* > *message*

An agent can send messages to an agent (*unicast*), to all the agents in a class (*multicast*), or to all the agents in the system (*broadcast*), using the primitive:

send(receiver,message), where the receiver can be:

- *this* - the message is sent to himself;

- *parent* or *authority* - the message is sent to the agent's current parent or authority (the agent that created the current agent);

- *agentName* - the message is sent to the specified agent;

- *all* - the message is sent to all the running agents;

- *?Ag:className* - the message is sent to all the agents that have been instantiated from the specified class of agents;

In CLAIM there are three types of messages:

1. *propositions*, defined by the designer to suit the current application and used to activate capabilities;

2. the **messages concerning the knowledge**, used by agents to exchange information about their knowledge and capabilities. These messages have a predefined treatment, but a designer can write capabilities to treat them in a different manner:

- *tell(knowledge)* - to give an agent a piece of information; the specified knowledge is added in the agent's knowledge base.

- *askAllCapabilities()* - an agent requests all the capabilities of another agent; The later inform the first agent about all his capabilities, using the **tell** primitive.

- *askIfCapability(capabilityName)* - an agent asks another agent if he has the specified capability; If the later has this capability, he confirms using the **tell** communication primitive.

- *achieveCapability(capabilityName)* - an agent requests from another agent the execution of the specified capability; if this capability's condition is verified, it is executed.
- *askEffect(effect)* - to ask the achievement of an effect from another agent.
- *doneEffect(effect)* - to confirm the accomplishment of an effect.

3. the **mobility messages** are used by the system during the mobility operations, for asking, granting or not granting mobility permissions. Their treatment can be redefined by the designer in order to control the mobility. They are represented at the semantical level by co-actions. In the *ambient calculus*, the only condition for the mobility operations is a structure condition (*e.g.* for the *enter* operation, the involved agents must be on the same level in the agents' hierarchy). In CLAIM, we kept this condition, but we added the mobility messages for an advanced security and control.

The **capabilities** are the main elements of an agent and dictate his behavior. They represent the actions an agent can do in order to achieve his goals or that he can offer to other agents. A *capability* has a message of activation, a condition, the process to execute in case of activation and a set of possible effects:

capability ::= capabilityName {
   message = null; | message;
   condition = null; | condition;
   do { process }
   effects = null; | { (effect;)+ }
}

To execute a capability, the agent must receive the activation message and verify the condition. If the message is *null*, the capability is executed whenever the condition is verified. If the condition is *null*, the capability is executed when the message is received. A condition can be a Java function that returns a *boolean*, an achieved effect, a condition about agent's knowledge or sub-agents, or a logical formula:

condition ::=   Java(*objectName.function(args)*)
       | *agentName.effect*
       | *hasKnowledge(knowledge)*
       | *hasAgent(agentName)*
       | *not(condition)*
       | *and(condition,(condition)+)*
       | *or(condition,(condition)+)*

An agent concurrently executes several **processes**. One of these concurrent processes can be a sequence of processes, an instruction, a variable's instantiation, a method implemented in other programming language (*e.g.* Java), the invocation of a known Web Service, the creation of a new agent or the removal on an existing one, a mobility operation or a message transmission:

```
process ::=   process.process
          |   instruction
          |   ?x = (value | Java(obj.method(args)))
          |   Java(obj.method(args))
          |   WebService(address,method(args))
          |   newAgent agentName:className( (arg,)*)
          |   kill (agentName)
          |   open (agentName)
          |   acid
          |   in (mobilityArgument,agentName)
          |   out (mobilityArgument,agentName)
          |   move (mobilityArgument,agentName)
          |   send (receiver,message)
```

We defined two instructions:

forAllKnowledge(knowledge) { process } - execute the process for all agent's knowledge that satisfy a criteria (*e.g.* all agent's knowledge about a certain agent).

forAllAgents(agentName) { process } - execute the process for all the agent's sub-agents that satisfy a criteria (*e.g.* all the agent's sub-agents that belong to a certain class).

The mobility primitives have the same utilization as in the ambient calculus but they have been adapted to intelligent agents. Hence, an agent can open the borders of one of his sub-agents (*open*) or can open his own borders (*acid*); in both cases, the parent of the open agent inherits knowledge, capabilities, processes and sub-agents from the open agent. Also, an agent can enter an agent form the same level in the hierarchy, *i.e.* having the same parent (*in*), can exit the current parent (*out*) or can migrate into another agent (*move*). With respect to the hierarchical representation of agents, these operations allow flexible reconfiguring of MAS and dynamic gathering of capabilities and knowledge.

An important problem is the migration's granularity, and the question is "who can migrate?". We specify this using the mobility argument that allows the migration of the agent himself, of a clone of the agent or of a process:

*mobilityArgument = **this** | **clone** | process*

The **agent** component represents the agent's current sub-agents.

The CLAIM language offers to the agents' designer the possibility to define two types of behavior for the agents:

The *reactive behavior* (or forward reasoning):

- get a message from the queue (the first or using a selection heuristic);

- find the capabilities that have this message of activation and replace the variables in the body of the capability;

- verify the conditions of the chosen capabilities;

- execute the process of the verified capabilities; let us note that several capabilities can be concurrently activated.

The *pro-active behavior* (or backward reasoning):

- get a goal from the list of goals (the first or using a selection heuristic);

- find the capabilities that allow to achieve this goal;

- verify the conditions of the chosen capabilities; if the condition is an agent's effect, add this effect in his list of goals; if the condition is other agent's effect, request the execution of the corresponding capability;

- execute the process of the verified capabilities.

Before reading the next section, about CLAIM's semantics, the reader can see in section 4.4 a list of applications implemented in CLAIM, one of them presented in details in order to illustrate the language's specifications.

4.2.2   Semantics and Verification

The specifications of the CLAIM programming language, presented in the previous section, are used by the programmer to define agents and classes of agents. Nevertheless, these specifications are complex and the reduction rules of the semantics using the same notations are difficult to read and understand. That's why we are using another formalism (equivalent with the specifications) to re-write the syntax and the operational semantics of the language, semantics that must take into account the mobility, the communication and the specificity of cognitive agents. All the components presented at the specification level will be also represented at the semantical level, with a different notation, to facilitate the understanding and the readability of the reduction rules.

A MAS in CLAIM is a set of connected hierarchies of agents. At the semantical level, a MAS (or a CLAIM program) is a set Π of running agents (deployed on several sites).

We consider that $\alpha, \beta, \pi, \ldots$ are agents' names. We also consider that $a_1, a_2,$ ... are agents (with all the components) belonging to Π. The goals, the messages, the capabilities' effects and the pieces of information about the world are propositions containing a name and a list (possibly empty) of arguments, denoted by: $\rho = n(t_1, t_2, ..., t_m)$. The other notations will be explained as they are introduced.

A program is: $\Pi = a_1 \parallel a_2 \parallel ... \parallel a_n, n \geq 0$. The notation $\parallel$ represents concurrent agents inside the MAS, running on the same computer or on different connected computers.

An agent: $a_i = \langle \alpha, \pi, K, G, G', M, C, P, S, E \rangle$, where:

- α is the agent's name;
- π is the name of the agent's current parent;
- K is the knowledge base, containing pieces of information about the world (represented as propositions) or about other agents' capabilities (containing the name, the message and the effect) or classes.

$$K = \{k_1, k_2, ..., k_n\}, k_i = \rho_i \mid \alpha_i(n_i, m_i, E_i) \mid \alpha_i : cl_i$$

- G is the agent's set of current goals (not treated yet); this list can contain not only agent's goals, but also goals requested by other agents, denoted by e.g. $\beta.g$
- G' is the agent's set of currently processing goals;
- M is the messages queue containing a set of pairs representing the sender and the message. The received messages are treated sequentially:

$$M = \oslash \mid \alpha_1\{m_1\}.\alpha_2\{m_2\}.... ;$$

- C is the agent's list of capabilities. A capability has a name (n_i) and triggers a process (p_i) according to a message (m_i) if a (optional) pre-condition (Ω_i) is verified. A capability may have eventual effects (post-conditions) (E_i):

$$c_i = \langle n_i, m_i, \Omega_i, p_i, E_i \rangle \in C$$

A condition can be a Java method that returns a boolean, an effect (used for the goal-driven behavior), a condition about the agent's knowledge, sub-agents or effects, or a logical formula. We defined a function $V : (\Omega, \Pi) \rightarrow \{true, false\}$ (detailed later), that evaluates the boolean value of a CLAIM agent condition in the context of a running MAS.

- P is the list of the agent' concurrent running processes (the notation $\mid$ represents concurrent processes inside an agent): $P ::= p_i \mid p_j \mid ... \mid p_k$

- S is the set of names of the agent's sub-agents;
- E is the list of achieved goals or effects.

A process may be executed either if it is explicitly coded in the agent or as a result of a triggered capability or in order to achieve a goal. Several processes can be concurrently executed by an agent. One of these concurrent processes can be, as seen in the previous section, a (possibly empty) sequence of processes, a message transmission, the creation of a new agent (belonging to an already defined class) or the removal of an existing one, a mobility operation (we added co-actions, represented in the previous section as mobility messages), an effect achievement, a variable instantiation or an instruction (the last two). We do not treat at the semantic level the Java methods and the Web Services invocations.

$$p_i ::= \quad \oslash \mid p_j.p_k \mid send(\alpha, m) \mid$$
$$newAgent\langle \alpha, \oslash, K, G, \oslash, \oslash, C, P, \oslash, \oslash \rangle \mid$$
$$kill(\beta) \mid$$
$$in(\beta) \mid \overline{in}(\alpha) \mid$$
$$out(\beta) \mid \overline{out}(\alpha) \mid$$
$$move(\beta) \mid$$
$$open(\beta) \mid \overline{open}(\alpha) \mid$$
$$acid \mid \overline{acid}(\beta) \mid$$
$$addEffect(e_i) \mid$$
$$?x = value \mid$$
$$forAllKnowkedge(k)\{p_j\} \mid$$
$$forAllAgents(\alpha_i)\{p_j\}$$

Additional notations

Propositions are important notions in our language. A proposition has a name and contains a set of arguments: $\rho = n(t_1, t_2, ..., t_m)$. They are used to represent goals, messages, information about the world and effects. The propositions may contain variables (denoted by $?x$) as arguments. We say that a proposition is *instantiated* if it contains no variables (all the arguments are instantiated).

DEFINITION 4.1 *A proposition* $\rho = n(t_1, t_2, ..., t_m)$ *is* equal *with another proposition* $\rho' = n'(t'_1, t'_2, ..., t'_o)$ *(notation* $\rho = \rho'$*) if* ρ *and* ρ' *are instantiated and* $n = n'$, $m = o$ *and* $\forall i \in \{1, ..., m\}, t_i = t'_i$.

DEFINITION 4.2 *A proposition* ρ belongs to *a set* Λ *(e.g. G, E) of propositions (notation* $\rho \in \Lambda$*) if* $\exists \rho' \in \Lambda$ *and* $\rho = \rho'$.

DEFINITION 4.3 *A proposition* $\rho = n(t_1, t_2, ..., t_m)$ corresponds to *another proposition* $\rho' = n'(t'_1, t'_2, ..., t'_o)$ *(notation* $\rho \cong \rho'$*) if* ρ' *is instantiated and* $n = n'$, $m = o$ *and* $\forall i \in \{1, ..., m\}, t_i = t'_i$ *or* t_i *is a variable.*

DEFINITION 4.4 *A proposition* ρ has a correspondent *in a set* Λ *(e.g. G, E) of propositions (notation* $\rho \sim\in \Lambda$*) if* $\exists \rho' \in \Lambda$ *and* $\rho \cong \rho'$.

These definitions also apply to all types of knowledge, with slight differences and with the same notations.

Conditions

The function V (as seen before, $V : conditions \rightarrow \{true, false\}$) evaluates the boolean value of a capability condition in the context of a running MAS. We will use the notation $V(\Omega)$.

$V(null) = true$

$V(Java(Obj.func)) = \begin{cases} true & \text{if Java returns true} \\ false & \text{else} \end{cases}$

$V(this.e_k) = \begin{cases} true & \text{if } e_k \sim\in E \\ false & \text{else} \end{cases}$

$V(\beta.e_k) = \begin{cases} true & \text{if } \exists a_j = \langle \beta, ..., E_j \rangle \in \Pi \\ & \text{and } e_k \sim\in E_j \\ false & \text{else} \end{cases}$

$V(hasKnowkedge(k)) = \begin{cases} true & \text{if } k \sim\in K \\ false & \text{else} \end{cases}$

$V(hasAgent(\beta)) = \begin{cases} true & \text{if } \beta \in S \\ false & \text{else} \end{cases}$

$V(not(\Omega)) = \neg(V(\Omega))$

$V(and(\Omega_1, \Omega_2, ..., \Omega_m)) = V(\Omega_1) \wedge V(\Omega_2) \wedge ... \wedge V(\Omega_m)$

$V(or(\Omega_1, \Omega_2, ..., \Omega_m)) = V(\Omega_1) \vee V(\Omega_2) \vee ... \vee V(\Omega_m)$

Reduction rules

We recall that a program in CLAIM contains a set of concurrent running agents: $\Pi = a_1 \parallel a_2 \parallel ...a_n$, where the notation $\parallel$ represents concurrent running agents in the MAS. For representing the semantics of CLAIM programs we choose an operational approach [169] consisting in a transition relation $\rightarrow$ between states of a program. We use a different notation, giving a set of reduction rules, from an initial state of a program, verifying certain conditions, to another stable state, after the execution of actions by agents in the program: $\frac{\Pi}{\Pi'}$ (instead of $\Pi \rightarrow \Pi'$).

For readability reasons we omit the unchanged components of agents. All the actions are considered to be atomic. At each step of an agent's execution, either a message is treated via a capability or a running process is executed or a goal is processed.

Terminal configuration

A very important notion for studying a program behavior is the terminal configuration. We give two related definitions, appropriate for CLAIM programs. The first one defines the termination of a CLAIM program, using the second definition that defines the termination of a CLAIM agent.

DEFINITION 4.5 (PROGRAM TERMINATION) *A CLAIM program is in a terminal configuration (denoted by Π_t) if it contains no agents (i.e. $\Pi_t = \oslash$) or if all its agents are in terminal configurations (see next definition).*

DEFINITION 4.6 (AGENT TERMINATION) *A CLAIM agent is in a terminal configuration if he has no message or goal to treat and no running process.*

Ex. $a_i = \langle \alpha, \pi, K, \oslash, \oslash, \oslash, C, \oslash, S, E \rangle$

Even if an agent can still receive messages that activate capabilities, we call this kind of configuration a terminal configuration.

Message transmission

Using the *send* primitive and the language's possibilities, an agent can send a message to himself or to another agent, to all the agents belonging to a class (multicast), or to all the agents in the MAS. The message is added at the end of the messages queue M (rule 4.1).

$$\langle \alpha, send(\beta, m) \rangle \quad \| \quad \langle \beta, M \rangle \quad \rightarrow \quad \langle \alpha, \oslash \rangle \quad \| \quad \langle \beta, M.\alpha\{m\} \rangle \tag{4.1}$$

Message processing

The arrived messages are processed sequentially, following a FIFO policy. The language offers to the designer the possibility to create his own messages, or to use several pre-defined messages (*e.g. tell, askIfCapability, askAllCapabilities, achieveCapability, askEffect, doneEffect*), that can be used by agents to exchange information about their capabilities, effects and knowledge base. These messages have a pre-defined treatment. We present next (rule 4.2) the treatment of the *tell* message, used by an agent to send a piece of information to another agent. By default, the information is added in the knowledge base. Nevertheless, the agent's designer can write a capability having this message of activation, for treating it someway else (*e.g.* verifying the trust level of the sender).

$$\langle \beta, K, \alpha\{tell(k)\} \rangle \quad \rightarrow \quad \langle \beta, K \cup \{k\}, \oslash \rangle \tag{4.2}$$

If the triggering message of a capability arrives and its condition is verified, the associated processes are executed and the effects are updated (rule 4.3). When a message arrives, the variables in the condition, process or effects are replaced with the corresponding values sent in the message. In the next reduction rule (4.3), we consider that if the capability's message m_i has a list of variables-attributes instantiated with real values in the received message, and if Ω_i, p_i and $e_i \in E_i$ contains as attributes some of the variables x_k from m_i, then Ω_i', p_i' and $e_i' \in E_i$ will have the variables replaced with the corresponding values from the received message.

$$\frac{\langle \beta, \alpha\{m\}, C, \oslash \rangle, \text{ and } \exists \langle n_i, m_i, \Omega_i, p_i, E_i \rangle \in C, m_i \cong m \text{ and } V(\Omega_i') = true}{\langle \beta, \oslash, C, p_i'.addEffect(e_1')....addEffect(e_j') \rangle, \ e_1'...e_j' \in E_i'} \tag{4.3}$$

If there are several capabilities activated by a message, the rule above is applied concurrently for each of these capabilities.

A message that does not have a corresponding capability or whose condition is not verified is simply removed from the queue, without any change in the agent's state.

Capabilities without messages

The CLAIM language gives the possibility to the agents to have capabilities that are not started by a received message, but only by a condition (*e.g.* concerning the internal state, a certain moment in time, etc.). If a capability does not have a message, it is executed whenever the condition is verified (rule 4.4).

$$\frac{\langle \beta, C, \oslash \rangle, \text{ and } \exists \langle n_i, \oslash, \Omega_i, p_i, E_i \rangle \in C, V(\Omega_i) = true}{\langle \beta, C, p_i.addEffect(e_1)....addEffect(e_j) \rangle, \ e_1...e_j \in E_i} \tag{4.4}$$

Agents' creation and removal

When an agent is created using the *newAgent* operation, his components are instantiated from an already defined class (rule 4.5).

$$\frac{\langle \alpha, newAgent \langle \beta, \oslash, K, G, \oslash, \oslash, C, P, \oslash, \oslash \rangle, \oslash \rangle}{\langle \alpha, \oslash, \{\beta\} \rangle \ \| \ \langle \beta, \alpha, K, G, \oslash, \oslash, C, P, \oslash, \oslash \rangle} \tag{4.5}$$

An agent can completely remove one of his sub-agents:

$$\frac{\langle \alpha, \pi, kill(\beta), S_\alpha \rangle \ \| \ \langle \beta, \alpha \rangle, \text{where } \beta \in S_\alpha}{\langle \alpha, \pi, \oslash, S_\alpha - \{\beta\} \rangle} \tag{4.6}$$

Mobility operations

The mobility primitives are inspired from the ambient calculus. The reduction rules will be accompanied for these operations by a graphical representation that emphasizes the changes in the MAS hierarchy. Using *in*, an agent can enter another agent from the same level in the hierarchy (rule 4.7 and Figure 4.1) and using *out*, an agent can exit his parent (rule 4.8 and Figure 4.2). Unlike the ambient calculus, where there is no control, we added an asking/granting permission mechanism, represented in term of co-actions, in the same spirit with the *safe ambients* [136], with the main difference that one can specify the agent to whom he will grant a permission. By default, a CLAIM agent will receive these permissions, unless another agent is explicitly programmed to refuse to give them.

$$\frac{\langle \pi, S_\pi \rangle \ \| \ \langle \alpha, \pi, in(\beta) \rangle \ \| \ \langle \beta, \pi, \overline{in}(\alpha), S_\beta \rangle, \alpha, \beta \in S_\pi}{\langle \pi, S_\pi - \{\alpha\} \rangle \ \| \ \langle \alpha, \beta, \oslash \rangle \ \| \ \langle \beta, \pi, \oslash, S_\beta \cup \{\alpha\} \rangle} \tag{4.7}$$

$$\frac{\langle \pi, S_\beta \rangle \ \| \ \langle \alpha, \beta, out(\beta) \rangle \ \| \ \langle \beta, \pi, \overline{out}(\alpha), S_\beta \rangle, \beta \in S_\pi, \alpha \in S_\beta}{\langle \pi, S_\pi \cup \{\alpha\} \rangle \ \| \ \langle \alpha, \pi, \oslash \rangle \ \| \ \langle \beta, \pi, \oslash, S_\beta - \{\alpha\} \rangle} \tag{4.8}$$

In both cases, if the structural condition is not verified or if the agent does not receive the permission (*i.e.* the other does not have the correspondent co-action), the mobility process waits until the operation is possible.

The *move* mobility operation is a direct migration to another agent, without verifying a structure condition (rule 4.9 and Figure 4.3). Nevertheless, the operation is subject to the $\overline{in}$ and $\overline{out}$ permissions.

$$\frac{\langle \pi, \overline{out}(\alpha), S_\pi \rangle \ \| \ \langle \alpha, \pi, move(\beta), S_\alpha \rangle \ \| \ \langle \beta, \overline{in}(\alpha), S_\beta \rangle, \alpha \in S_\pi}{\langle \pi, \oslash, S_\pi - \{\alpha\} \rangle \ \| \ \langle \alpha, \beta, \oslash, S_\alpha \rangle \ \| \ \langle \beta, \oslash, S_\beta \cup \{\alpha\} \rangle} \tag{4.9}$$

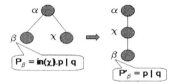

Figure 4.1.   The enter operation   *Figure 4.2.*   The exit operation

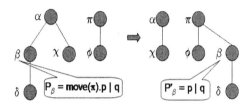

Figure 4.3.   The move operation

The *open* and *acid* actions are used as in the original ambient calculus, respectively for opening one of the sub-agents (rule 4.10 and Figure 4.4), and for opening his own boundaries (rule 4.11 and Figure 4.5). Nevertheless, they have been adapted to intelligent agents. Hence, not only the running processes and the sub-agents of the open agent, but also his knowledge base and capabilities, become components of his parent. In this way, an agent can dynamically gather new knowledge and capabilities and can adapt himself to the requirements of an application. These operations are controlled by co-actions and allow a dynamic reconfiguration of a MAS.

$$\frac{\langle \alpha, K_\alpha, C_\alpha, P \mid open(\beta), S_\alpha \rangle \parallel \langle \beta, \alpha, K_\beta, C_\beta, Q \mid \overline{open}(\alpha), S_\beta \rangle \parallel a_\beta}{\langle \alpha, K_\alpha \cup K_\beta, C_\alpha \cup C_\beta, P \mid Q, S_\alpha \cup S_\beta \rangle \parallel a_\beta, \text{where } a_\beta = \langle \gamma_\beta, \alpha \rangle, \forall \gamma_\beta \in S_\beta} \quad (4.10)$$
where $\beta \in S_\alpha, a_\beta = \langle \gamma_\beta, \beta \rangle, \forall \gamma_\beta \in S_\beta$

$$\frac{\langle \alpha, K_\alpha, C_\alpha, P \mid \overline{acid}(\beta), S_\alpha \rangle \parallel \langle \beta, \alpha, K_\beta, C_\beta, Q \mid acid, S_\beta \rangle \parallel a_\beta}{\langle \alpha, K_\alpha \cup K_\beta, C_\alpha \cup C_\beta, P \mid Q, S_\alpha \cup S_\beta \rangle \parallel a_\beta, \text{where } a_\beta = \langle \gamma_\beta, \alpha \rangle, \forall \gamma_\beta \in S_\beta} \quad (4.11)$$
where $\beta \in S_\alpha, a_\beta = \langle \gamma_\beta, \beta \rangle, \forall \gamma_\beta \in S_\beta$

All these mobility operations are considered atomics at the semantical level and are executed in one step.

Instructions

There are two instructions in CLAIM. The first one, *forAllKnowledge*, allows to sequentially execute a process for all the elements in the knowledge base verifying a criterion (rule 4.12). The second instruction, *forAllAgents*, allows to execute a process for all the sub-agents verifying a certain criterion (*e.g.* all sub-agents - rule 4.13, or all sub-agents belonging to a specific class

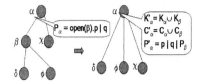 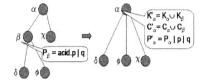

Figure 4.4. The open operation   *Figure 4.5.* The acid operation

- rule 4.14). The notation $p_i\{x_i/x\}$ symbolizes the substitution of all the occurrences of x with x_i (or of the variables in x with corresponding values from x_i) in p.

$$\frac{\langle \alpha, K, forAllKnowledge(k)\{p_i\}\rangle}{\langle \alpha, K, p_i\{k_1/k\}....p_i\{k_j/k\}\rangle, \forall k_i \in K, 1 \le i \le j, k \cong k_i} \quad (4.12)$$

$$\frac{\langle \alpha, K, forAllAgents(?x)\{p_i\}, S\rangle}{\langle \alpha, K, p_i\{\gamma_1/\gamma\}....p_i\{\gamma_n/\gamma\}, S\rangle, \forall \gamma_i \in S, 1 \le i \le n} \quad (4.13)$$

$$\frac{\langle \alpha, K, forAllAgents(?x:cl)\{p_i\}, S\rangle, S_{cl} \subseteq S, \forall \gamma_i \in S_{cl}, \gamma_i : cl, \gamma_i \text{ belongs to the class } cl}{\langle \alpha, K, p_i\{\gamma_1/\gamma\}....p_i\{\gamma_j/\gamma\}, S\rangle, \forall \gamma_i \in S_{cl}, 1 \le i \le j} \quad (4.14)$$

Updating effects

The effects are added in the effect list after the successful execution of the capability's process. If the achieved effects correspond to goals, they will be removed from the lists of not treated and processing goals.

$$\frac{\langle \alpha, G, G', addEffect(e_i), E\rangle}{\langle \alpha, G - \{e_i\}, G' - \{e_i\}, \oslash, E \cup \{e_i\}\rangle} \quad (4.15)$$

The goal-driven behavior

Concurrently with the reactive behavior, in which processes are executed when messages are received, an agent has a proactive behavior, accomplished using the capabilities' effects. When a capability has an effect corresponding to one of his goals, the agent will try to execute the capability. If its condition is true, the corresponding process is executed, (rule 4.16, where p_i', Ω_i' and $e_1'...e_j'$ have the variables replaced with values from g).

$$\frac{\langle \alpha, \{g\}, \oslash, C, \oslash\rangle, \exists \langle s_i, m_i, \Omega_i, p_i, E_i\rangle \in C, \exists e_i \in E_i, e_i \cong g, V(\Omega_i') = true}{\langle \alpha, \oslash, \{g\}, C, p_i'.addEffect(e_1')....addEffect(e_j')\rangle, e_1'...e_j' \in E_i} \quad (4.16)$$

If the condition allowing to achieve the goal contains an agent' effect not achieved yet, the agent will try first to achieve this effect, by adding it in his goals list. In the same time, the fist goal is moved from the current goals list to the processing goals (rule 4.17).

$$\frac{\langle \alpha, \{g\}, \oslash, C \rangle, \exists \langle s_i, m_i, \Omega_i, p_i, E_i \rangle \in C, \exists e_i \in E_i, e_i \cong g,}{\langle \alpha, \{e_i'\}, \{g\}, C \rangle} \quad V(\Omega_i) = false, \Omega_i \text{ contains } this.e_i} \tag{4.17}$$

If the condition allowing to achieve the goal contains an effect of another agent, the effect is requested to the other agent using a specific message, $askEffect$ (rule 4.18).

$$\frac{\langle \alpha, \{g\}, \oslash, C, \oslash \rangle, \exists \langle s_i, m_i, \Omega_i, p_i, E_i \rangle \in C, \exists e_i \in E_i, e_i \cong g,}{\langle \alpha, \oslash, \{g\}, C, send(\beta, askEffect(e_i')) \rangle} \quad V(\Omega_i) = false, \Omega_i \text{ contains } \beta.e_i} \tag{4.18}$$

When an agent receives an $askEffect$ message, if he does not have a capability with this message, meaning that the agent is programmed to treat differently the requests for services from other agents, he will add the demanded effect to his list of goals (rule 4.19).

$$\langle \beta, \oslash, \alpha\{askEffect(e_i)\} \rangle \quad \rightarrow \quad \langle \beta, \{\alpha.e_i\}, \oslash \rangle \tag{4.19}$$

The treatment of this new goal, resulting from another agent's demand, is done in the same way as his own goals. The only difference is that after the successful achievement of this external goal, a $doneEffect$ message is sent to the agent that requested it (rule 4.20).

$$\frac{\langle \beta, G, G', addEffect(e_i), E \rangle, \text{ and } \exists \alpha.e_i \in G \text{ or } \exists \alpha.e_i \in G'}{\langle \beta, G - \{e_i\}, G' - \{e_i\}, send(\alpha, doneEffect(e_i)), E \cup \{e_i\} \rangle} \tag{4.20}$$

The treatment of a $doneEffect$ message consists in removing the effect from the goals lists and adding it in the effect list, similar with the $addEffect$ process.

Variable instantiation

The language allows to instantiate variables that will be used in the following processes in the current sequence (rule 4.21).

$$\langle \alpha, ?x = v.p_i \rangle \quad \rightarrow \quad \langle \alpha, p_i\{v/?x\} \rangle \tag{4.21}$$

Sequence

If an agent can evolve from a state containing a process p_i into another state containing the process p_i', then the agent containing p_i followed (in sequence) by another process q is able to evolve into p_i' followed by q.

$$\text{if } \langle \alpha, p_i \rangle \rightarrow \langle \alpha, p_i' \rangle \text{ then } \langle \alpha, p_i.q \rangle \rightarrow \langle \alpha, p_i'.q \rangle \tag{4.22}$$

Java and Web Services

As seen in the previous section, the programming language offers additional features, for calling Java methods or for invoking Web Services, that cannot change the components of an agent and we do not treat them at the semantical level.

Verification of programs: a discussion

The operational semantics presented above is just a first necessary step towards the formal verification of multi-agent programs written in CLAIM. The formal definition of an agent is more complex than the other formalisms treating mobile processes and the verification become much more complicated. We are currently studying aspects as programs' correctness (desirable properties that programs should verify [5]) and verification and we provide here a brief discussion about the characteristics of CLAIM programs. A CLAIM program is distributed and concurrent, containing agent communicating asynchronously and that do not share common variables. We have already presented the notion of program termination. We continue in this section with other important properties.

Determinism: A program is determinist if for any given state, there is exactly one next possible computational state. CLAIM programs are implicitly non-deterministic, because starting from a state, a program can evolve in several different states (see below).

The next configuration is a valid CLAIM program.

$$\langle \tau, S_\tau \cup \{\pi\}\rangle \quad \| \quad \langle \pi, \overline{out}(\beta).p_k, S_\pi \cup \{\alpha, \beta\}\rangle \quad \|$$
$$\langle \alpha, \pi, in(\beta).p_i\rangle \quad \| \quad \langle \beta, \pi, out(\pi).p_l \mid \overline{in}(\alpha).p_j, S_\beta\rangle$$

This configuration can evolve (with equal probabilities) in two different configurations. If α executes *in*:

$$\langle \tau, S_\tau \cup \{\pi\}\rangle \quad \| \quad \langle \pi, \overline{out}(\beta).p_k, S_\pi \cup \{\beta\}\rangle \quad \|$$
$$\langle \alpha, \beta, p_i\rangle \quad \| \quad \langle \beta, \pi, out(\pi).p_l \mid p_j, S_\beta \cup \{\alpha\}\rangle$$

or, if *out* is executed by β:

$$\langle \tau, S_\tau \cup \{\pi, \beta\}\rangle \quad \| \quad \langle \pi, p_k, S_\pi \cup \{\alpha\}\rangle \quad \|$$
$$\langle \alpha, \pi, in(\beta).p_i\rangle \quad \| \quad \langle \beta, \tau, p_l \mid \overline{in}(\alpha).p_j, S_\beta\rangle$$

In the first case, β will still be capable of executing $out(\pi)$, but in the second case, α no longer can enter β, because he is not at the same level in the hierarchy anymore. Nevertheless, we guarantee at the implementation level that this kind of program will evolve in a stable state (one of the two in our example), in concordance with the reduction rules.

Deadlock: A configuration of a program is called deadlock if the configuration is non-terminal and there is no possible successor configuration (using a reduction rule). In CLAIM, because of the needed structure condition for the mobility operation, an agent may try infinitely to execute an *in* operation, for entering an agent that is not in his neighborhood (and may never be), and consequently the next processes (in the same sequence) are blocked. However, we are not considering this as being a deadlock configuration, because the destination agent may be sometimes in the future in the neighborhood thus verifying the structural condition and unblocking the execution.

Correctness: A program is correct if it satisfies the intended input-output relation. To prove the correctness of CLAIM programs in syntax-directed manner, we are using a proof system. A proof system is a finite set of axiom schemas and proof rules. An axiom is a correctness formula representing the intended next states of a program starting from initial states. These axioms correspond to the reduction rules introduced earlier (note that we did not present in this chapter all the reduction rules; however, the proof system contains them all). A correctness formula is true with respect to the operational semantics reduction rules. Our current work tackles the soundness and the completeness of the proof system.

Structural congruence: As a first step towards the verification of MAS built using CLAIM, we studied the structural congruence of programs. We defined a CLAIM program as a set of running agents. Two *programs* are equivalent if they exhibit an identical behavior for an external observer. Following this reasoning, two programs are equivalent if they have *equivalent running agents*. That is, the same agents, with the same name, parent, knowledge base, goals, messages, capabilities and with *equivalent running processes*. So, the equivalence between programs is reduced at equivalence between processes inside agents. Processes are grouped into equivalence classes using the structural congruence relation $\equiv$. Its properties are presented below.

$$
\begin{array}{ll}
p \equiv p & p \mid q \equiv q \mid p \\
p \equiv q \Rightarrow q \equiv p & (p \mid q) \mid r \equiv p \mid (q \mid r) \\
p \equiv q, q \equiv r \Rightarrow p \equiv r & p \equiv q \Rightarrow p \mid r \equiv q \mid r \\
p \mid 0 \equiv p & p \equiv q \Rightarrow p.r \equiv q.r \\
p.0 \equiv p & p \equiv q \Rightarrow r.p \equiv r.q
\end{array}
$$

4.2.3   Software Engineering Issues

The language includes the notion of class of agents. Generic classes can be defined and instantiated later. In this version of the language there is no inheritance as in object-oriented programming, but we intend to offer the possibility to define classes of agents that are sub-classes (specializations) of other classes. Nevertheless, at the agent level, CLAIM offers two primitives, *open* and *acid*, allowing an agent to gather sub-agents, processes, knowledge and capabilities from an open sub-agent, thus allowing a dynamic reconfiguring and adaptability of a MAS. We also developed several libraries of classes of agents for different domains, that can be parameterized and used by designers.

The CLAIM agents can invoke Java methods or Web Services for computational purposes. In the future, we intend to give the agents the possibility to invoke methods or programs implemented in other programming languages.

4.2.4 Other features of the language

The lack of formalisms to deal with both intelligent and mobile agents was one of our main motivations in developing CLAIM. The agents' mobility is a central aspect in our framework. We can easily model agents' reasoning, but our target applications must take advantage of both mobility and cognitive skills. There is a strong mobility at the agents' processes level and a week mobility for the invoked Java methods.

Concerning the extensibility of the language, the main constructs of CLAIM (*e.g.* agents' creation, mobility and communication primitives) are fixed. Nevertheless, the language offers the possibility to the agents' designer to develop his own ontology for representing knowledge or goals and for creating his own messages, with a specific treatment (represented by capabilities), to suit the current application.

4.3 Platform

The CLAIM language is supported by a dedicated platform, called SyMPA (French: Système Multi-Plateforme d'Agents), implemented in Java and that offers all the necessary mechanisms needed for the design and the secure execution of a distributed MAS.

4.3.1 Available tools and documentation

There are many platforms for mobile agents nowadays. The main difference of SyMPA with respect to other mobile agents platforms is that it supports agents implemented in CLAIM, an agent-oriented programming language while the other platforms support agents implemented using mainly object-oriented languages (*e.g.* Java in most cases). In addition, a CLAIM agent deployed in SyMPA can use Java methods. SyMPA is compliant with the specifications of the MASIF [151] standard from OMG, that provides a set of interfaces and definitions for the mobile agents' management, identification, authentication, localization, tracking, communication, mobility and security.

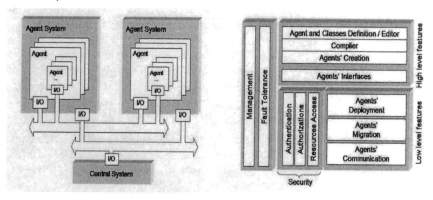

Figure 4.6. SyMPA's Architecture   *Figure 4.7.* SyMPA's features

SyMPA can be deployed on a set of connected computers. It provides installation and deployment guidelines and a tutorial is currently developed. The platform's architecture is presented in Figure 4.6. There is a central system providing management functions. An agent system is deployed on each computer connected to the platform. It provides a graphical interface for defining and creating agents and for visualizing their execution, a compiler, mechanisms for agents' deployment, communication, migration and management (conf. Figure 4.7), all of these in a secure and fault tolerant environment. The compiler was implemented using JavaCC (Java Compiler Compiler) [84].

The agent system is also in charge of the communication with other agent systems or with the central system and of the mobility. The communication and the mobility are implemented using Java on top of the TCP/IP protocol. For each running agent, a optional graphical interface (Figure 4.8) can be used to monitor his behavior, communication or mobility.

Mobility

Due to the hierarchical representation of the agents and the distributed deployment of an MAS, we distinguish local and remote migrations. The local migration takes place inside a hierarchy, while the remote migration is the migration between hierarchies, using the *move* primitive.

The remote mobility in SyMPA can be considered at two levels. First, there is a strong migration at the language level, because, before the migration, the state of an agent is saved and then transferred to the destination. The agent's

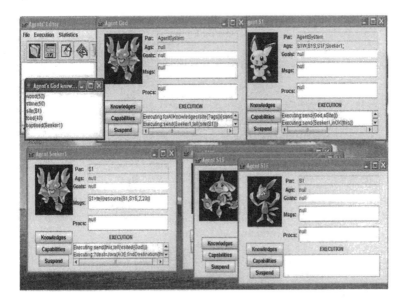

Figure 4.8. Agents' interfaces

language-specific processes are resumed from their interruption point. An agent can be at any moment saved in a format similar to the definition, containing the current state (*e.g.* knowledge, messages, running processes). This representation is sent through the network to the destination agent system, in an encrypted format and the agent's execution is resumed from the saved state.

At the Java level, we use its mobility facilities, so there is a weak migration. A Java method that has begun before the migration will be reinvoked after the arrival at the destination. Since the migration is achieved using the language's primitives, unlike in other platforms, where there are Java objects that migrate during their execution, a solution can also be to let all the agent's running Java methods terminate before his migration.

Security

The mobile agents are programs running in a distributed and insecure environment (*e.g.* the Internet) where there are possible different attacks from the agents against the host agent system or attacks against an agent during the migration or during his execution. Several solutions exist against these attacks [101]. For the agent systems' protection, we are using agents' authentication, the control of the access to the system's resources in accordance with a set of permissions given to agents with regard to their authority, and audit techniques. For the agents' protection, we are using encryption during the migration and during the execution on a agent system (when the agent is stored on the disk), and also fault-tolerance mechanisms. The reader can find in [211] a detailed description of these security aspects.

4.3.2 Standards compliance, interoperability and portability

The SyMPA platform is implemented in Java and takes advantage of the portability and the platform-independence of this language. The SyMPA environment is composed of an ensemble of packages that can be installed on every computer with an operating system supporting *Java Virtual Machine*. After installing the packages, a few configuring operations are needed and the CLAIM language supported by the platform is ready to be used to implement MAS applications. We easily installed and tested the platform on Windows, Unix-based or Macintosh systems.

As we have already specified, SyMPA is compliant with the specifications of the MASIF [151] standard from the OMG, that provides a set of interfaces and definitions for the mobile agents' management, identification, authentication, localization, tracking, communication, mobility and security.

We have seen that CLAIM offers a set of agent-specific concepts and primitives for the agents' reasoning, communication and mobility. In addition, an agent can use Java methods or Web Services invocations for computational purposes.

Considering that the interoperability between heterogenous agents is a very important aspect in the MAS applications, we used the Web Services approach to develop an interoperability environment, called Web-MASI [80]. This environment is based on two key elements: an architecture that includes the MAS in the functional model of the Web Services and an interoperability module playing the role of interface between the agents and the Web Services layer. Using this plug-in module, the agents can publish their capabilities as Web Services, that can be invoked by other agents, independently from conceptual (agent architecture, interaction model) or technical (platform, programming language) characteristics.

4.3.3 Other features of the platform

The implementation of the platform is in a prototype stage, in continuous development and optimization and has already been used to implement several applications, presented in the next section. The results are very promising and an open-source version will be available soon, that will allow us to improve our implementation and to detect the expressiveness and the power but also the limits of the language and of the platform.

The developed applications cover a wide area, starting from simple applications with a small number of agents to largely distributed applications, with big number of highly communicating mobile agents. Concerning the reached performances, we could deploy up to 30 agents on one computer, but this number could easily increase if the resources consuming graphical interfaces of agents are not used. Nevertheless, in our current applications we used the interfaces to monitor the agents' execution, behavior, communication and migration. Concerning the scale of tests, until now we developed application using agents deployed on up to 10 connected computers.

As specified before, there is a central system with management functions in our environment. In the first phases, the central system had some problems with treating a great number of messages, but after adding fault-tolerance techniques and optimizations, the communications proceeded in a satisfying manner. Nevertheless, we are studying the possibility to introduce different management solutions (*e.g.* distributed, non-centralized) that the developer can choose in function of the current application's requirements.

The code reutilization is another of our priorities. The notion of class in central in our framework. Our long term goal is to have different already defined classes of agents for different types of applications that can be only parameterized and easily used by the designers.

4.4   Applications supported by the language and/or the platform

The CLAIM language supported by the SyMPA platform has been used to develop several applications, summarized below, that emphasize the main features of the framework, show the expressiveness and the facility of usage of the language and the robustness of the platform.

Translations

In the first phase of development of the CLAIM language, applications from other agent-oriented programming languages, such as *Airline reservations* from *AGENT-0* [206] or *Bolts Make Scenario* from *AgentSpeak* [233], were translated. FIPA protocols were also programmed using CLAIM. There is no mobility in these applications, but the agents' reasoning and communication were easily translated.

Research of information

One of the first applications implemented was the research of information on a network [82] using mobile agents. Receiving requests from users, these agents migrate to all the available connected sites searching for pieces of information corresponding to a request.

Electronic commerce

A more complex application, that justified the hierarchical representation of agents, was an e-commerce application [81], where there are several electronic markets distributed on a network. Each e-market has various departments (represented as sub-agents of a market), for different types of products. The markets can move with all the sub-departments to other sites in order to find clients and the clients can move to different markets searching for products.

Load balancing

In the two applications previously presented, the intelligent elements of the agents were central. An application focused on the computational aspects was implemented next. Thus, CLAIM and SyMPA served for programming an application of load balancing and resource sharing [212]. The connected computers' characteristics are gathered by mobile agents and the computers are classified using different criterions. The users' tasks are executed on computers satisfying some requirements and can dynamically migrate during the execution in order to finish the execution in the fastest way possible.

E-libraries network

The next step was to combine the intelligent features of the agents with the results of the load balancing application in an application containing a network of distributed cooperative digital libraries [129]. The libraries have sections and are used by customers searching for various documents. The libraries manage the subscribers, the documents and have information about other libraries, as the goal is to satisfy the customers, even if this means to direct them towards other libraries. A library can also distribute one or several sections to another site when there are too many clients on the local computer, using results from the load-balancing application.

Veracruz coffee market

Another complex application developed using CLAIM was the modelling of the coffee market in Veracruz, Mexico [213]. Using our framework, all the involved actors were designed, proposing an agent-based application able to deal with the different types of transaction negotiations and covering the entire value chain of coffee.

A Case Study

In order to illustrate the language's specifications, we present here an application inspired from strategy games, such as *Age of Empires*[4]. As a simplified version, there is a village of people in a prehistoric era, trying to survive by gathering resources. There are sites of resources distributed on several computers of a network. Each site can contain three types of resources: wood, stone and food. The population is represented by a *Creator* agent that can create *Seeker* agents and resource gatherer agents for each type of resource (resources are consumed when creating new agents): *WoodCutter*, *Miner* and *Hunter*. Each type of agent has capabilities for gathering only his corresponding resource. The goal is to gather all the resources. We implemented several strategies, in order to observe the agents' behavior in different situations. Since the goal here is only to show examples of agents implemented in CLAIM, we focus on one scenario.

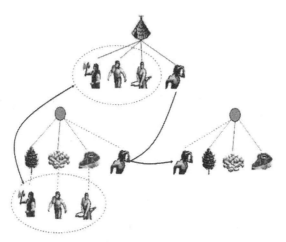

Figure 4.9. Application's schema

The *Creator* agent creates (using **newAgent**) a *Seeker* agent, finds out the list of the existing sites and tells to the *Seeker* to migrate to each of them (using **move**). When the *Seeker* arrives on a site, he "counts" the available

---

[4]http://www.microsoft.com/games/empires/

resources and asks (using **send**) specialized agents from the *Creator*, who will create (using **newAgent**) one specialized agent for each type of resource, agents that migrate to the specific resource agents on the site. After gathering the resources, they return to the village, give the resources to the *Creator* and wait for other calls. Meanwhile, the *Seeker* moves to other sites, searches for resources and asks for specialized agents. If there is no specialized agent available at the *Creator* when a new ask for help arrives, a new specialized agent is created.

We present only some of the most important capabilities of our agents. Every identified actor of our scenario will be represented as a class of agents. When programming a CLAIM class, one must identify the possible parameters of the class, the knowledge ontology (that can evolve during the execution), the chosen type of reasoning (forward reasoning or proactive or both), the goals (for agents with a proactive behavior), the capabilities, the messages to be exchanged with other agents and the necessary Java methods used for various computations.

The agents in the presented scenario use a forward reasoning, *i.e.* they execute actions when specific messages arrive and some (optional) conditions are verified. The *Creator* has an initial amount of resources, given as parameters for the class and represented in the knowledge base as $wood(?woodQuant)$, $stone(?stoneQuant)$ and $food(?foodQuant)$. The quantities of resource evolve during the execution (decrease when new agents are created and increase when resources are brought by agents). Other manipulated knowledge represents the found sites (not known *a priori*). Several Java methods were needed for verifying if the agent has sufficient resources when he tries to create a new agent, for waiting an amount of time, for updating the quantities of resources, etc.

```
defineAgentClass Creator(?w,?s,?f) {
    authority=null;    parent=null;
    knowledge={wood(?w);stone(?s);food(?f);}
    goals=null;    messages=null;
    capabilities {
    findSites {
```
capability for sending to all the existing *Site* agents a message for asking their names; the *Site* agents which answer to this messages are added in the *Creator*' knowledge base
```
        message=findSites();
        condition=null;
        do(send(?agS:Site(),askSiteName()).Java(AOE.wait(30)).send(this,initSearch()))
        effects=null;
    }
    createSeeker {
```
capability for creating a *Seeker* (if there are sufficient resources), for telling him the names of the known sites and for

requesting his departure

```
message=initSearch();
condition=Java(AOE.hasResources(this,0,0));
do{?n=Java(AOE.baptise(this,0)).newAgent ?n:Seeker().
    forAllKnowledge(site(?ags)){send(?n,tell(site(?ags)))}.send(?n,seek())}
effects=null;
} ...
```

the class has several other capabilities for creating specialized agents when the *Seeker* arrives on a site and requests help and for updating the resources when these agents return.

```
}
processes={send(this,findSites())}
agents=null;
}
```

The *Site* class has parameters representing the amount of each resource (the knowledge base contains pieces of information similar with those of a *Creator*) and capabilities for creating the sub-resource agents and for answering the questions concerning his names and his resources. The sub-resource agents are represented in a simple class (named *Resource*) that can receive agents and updates the amount of resources after a gatherer agent's passage.

A *Seeker* manipulates pieces of information about the known sites, about the visited sites and about the sites' resources. When created, he selects a destination site (known and not visited already; he uses a Java method for this), migrates to this site, finds out the amount of available resources (by communicating with the site agent) and then requests specialized agents from the *Creator*.

```
defineAgentClass Seeker() {
    authority=null;  parent=null;  knowledge=null;  goals=null;  messages=null;
    capabilities {
    seek {
```

capability for migrating to a not visited site and for asking the amount of available resources

```
message=seek();
condition=null;
do{?d=Java(AOE.findDestination(this)).move(this,?d).send(?d,needResources(?d))}
effects=null;
} ...
```

he requests next specialized agents and continues the search migrating to other sites.

```
}
processes=null;  agent=null;
}
```

The specialized gatherer agents (*WoodCutter, Miner* and *Hunter*) can migrate to specific *Resource* agents, return to the *Creator*, give him the gathered resources and await for new requests.

After defining all the classes of agents for our scenario (but also for the other considered scenarios) and writing all the necessary Java methods, the SyMPA platform was deployed on several computers of the network. Several sites of resources were started on different computers and a *Creator*. We observed the behavior of all the agents in our application (not only for presented scenario) that migrate in order to gather resources and we also counted the times for gathering all the resources and the *Creator'* resource variation for different scenarios.

4.5   Final Remarks

In this chapter, we argue that the development of MAS applications needs specific languages (*i.e.* agent-oriented) in order to reduce the gap between the design and the implementation phases.

The presented language, CLAIM, frees the designer from time-consuming implementation aspects and combines in a unified framework the advantages of the intelligent agents with those of the ambient calculus (particularly suitable for mobile computation). Hence, both computational aspects (communication, mobility, processing) and cognitive features (knowledge, goals and reasoning) of agents are easily represented thanks to CLAIM.

For using the language in real-life applications, we would like to be able to verify some important aspects of the built MAS, using a formal operational semantics, whose main elements were also presented in this chapter.

Using a flexible hierarchical topology of the MAS, a goal-driven behavior and a mental state of agents that continuously evolves in an autonomous manner, CLAIM allows a dynamic re-configuring of the built MAS in order to give the system the full scope to adapt its structure and to meet the requirements of target applications.

The language is supported by a distributed platform, SyMPA, that offers all the necessary mechanisms for creating and deploying CLAIM agents and for a secure execution of a distributed MAS.

CLAIM and SyMPA have been used for developing several complex applications that showed the expressiveness of the language and the robustness and the strength of the platform, such as an application for information research on the Web, electronic commerce applications, a load balancing and resource sharing application using mobile agents or an application of a digital libraries network. All the results were very promising.

The current work tackles the verification of CLAIM programs, using the defined operational semantics, the optimization of the platforms and the adaptability and interoperability issues. We would like to deploy SyMPA on mobile devices in order to fulfill the ambient intelligence requirements.

II

JAVA-BASED AGENT PROGRAMMING LANGUAGES

Chapter 5

JADE — A JAVA AGENT DEVELOPMENT FRAMEWORK

Fabio   Bellifemine,[1]   Federico   Bergenti,[2]   Giovanni   Caire,[1]   and
Agostino Poggi[2]

[1] *Telecom Italia Lab*
Via G. Reiss Romoli, 274
10148, Torino, Italy
{ fabio.bellifemine,giovanni.caire } @tilab.com

[2] *DII · University of Parma*
Parco Area delle Scienze 181A
43100, Parma, Italy
{ bergenti,poggi } @ce.unipr.it

Abstract   JADE (Java Agent Development Framework) is a software environment to build agent systems for the management of networked information resources in compliance with the FIPA specifications for interoperable multi-agent systems. JADE provides a middleware for the development and execution of agent-based applications which can seamless work and interoperate both in wired and wireless environment. Moreover, JADE supports the development of multi-agent systems through the predefined programmable and extensible agent model and a set of management and testing tools. Currently, JADE is one of the most used and promising agent development framework; in fact, it has a large user group, involving more than two thousands active members, it has been used to realize real systems in different application sectors, and its future development is guided by a governing board involving some important industrial companies.

Keywords: Agent development framework, FIPA compliant agent platform, Middleware for heterogeneous networks, Java

5.1   Motivation

Since ten years ago, agents are considered one of the most promising information technologies, in particular, to realize distributed interoperable systems [95, 239, 123, 238]. However, researchers realized that agent-based technologies could not keep their promises and become wide-spread, until there were no suitable standards to support agent interoperability and adequate environments for the development of agent systems. Therefore, in those years, different groups of researchers started working towards the definition of standards for agent technologies and the realization of development environments for multi-agent systems.

FIPA specifications [89] and the JADE software framework [12, 10, 119] may be considered two of most interesting results in these two fields. FIPA specifications define the reference model of an agent platform and a set of services that should be provided to realize truly interoperable multi-agent systems. JADE (Java Agent Development framework) is a software environment to build agent systems for the management of networked information resources in compliance with the FIPA specifications.

The focus of this chapter is the JADE software framework. In particular, we describe the main features of this framework and give a short description of some applications realized with it.

5.2   Platform

The JADE framework is based on a middleware that facilitates the development of distributed multi-agent applications based on a peer-to-peer communication architecture [12, 10, 119]. The intelligence, the initiative, the information, the resources and the control can be fully distributed on mobile terminals as well as on hosts in the fixed network. The environment can evolve dynamically with agents that appear and disappear in the system according to the needs and the requirements of the context. Communication between agents, regardless of whether they are running in the wireless or wireline network, is completely symmetric with each agent is able to play both the initiator and the responder role.

JADE is fully developed in Java and is based of the following main principles:

- Interoperability. JADE is compliant with FIPA specifications [89]. As a consequence a JADE agent can interoperate with other peers not running on the JADE run-time (provided that they comply with the same standard).

- Uniformity and portability. JADE provides applications with a homogeneous set of APIs that are independent from the underlying network and Java version. More in details, the JADE run-time provides the same APIs both for the J2EE, J2SE and J2ME environment. In theory, developers could decide the Java run-time environment at deploy-time.

- Ease of use. The complexity of the middleware is hidden behind a simple and intuitive set of APIs.

- Pay-as-you-go philosophy. Programmers do not need to use all the features provided by the middleware. Features that are not used do not require programmers to know anything about them, neither add any computational overhead.

JADE includes both the libraries of Java classes required to develop application agents and the run-time environment that provides the basic services and that must be active on a given device before one or more agents can be executed on that device. Each instance of the JADE run-time is called container (since it "contains" agents). The set of all containers is called platform and provides a homogeneous layer that hides completely from agents (i.e., from applications) the complexity and the diversity of the underlying tires (hardware, operating systems, types of network, JVM).

As depicted in figure 5.1, JADE framework is compatible with Java J2ME CLDC/MIDP1.0 environment and it has already been tested on the fields over the GPRS network with different mobile terminals among which: Nokia 3650 and 6600, Motorola Accompli008, Siemens SX45, PalmVx, Compaq iPaq, Psion5MX, HP Jornada 560. The JADE run-time memory footprint in a MIDP1.0 environment is around 100 KB, but can be further reduced until 23 KB using the ROMizing technique [14], i.e., compiling JADE together with the JVM. The limited memory footprint allows installing JADE on mostly all cell phones provided that they are Java-enabled.

JADE is extremely versatile and therefore, not only it fits the constraints of environments with limited resources, but it has already been integrated into complex architectures such as .NET or J2EE [17] where JADE becomes a service to execute multi-party proactive applications.

From the functional point of view, JADE provides the basic services necessary to distributed peer-to-peer applications in the fixed and mobile environment. JADE allows each agent to dynamically discover other agents and to communicate with them according to the peer-to-peer paradigm. From the application point of view, each agent is identified by a unique name and provides a set of services. It can register and modify its services and/or search for agents providing new services, control its life cycle and, most of all, communicate with all other peers.

Agents communicate by exchanging asynchronous messages, a communication model suitable for distributed and loosely-coupled communications ,

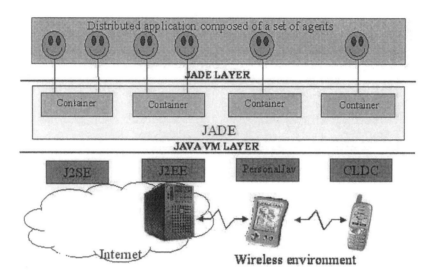

Figure 5.1. The JADE architecture.

i.e., between heterogeneous entities that do not know anything about each other. In order to communicate, an agent just sends a message to a destination. Agents are identified by a name (no need for the destination object reference to send a message) and, as a consequence, there is no temporal dependency between communicating agents. The sender and the receiver could not be available at the same time. The receiver may not even exist (or not yet exist) or could not be directly known by the sender that can specify, e.g., "all agents interested in football" as a destination.

Despite this type of communication, security is preserved, since (for applications that require it) JADE provides proper mechanisms to authenticate and verify "rights" assigned to agents. When needed, an application can verify the identity of the sender of a message and prevent actions that it is not allowed to perform (for instance an agent may be allowed to receive messages from the agent representing its boss, but not to send messages to it). All messages exchanged between agents are carried out within an envelope including only the information required by the transport layer. This allows, among others, to encrypt the content of a message separately.

The structure of a message complies with the ACL language defined by FIPA [89] and includes fields, such as variables indicating the context a message refers to and timeout that can be waited before an answer is received, aimed at supporting complex interactions and multiple parallel conversations.

To further support the implementation of complex conversations, this development framework provides a set of skeletons of typical interaction patterns associated with specific tasks such as negotiations, auctions and task delegation. By using these skeletons (implemented as Java abstract classes), programmers can get rid of the burden of dealing with synchronization issues, timeouts, error conditions and, in general, all those aspects that are not strictly related to the application logic.

To facilitate the creation and handling of messages content, JADE provides a rich support for automatically converting back and forth between a string formats including XML and RDF (suitable form to transfer information) and Java objects (suitable form to manipulate information). This support is integrated with existing ontology creation tools allowing programmers to graphically create their ontology and then work with Java objects to handle message contents conformant to it.

To increase scalability or to meet the constraints of environments with limited resources, JADE provides the opportunity of executing multiple parallel tasks within the same Java thread. Several elementary tasks may then be combined to form more complex tasks structured as concurrent Finite States Machines.

In the J2SE and Personal Java environments, JADE supports code and execution-state mobility. That is an agent can stop running on a host, migrate on a different remote host (without the need to have the agent code already installed on that host) and restart its execution there from the very point it was interrupted. This functionality allows for example to distribute computational load at runtime by moving agents on less loaded machines without any impact on the application.

The platform also includes a naming service (ensuring each agent has a unique name) and a yellow pages service that can be distributed across multiple hosts. Federation graphs can be created to support the definition of agent services domains.

As already mentioned, the JADE run-time can be executed on a wide class of devices ranging from servers to cell phones with the only requirement to support Java MIDP1.0 (or higher versions). In order to properly address the memory and processing power limitations of mobile devices and the characteristics of wireless networks (GPRS in particular) in terms of bandwidth, latency, intermittent connectivity and IP addresses variability, and at the same time to be efficient when executed on fixed network hosts, JADE can be configured to adapt to the characteristics of the deployment environment. JADE architecture is completely modular and, by activating certain modules instead of others, it is possible to meet different requirements in terms of connectivity, memory and processing power.

More in details, a module called LEAP allows optimising all communication mechanisms when dealing with devices with limited resources and connected through wireless networks. By activating this module, a JADE container is "split", as depicted in figure 5.2, into a front-end, actually running on the mobile terminal, and a back-end, running in the fixed network. A proper architectural element, called mediator, must be already active. It is in charge of instantiating and holding the back-ends (that basically are entries in the mediator itself). To face work-load problems it is possible to deploy several mediators each one holding several back-ends. Each front-end is linked to its corresponding back-end by means of a permanent bi-directional connection. It is important to note that there is no difference at all for application developers depending on whether an agent is deployed on a normal container or on the front-end of a split container, since both the available functionality and the APIs to access them are exactly the same.

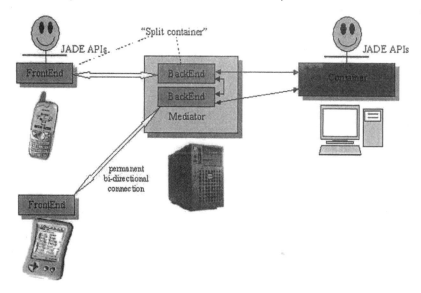

Figure 5.2. JADE architecture in the wireless environment.

The described approach has a number of advantages:

- Part of the functionality of a container are delegated to the back-end, thus making the front-end extremely lightweight in terms of required memory and processing power.

- The back-end masks the actual IP address assigned to the wireless device to other containers (no matter whether they are normal or split). This allows hiding a possible change of IP address from the rest of the platform.

- The front-end is able to detect a loss of connection with the back-end (for instance due to an out of coverage condition) and to re-establish it as soon as possible.

- Both the front-end and the back-end use a store-and-forward mechanism to buffer messages, that cannot be transmitted due to a temporary disconnection, and then deliver as soon as the connection is re-established.

- Several information that containers exchange (for instance to retrieve the container where an agent indicated as the receiver of a message is currently running) are handled only by the back-end. This approach, together with a bit-efficient encoding of communications between the front-end and the back-end, allows optimising the usage of the wireless link.

5.2.1   Available tools and documentation

JADE offers a set of documents (manuals and tutorials) and code examples to help users to install and use it; they are all available from the official JADE Web site [119]. Moreover, JADE provides a rich suite of graphical tools supporting both the debugging, management and monitoring phases of the application life cycle. (figure 5.3 shows their graphical interfaces). By means of these tools, for instance, it is possible to emulate remote conversations, "sniff" messages exchanged by agents, monitor tasks executed by a specific agent and view its life cycle. As far as deployed applications management and monitoring is concerned, it is also possible to control agents running in the system, start, suspend and terminate agents even on remote hosts, inspect and modify the services published in the yellow pages and generate suitable logs. All these tools are implemented as agents themselves. They require no special support to perform their tasks and they simply rely on JADE AMS (Agent Management System). The general management console for a JADE agent platform is called RMA (Remote Management Agent). The RMA acquires information about the platform and executes the GUI commands to modify the status of the platform (creating new agents, shutting down peripheral containers, etc.) through the AMS. On one hand, the RMA asks the AMS to be notified about changes of state of platform agents, on the other hand, it transmits to the AMS the requests for creation, deletion, suspension and restart received by the user. The Directory Facilitator agent also has a GUI of its own, with which the DF can be administered, adding or removing agents and configuring their advertised services.

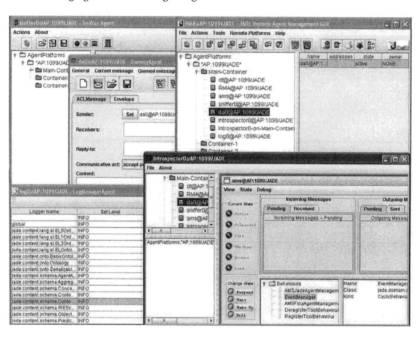

Figure 5.3. Graphical interfaces of JADE tools.

The graphical tools with which JADE users can debug their agents are the Dummy Agent, the Sniffer Agent, the Introspector Agent and the Log Manager Agent. The Dummy Agent is a simple, yet very useful, tool for inspecting message exchanges among agents. The Dummy Agent facilitates validation of an agent message exchange pattern before its integration into a multi-agent system and facilitates interactive testing agents. The graphic interface provides support to edit, compose and send ACL messages to agents, to receive and view messages from agents, and, eventually, to save/load messages to/from disk. The Sniffer Agent makes it possible to track messages exchanged in a JADE agent platform. When the user decides to sniff a single agent or a group of agents, every message directed to or coming from that agent or group of agents is tracked and displayed in the sniffer window, using a notation similar to UML Sequence Diagrams. Every ACL message can be examined by the user, that can also save and load every message track for later analysis. The Introspector Agent, finally, is a very powerful tool that allows to debug and introspect a running agent through the following functionalities: a) monitor and control the agent life-cycle; b) inspect all its exchanged messages, both the queue of sent and received messages; c) monitor the queue of behaviours, including the possibility of executing a behaviour step-by-step, in a similar way to a code debugger. Finally, the Log Manager Agent tracks and stores events happening during the life of multi-agent systems.

Moreover, different "add-ons" to the JADE framework are provided by both the JADE team and other JADE users (all these add-ons are available from the official JADE Web site [119]). In particular, tools and software libraries have been developed and made available for the management of: the persistence of agents, the security of systems, the exchange of messages and the management of ontologies, etc. Add-ons are also available for the integration of JADE with other technologies, such as Servlets, JSP, Applets, the JESS rule engine, and the Protege ontology tool.

5.2.2 Standards compliance, interoperability and portability

JADE is written in Java language and comprises various Java packages, giving application programmers both ready-made pieces of functionality and abstract interfaces for custom, application-dependent tasks. Java was the chosen programming language because of its many attractive features, which are particularly geared towards object-oriented programming in distributed heterogeneous environments.

JADE is available on all the Java versions from J2EE to J2ME. Moreover, JADE facilities the ŠportingŠ of applications among different Java versions and allows the bi-directional communication between agents acting on different wired and wireless networks. This last feature allows, for example, the communication of an agent acting on a network server with an agent acting on a mobile phone.

JADE allows to build agent systems in compliance with FIPA specifications [89]. Therefore, JADE allows the interoperability with agents acting on different agent platforms with the constraint that they must be FIPA-compliant. For this purpose, JADE participated to the bake-off organized by FIPA where the interoperability with the other FIPA based middleware has been verified.

5.2.3 Other features of the platform

The whole JADE source code is distributed under an open source policy, the Lesser GNU Public License (LGPL for short). LGPL enables full exploitation of JADE, even in a business environment, while enforcing the constraint that any modification of JADE source code and any derivative work be returned to the community under the LGPL license itself. No restrictions, instead, are put on applications and other categories of software that simply uses JADE. TILAB, as project initiator, holds the exclusive right to re-release JADE under different or additional license terms.

The different releases of the JADE software (including the last one: 3.2) are stable and used in different research and application projects in different part of world. Moreover, different agent development platforms derive from JADE (see, for example, JADEX [120] and BlueJADE [17]).

A JADE system is based on a set of agent platforms each of them composed of a set of agent containers deployed on an heterogeneous network. Moreover, message exchanges between agents is managed efficiently using different techniques for intra- and inter-container (i.e., Java Virtual Machine) communication. Therefore, a JADE system may contain thousands of agents exchanging a huge amount of messages (a more detailed study on Jade scalability and performance is given in [48]).

A JADE system provides a centralized control. Following the FIPA standard, each JADE platform is controlled by the AMS. However, JADE offers a fault tolerance mechanism that allows an agent platform to survive the failure of its AMS. In fact, each agent platform may have different AMSs usually on different containers: one is active, the others are in backup ready to replace it when it fails.

5.2.4   Realizing multi-agent systems with the platform

A JADE multi-agent application is composed of the FIPA standard agents, provided by the JADE platform, and of a set of application dependent agents realized by the application developer. Agents are implemented through a Java class containing a set of inner classes that realize the different behaviours of the agent. Agent behaviours can be composed of other behaviours and can be executed either a single time (one-shot behaviours) or different times (cyclic behaviours).

Agent classes are based on a method, called *setup*, that performs the agent initialization, and another method, called *takedown*, that performs cleanup operations at the end of its execution. Agent behaviours are based on a method, called *action*, that defines the operations to be performed when the behaviour is in execution. Moreover, cyclic behaviours may have another method, called *done*, that returns a Boolean value indicating whether or not this behaviour has completed its iterative execution.

Therefore, the code of an agent class has the following structure:

```
public class AgentClassName extends Agent {

 Ě variables definition Ě

 protected void setup() {
    ... initialize the agent ...
 }

 protected void takeDown() {
    ... clean-up operations ...
 }

 private class RBehaviourClassName extends Behaviour {

  ... variables definition ...

  public void action() {
   ... behaviour execution ...
  }

  // optional method for cyclic behaviours
  public boolean done() {
   ... return true if execution is completed
  }
 }

 ... other behaviour inner classes ...

}
```

As an example of how is possible to realize a multi-agent system with JADE, we illustrate how to implement a simple book trading multi-agent system showing also some parts of its Java code [1].

This system is based on some seller and buyer agents. Each buyer agent receives the title of the book to buy as a command line argument from its user and periodically requests all known seller agents to provide an offer. As soon as an offer is received, the buyer agent accepts it and issues a purchase order. If more than one seller agent provides an offer the buyer agent accepts the best one (lowest price). Having bought the target book the buyer agent terminates. Each seller agent has a minimal GUI by means of which the user can insert new titles and the associated price) in the local catalogue of books for sale. Seller agents continuously wait for requests from buyer agents. When asked to provide an offer for a book, they check if the requested book is in their catalogue, and in this case reply with the price; otherwise they refuse.

---

[1] The complete code can be found in the JADE software distribution

When they receive a purchase order they serve it and remove the requested book from their catalogue.

A buyer agent is implemented by the *BookBuyerAgent* class. Given that a buyer agent has the only goal of buying books on the behalf of its user, then it needs to realize a single behaviour implemented by the *RequestPerformer* inner class. This behaviour has to send a call for proposal (CFP) message to the known seller agents, get back all the replies and, in case at least a reply proposing a bid for the request is received, send a further message accepting the proposal to the seller agent that made the best proposal and, finally, get back the response.

A seller agent is implemented by the *BookSellerAgent* class. This agent needs to wait for book requests from buyer agents and serves them; these requests can be requests to provide an offer for a book or purchase orders. This is done through two different cyclic behaviours: one dedicated to serve offer requests, implemented by the *OfferRequestsServer* inner class, and the other dedicated to serve purchase orders, implemented by the *PurchaseOrdersServer* inner class. Moreover, the seller agent needs to execute a one-shot behaviour updating the catalogue of books available for sale whenever its user adds a new book from the GUI. This is done through a method, called *updateCatalogue*, that creates the behaviour the agent needs and adds it to the list of running behaviours.

In particular, the code of the *RequestPerformer*, *OfferRequestsServer* and *PurchaseOrdersServer* action methods has the following structure[2]:

```
public void action() { // RequestPerformer
 switch (step) {
  case 0: // Send the cfp to all sellers
   Ě CFP message construction Ě
   myAgent.send(cfp);
   ... message type reception setting ...
   step = 1;
   break;
  case 1: // Receive all proposals/refusals
   ACLMessage reply = myAgent.receive(mt);
   if (reply != null) { // Reply received
     ... update the best offer ...
   }
   }
   repliesCnt++;
   if (repliesCnt >= sellerAgents.length) {
   // We received all replies
   step = 2;
   }
```

---

[2]Note that the *block* method blocks a behaviour until a new message arrives.

```
   else { block(); }
   break;
 case 2: // Send the purchase order
  ... order message construction ...
  myAgent.send(order);
  ... message type reception setting ...
  step = 3;
  break;
 case 3: // Receive the purchase order reply
  reply = myAgent.receive(mt);
  if (reply != null) { // Purchase order reply received
   if (reply.getPerformative() == ACLMessage.INFORM) {
    ... inform the user about success and exit ...
   }
   else {
    ... print: requested book already sold ...
   }
   step = 4;
  }
  else { block(); }
  break;
 }
}

public void action() { // RequestPerformer
 ... message type reception setting ...
 ACLMessage msg = myAgent.receive(mt);
 if (msg != null) { // CFP Message received. Process it
  String title = msg.getContent();
  ACLMessage reply = msg.createReply();
  Integer price = (Integer) catalogue.get(title);
  if (price != null) {
   // The requested book is available: reply with the price
   reply.setPerformative(ACLMessage.PROPOSE);
   reply.setContent(String.valueOf(price.intValue()));
  }
  else { // The requested book is not available
   reply.setPerformative(ACLMessage.REFUSE);
   reply.setContent("not-available");
  }
  myAgent.send(reply);
 }
 else { block(); }
}

public void action() { // PurchaseOrdersServer
 ... message type reception setting ...
 ACLMessage msg = myAgent.receive(mt);
 if (msg != null) {
  // ACCEPT_PROPOSAL Message received. Process it
```

```
String title = msg.getContent();
ACLMessage reply = msg.createReply();
Integer price = (Integer) catalogue.remove(title);
if (price != null) {
 reply.setPerformative(ACLMessage.INFORM);
 ... print: information about the sold book ...
 }
else {
 // The requested book has been already sold
 reply.setPerformative(ACLMessage.FAILURE);
 reply.setContent("not-available"); }
 myAgent.send(reply);
 }
else { block(); }
}
```

5.3 Applications supported by the platform

JADE is being used in a plethora of projects and applications, both from the academic and the industrial communities (see, for example, [11]). JADE applications cover different domains: collaborative work support, e-learning, e-tourism, network management, entertainment, knowledge management, manufacturing and supply-chain management and simulation.

In the following, we present some applications that have been realized taking advantage of JADE: the CoMMA system [93], the Agentcities agent network [1] and the RAP system [146].

5.3.1 CoMMA

CoMMA (Corporate Memory Management through Agents) is a FIPA compliant multi-agent system for the management of a corporate memory, implemented by using JADE [93]. It is the result of an international project funded by the European Commission. The project started in January 2000 and ended in Jannuary 2002. The CoMMA system was completely implemented and tested in different companies to offer a helping service for enhancing the insertion of new employees and as a support system for technology monitoring.

The innovative aspect of the system is the integration of several emerging technologies that were generally used separately in the former information retrieval and management systems. These technologies are: agent technology, knowledge modelling, XML technology, information retrieval techniques and machine learning techniques [56, 87, 16, 177]. The multi-agent approach, relying on loosely-coupled software components, is naturally prone to facilitate integration of different and heterogeneous technologies in one system. CoMMA developers therefore decided to use agents for wrapping information repositories defining the corporate memory, for the retrieval of information, for enhancing scaling, flexibility and extensibility of the corporate memory and to adapt the system interface to the users. One of the points that makes CoMMA system different from the majority of former multi-agent information systems is that agents are not only used for the retrieval of information, but also for the insertion of new information in the corporate memory. The use of JADE increases system modularity and flexibility. The separation between the software platform infrastructure managing agent life-cycle, distribution and communication and the software implementing agent tasks decouples modifications in these two parts. The behaviour based agent model, that JADE offers, allows to separate the software code realizing the different tasks of the agents; therefore, the modification of a task or the introduction of new tasks usually do not cause the modification of other parts of agent code. Moreover, given that the main complexity of the CoMMA system is given by the interaction between the different types of agents cooperating in the different tasks of the system, the availability in JADE of a FIPA ACL library for agent communication and a set of predefined behaviours for the management of FIPA communication protocols much reduces the cost of realizing the multi-agent system.

The CoMMA system aims at helping users in the management of an organization corporate memory and in particular at facilitating the creation, dissemination, transmission and reuse of knowledge in an organization. The services offered by the CoMMA system are the result of three main tasks: insertion of XML annotations of new or updated documents, search of existing documents, and autonomous document delivery in a push fashion to provide her/him with information about new interesting documents (figure 5.4 shows a schematic view of the CoMMA multi-agent system). These tasks are performed through the cooperation among different kinds of agents that can be divided in four sub-societies: document and annotation management; ontology (enterprise and user models) management; user management; agent interconnection and matchmaking.

The agents belonging to the document dedicated sub-society are concerned with the exploitation of documents and annotations composing the corporate memory, they search and retrieve the references matching the query of the user with the help of the ontological agents. A hierarchical organization of the document sub-society has been chosen since separates the task of maintaining document repositories from the task of intelligent interface towards the other agents of the system. The agents belonging to the ontology dedicated sub-society are concerned with the management of the ontological aspects of the information retrieval activity, especially the queries about the hierarchy of concepts and the different views. The ontology repository, composed of RDF schema forms, maintains a set of concepts

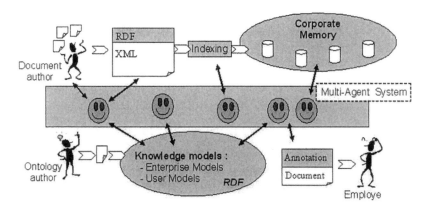

Figure 5.4. Schematic view of the CoMMA multi-agent system.

and their relationships. Documents of the community are annotated using these ontologies and the same ontologies are used to search documents into the corporate memory and to navigate into it. In particular, the CoMMA ontology describes the documents maintained in the organization corporate memory and the enterprise model describes the structure of the organization ruling, for example, the access to the different type of documents of the corporate memory. A replicated organization of the ontology sub-society has been chosen since ontologies shared by users should be quite stable and most of the queries will need the whole ontology to apply inference algorithms. Agents belonging to the user dedicated sub-society are concerned with the interface, the monitoring, the assistance and the adaptation to the user. Moreover, they maintain the user profile repository and distribute information about user profiles to the agents needing it. Finally agents belonging to the interconnection dedicated sub-society are in charge of the matchmaking of the other agents based upon their respective needs.

5.3.2   Agentcities

Agentcities is a network of FIPA compliant agent platforms that constitute a distributed environment to demonstrate the potential of autonomous agents. It started on the second half of 2001 as a research project funded by the European Commission [1]. One of the aims of the project is the development of a network architecture to allow the integration of platforms based on different technologies and models. It provides white pages and yellow pages services to allow the dynamic discovery of hosted agents and the services they offer. An important outcome is the exploitation of the capability of agent-based applications to adapt to rapidly evolving environments. This is particularly appropriate to dynamic societies where agents act as buyers and sellers negotiating their goods and services, and composing simple services offered by different providers into new compound services. To allow the integration of different applications and technologies in open environments, high level communication technologies are needed. The project largely relies on semantic languages, ontologies and protocols in compliance with the FIPA standards.

The Agentcities network grows around a backbone of 14 agent platforms, mostly hosted in Europe. These platforms are deployed as a testbed, hosting the services and the prototype applications developed during the lifetime of the project. The backbone is an important resource for other organizations, even external to the project, that can connect their own agent-based services, making the network really open and continuously evolving.

Currently, the Agentcities network counts 160 registered platforms. The platforms are based on more than a dozen of heterogeneous technologies, including Zeus [160], FIPA-OS [37] and Opal [175]. More than 2/3 of them are based on JADE and its derived technologies, as LEAP [133] and BlueJADE [17].

The main rationale for using agents is their ability to adapt to rapidly evolving environments and yet being able to achieve their goals. In many cases, this can only be accomplished by collaborating with other agents and leveraging on services provided by cooperating agents. This is particularly true when the desired goal is the creation of a new service to be provided to the community, as this scenario often calls for the composition of a number of simple services that are required to create the desired compound service. The Event Organizer is an agent-based prototype application showing the results that can be achieved using the services provided by the Agentcities project (figure 5.5 gives a graphical description of the event organizer). It allows a conference chair to organize an event, booking all needed venues and arranging all needed services, and then sell the tickets for the new event. Using the Web interface of the Event Organizer, users can list a set of needed services, fixing desired constraints on each individual service and among different services. The global goal is then split into sub-goals, assigned to skilled solver agents. The Event Organizer uses the marketplace infrastructure deployed on the Agentcities network to search for relevant venues. These are matched against cross-service constraints and, if found, a proper solution is proposed to the user as a list of services that allow the arrangement of the event. These services are then negotiated on the marketplace with their providers and a list of contracts is returned to the user. Finally, when the new event is successfully organized, the tickets for it can be sold, once again using the marketplace infrastructure. The process requires the cooperation of a number of partners. Each of them can exploit the directory services to dynamically discover the location of others. The Event Organizer directly interacts with a Trade House to search for venues and negotiate selected services. Other agents are responsible to offer goods (e.g., hotel and conference rooms) on the Trade House and to negotiate them on behalf of their users. A Banking Service takes care of managing the banking accounts of the involved partners, securing all requests against tampering and eavesdropping. An Auction House is used to create auctions and sell tickets of the new event. The interesting part of the process is that these tickets are available for other agent-based applications. In fact, an Evening Organizer helping its user to arrange an evening out (e.g., booking a restaurant and buying the tickets for a concert) can discover the new event and bid for some tickets on the Auction House.

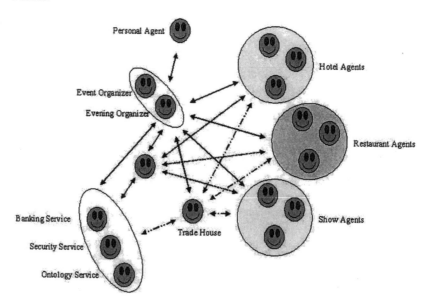

Figure 5.5.   Event organizer scenario.

5.3.3   RAP

RAP (Remote Assistant for Programmers) is a multi-agent system that integrates information and expert searching facilities for communities of students and researchers working on related projects developed in Java [146]. RAP associates a personal agent with each user, which helps her/him to solve problems proposing information and answers, extracted from some information repositories, and forwarding answers received by "experts" recommended on the basis of their expertise on the topic. A personal agent also maintains a profile of its user. This profile contains information about the competences and experience of its user and is built by using the answers sent to other users and the code written by the user.

The RAP system is based on seven different kinds of agents: Personal Agents, Code Documentation Managers, Answer Managers, User Profile Managers, Email Managers, Starter Agents and Directory Facilitators. Figure 5.6 gives a graphical representation of the architecture of the RAP platform; in particular, this figure presents the interactions of the personal agents and of the directory facilitator with the other agents of the platform.

Personal Agents are the agents that allow the interaction between the user and the different parts of the system and, in particular, between the users themselves. Moreover, this agent is responsible for building the user profile and maintaining it when its user is on-line. User-agent interaction can be performed in two different ways: when the user is active in the system, through a Web based interface; when it is off-line through emails. Usually, there is a Personal Agent for each on-line user, but sometimes Personal Agents are created to interact with off-line users via emails.

User Profile Managers are responsible for maintaining the profile of off-line users and for activating Personal Agents when it is necessary that they interact with their off-line users via emails.

Code Documentation Managers are responsible for maintaining code documentation and for finding the appropriate pieces of information to answer the queries done by the users of the system.

Answer Managers are responsible for maintaining the answers provided by users during the life of the system and for finding the appropriate answers to the new queries of the users. Besides providing answers to users, these agents are responsible for updating the score of the answer and forwarding the vote to either the Personal Agent or the user profile manager for updating the profile of the user that answered.

Email Managers are responsible for receiving emails from off-line users and forwarding them to the corresponding Personal Agents.

Starter Agents have the duty of activating a Personal Agent when either a user logs on or another agent requests it.

Directory Facilitators are responsible for informing an agent about the address of the other agents active in the system (e.g., a Personal Agent can ask about the address of all the other Personal Agents, of the code documentation managers, etc.).

A quite complete description of the behaviour of the system can be given showing the scenario where a user asks information to its personal agent to

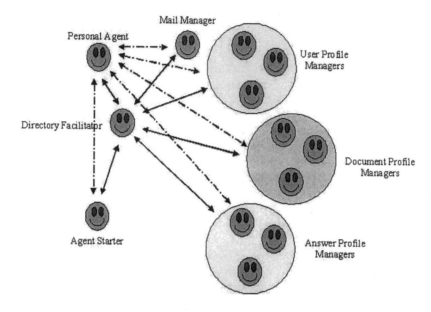

Figure 5.6. The RAP architecture.

solve a problem in its code and the personal agent finds one (or more) pieces of information that may help her/him. The description of this scenario can be divided in the following steps:

1) Select answer types. The user can receive: information extracted from code documentation, old answers stored in the answer repositories and new answers sent by the other users of the system. Therefore, before submitting the query, the user can select the types of answers (one or more) she/he likes to receive.

2) Submit a query. The user, through its user interface, provides the query to its personal agent. In particular, the user can query either about a class or an aggregation of classes for implementing a particular task or about a problem related to her/his current implementation. The query is composed of two parts. The first part (we call it "annotation") identifies the context of the query and can contains keywords provided by a system glossary and/or the identification of classes and/or methods in a univocal way (i.e., the user needs to specify the complete package name for a class and the class name for a method). The second part contains the textual contents of the query.

3) Find answers. The personal agents perform different actions and interact with different agents to collect the various types of answers. For getting code documentation, the personal agent asks the directory facilitator about all the code documentation managers. After receiving this information, the personal agent forwards the query to all these agents. These agents search pieces of code documentation related to the query and send them to the personal agent associating a score with each piece. For getting answers from the answer system repositories, the personal agent asks the directory facilitator about all the answer managers. After receiving this information, the personal agent forward the query to all these agents. These agents search answers related to the query and send them to the personal agent associating a score with each answer. The reception of new answers from the system users is a more complex activity and its description can be divided in four further steps:

3.1) Find experts. The personal agent asks the directory facilitator about the other active personal agents (i.e., the personal agents of the user that are available on-line) and all the user profile managers of the system (i.e., the agents managing the profile of the users that are off-line). After receiving this information, the personal agent forwards the query to these personal agents together to the user profile managers.

3.2) Receive expert rating. All these agents (personal agents and user profile managers) compute the rating of their users to answer to this query on the basis of the query itself and of the user profile. The agents that compute a positive score (i.e., its user may give an appropriate answer to the query) reply to the querying personal agent with the rating of its user (in the case of a personal agent) or its users (in the case of user profile manager).

3.3) Select experts. The personal agent divides on-line and off-line users, order them on the basis of their rating and, finally, presents these two lists to its user. The user can select more than one user and then the personal agent sends the query to the corresponding personal agents (for the on-line users) and to the corresponding user profile managers (for the off-line users).

3.4) Receive answers. The replying personal agents immediately present the query to their user and forward the answer as soon as the user provides it. User profile manager activates the personal agents of the involved users through the starter agent. These personal agents forward the query to their user via email and then terminate themselves. Users can answer either via email or when they log again on the system. In the case of email, the email manager starts the appropriate personal agent that extracts the answer from the email and forwards it. When the querying personal agent receives an answer, it immediately forward it to its user.

4) Rate answers. After the reception of all the queries, or when the deadline for ending them expired, or, finally, when the user has already found an answer satisfying its request, the personal agent presents the list of read answers to its user asking her/him to rate them. After the rating, it forwards each rating to the corresponding personal agent, code documentation manager, answer manager or user profile manager that provides to update the user profile and/or the answer rating (when a user rates an answer retrieved from the answer repository, this rating is also used to updated the user profile of the user that previously proposed the answer). Note that in the case of rating of users answers, the rating cannot be known by the user that sent the answer and users that did not send answers automatically received a negative rating.

The management of user and document profiles is performed in two different phases: an initialization phase and an updating phase.

In order to simplify, speed-up and reduce the possibility of inaccuracy due to peopleŠs opinions of themselves and to incomplete information, we decided to build the initial profile of the users and documents in an automated way that, for the users, is very similar to the one used by Expert Finder system [230].

Profiles are represented by vectors of weighted terms whose value are related to the frequency of the term in the document or to the frequency of the use of the term by the user. The set of terms used in the profiles is not extracted from a training set of documents, but it corresponds to those terms included in the system glossary, provided to the users for annotating their queries, and to the names of the classes and methods of the Java software libraries used by the community of the users of the system.

Document and user profiles are computed by using term frequency inverse document frequency (TF-IDF) [200] and profiles weighted terms correspond to the TF-IDF weight. Each user profile is built by userŠs personal agent through the analysis of the Java code she/he has written. The profile built by personal agents is only the initial userŠs profile, and it will be updated when the user writes new software and especially when the user helps other users answering their queries.

5.4   Final Remarks

In this chapter we presented JADE (Java Agent Development framework), a software framework to support the development of agent applications that is considered the reference implementation of the FIPA specifications.

JADE is written in Java and comprises various Java packages, giving application programmers both ready-made pieces of functionality and abstract interfaces for custom, application dependent tasks. Java was chosen because of its many attractive features, which are particularly geared towards object-oriented programming in distributed heterogeneous environments. Starting from the same assumption behind FIPA specifications, i.e., that only the external behaviour of system components should be specified, leaving the implementation details and internal architectures to agent developers, JADE provides a very general but primitive agent model that can serve as a useful basis to implement more sophisticated agent architectures. In addition, the behaviour abstraction of the JADE agent model permits an easy integration of external software and it was done with success allowing, for example, the integration of JADE with rules engines (JESS and DROOLS), Web technologies (servlets and JSP), ontology management tools (Protegè and Jena).

Three of the most important features of JADE are: heterogeneous device and network support, performance and scalability. In fact, JADE has been proved suitable to realize large and complex multi-agent systems composed of thousands of agents distributed on different heterogeneous networks, running on heterogeneous devices and exchanging huge amount of messages.

JADE is an open source project around which a community of users and contributors has grown up, and recently also an International Governing Board, called "JADE board" has been established. The JADE board is a no-profit organization that join five industrial companies (TILAB, Motorola, Whitestein Technologies, Profactor, and France Telecom), with the intent of promoting the evolution and the adoption of JADE by the mobile telecommunications industries as a Java-based de-facto standard middleware for agent-based applications in the mobile personal communication sector.

Acknowledgments

This work is partially supported by the European Commission through the contracts "@lis Technology Net (ALA/2002/049-055)" and by MIUR (Ministero dell'Istruzione, dell'Universitá e della Ricerca) through the COFIN project ANEMONE.

Chapter 6

JADEX: A BDI REASONING ENGINE

Alexander Pokahr,[1] Lars Braubach,[1] and Winfried Lamersdorf[1]

[1] *University of Hamburg*
Distributed Systems and Information Systems
22527 Hamburg, Germany
{pokahr|braubach|lamersd}@informatik.uni-hamburg.de

Abstract   This chapter presents Jadex, a software framework for the creation of goal-oriented agents following the belief-desire-intention (BDI) model. The Jadex project aims to make the development of agent based systems as easy as possible without sacrificing the expressive power of the agent paradigm. The objective is to build up a rational agent layer that sits on top of a middleware agent infrastructure and allows for intelligent agent construction using sound software engineering foundations. Fostering a smooth transition from traditional distributed systems to the development of multi-agent systems, well established object-oriented concepts and technologies such as Java and XML are employed wherever applicable. Moreover, the Jadex reasoning engine tries to overcome traditional limitations of BDI systems by introducing explicit goals. This allows goal deliberation mechanisms being realized and additionally facilitates application development by making results from goal-oriented analysis and design easily transferable to the implementation layer. The system is freely available under LGPL license and provides extensive documentation as well as illustrative example applications.

Keywords: BDI agents, FIPA standard, object-oriented software engineering, explicit goals.

6.1   Motivation

Today, a numerousness of different agent platforms is available for developing multi-agent applications [144]. Nevertheless, most of these platforms are developed with a specific technological focus such as the cognitive or infrastructural architecture. Hence, not all aspects of agent technology are covered equally well. General applicability of an agent platform for a great variety of domains demands that at least three categories of requirements are considered: openness, middleware, and reasoning. Openness is closely related to the vision of interconnected networks of originally unrelated applications whereas middleware aspects emphasize traditional software engineering concerns such as service management, security and persistency aspects. Reasoning, in turn, focuses on the agent's internal decision-making process and mostly tries to map this process from a natural archetype such as insects or humans.

According to these aspects, the existing platforms can be classified into two almost distinct groups. On the one hand, FIPA-compliant platforms mainly address openness and middleware issues by realizing the FIPA communication respectively platform standards [172]. On the other hand, reasoning-centered platforms exist, that focus on the behaviour model of a single agent, e.g. trying to achieve rationality and goal-directedness. This gap between middleware and reasoning-centered systems is one main motivation for the realization of the Jadex BDI (Belief-Desire-Intention) reasoning engine [30, 171], which aims to bring together both research strands.

Besides this overall objective to support both classical virtues from middleware and BDI reasoning, the design of the system is driven by two main factors. On the one hand, the development of the reasoning engine is accompanied by an ongoing effort of enhancing the BDI architecture in general. The system addresses shortcomings of earlier BDI agent systems, e.g. by providing an explicit representation of goals and a systematic way for the integration of goal deliberation mechanisms. On the other hand, the system respects the current state of the art regarding mainstream object-oriented software engineering, and is designed to be used not only by AI experts, but also by the normally skilled software developer. Therefore, agent development is based on established techniques such as Java and XML, and is further supported by software engineering aspects, such as reusable modules and development tools.

6.2   Architecture

This section presents the architectural underpinnings of the Jadex system. It starts with a short review of the BDI model and related systems. Subsequently, an overview of the architecture of Jadex is presented. The basic concepts – beliefs, goals, and plans – of the system are introduced by highlighting their main characteristics and differences to other BDI agent systems. Finally, the execution model is shortly sketched, showing how the components of the system interoperate.

6.2.1 BDI Models and Systems

The BDI model was initially conceived by Bratman as a theory of human practical reasoning [28]. Its success is based on its simplicity reducing the explanation framework for complex human behavior to the *motivational stance* [58]. In this model, causes for actions are only related to desires ignoring other facets of cognition such as emotions. Another strength of the BDI model is the consistent usage of folk psychological notions that closely correspond to the way people communicate about human behavior [157].

The BDI theory of Rao and Georgeff [182] defines beliefs, desires, and intentions as mental attitudes represented as possible world states. The intentions of an agent are subsets of the beliefs and desires, i.e., an agent acts towards some of the world states it desires to be true and believes to be possible. To be computationally tractable Rao and Georgeff also proposed several simplifications to the theory, the most important one being that only beliefs are represented explicitly. Desires are reduced to events that are handled by predefined plan templates, and intentions are represented implicitly by the runtime stack of plans to be executed.

According to Martha Pollack [96], work on BDI can be further subdivided into three categories: 1. General models for practical reasoning, based on BDI concepts. 2. Computational models based on the "Intelligent Resource-Bounded Machine Architecture" (IRMA) [27], exhibiting close correspondence to Bratman's philosophy. 3. The computational model employed in the PRS family of systems [98, 118], which found many uses in practice. Nowadays, current descendants of the PRS family, in particular commercial products and solutions such as Agent Oriented Software's JACK 7 and Agentis' AdaptivEnterprise Suite [127] have the most practical relevance concerning development of agent-based software systems.

In the next sections, the architecture of the Jadex reasoning engine, which basically follows the PRS computational model, will be described. Important differences to other representatives of the PRS family will be highlighted in the corresponding subsections.

6.2.2 Concepts within Jadex

In Fig. 6.1 an overview of the abstract Jadex architecture is presented. Viewed from the outside, an agent is a black box, which receives and sends messages. As common in PRS-like systems, all kinds of events, such as incoming messages or goal events serve as input to the internal reaction and deliberation mechanism, which dispatches the events to plans selected from the plan library. In Jadex, the reaction and deliberation mechanism is the only global component of an agent. All other components are grouped into reusable modules called capabilities.

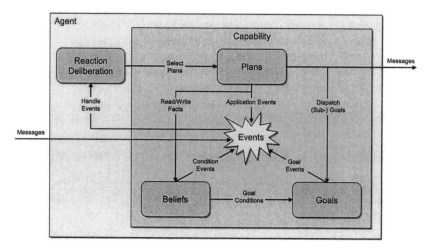

Figure 6.1.   Jadex abstract architecture

Beliefs

One objective of the Jadex project is the adoption of a software engineering perspective for describing agents. In other BDI systems, beliefs are represented in some kind of first-order predicate logic (e.g. Jason, described in chapter 1) or using relational models (e.g. JACK and JAM [114]). In Jadex, an object-oriented representation of beliefs is employed, where arbitrary objects can be stored as named facts (called beliefs) or named sets of facts (called belief sets). Operations against the beliefbase can be issued in a descriptive set-oriented query language. Moreover, the beliefbase is not only a passive data store, but takes an active part in the agent's execution, by monitoring belief state conditions. Changes of beliefs may therefore directly lead to actions such as events being generated or goals being created or dropped.

Goals

Goals are a central concept in Jadex, following the general idea that goals are concrete, momentary desires of an agent. For any goal it has, an agent will more or less directly engage into suitable actions, until it considers the goal as being reached, unreachable, or not wanted any more. In other PRS-like systems, goals are represented by a special kind of event. Therefore, in these systems the current goals of an agent are only implicitly available as the causes of currently executing plans. In Jadex, goals are represented as explicit objects contained in a goalbase, which is accessible to the reasoning

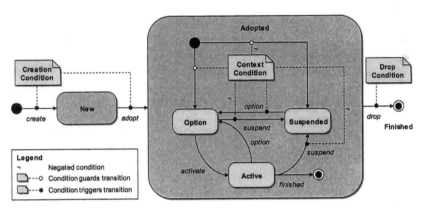

Figure 6.2. Goal lifecycle (from [32])

component as well as to plans if they need to know or want to change the current goals of the agent. Because goals are represented separately from plans, the system can retain goals that are not currently associated to any plan. As a result, unlike other BDI systems, Jadex does not require that all adopted goals are consistent to each other, as long as only consistent subsets of those goals are pursued at any time. To distinguish between just adopted and actively pursued goals, a goal lifecycle is introduced which consists of the goal states *option*, *active*, and *suspended* (see Fig. 6.2). When a goal is adopted, it becomes an option that is added to the agent's goalbase, either as top-level goal, or when created from a plan as subgoal of a plan's root goal. Application specific goal deliberation settings specify dependencies between goals, and are used for managing the state transitions of all adopted goals (i.e. deciding which goals are active and which are just options). In addition, some goals may only be valid in specific contexts determined by the agent's beliefs. When the context of a goal is invalid, it will be suspended until the context is valid again.

Jadex supports four types of goals, which extend the general lifecycle and exhibit different behaviour with regard to their processing as explained below. A *perform* goal is directly related to the execution of actions. Therefore, the goal is considered to be reached, when some actions have been executed, regardless of the outcome of these actions. An *achieve* goal is a goal in the traditional sense, which defines a desired world state without specifying how to reach it. Agents may try several different alternative plans, to achieve a goal of this type. A *query* goal is similar to an achieve goal, but the desired state is not a state of the (outside) world, but an internal state of the agent, regarding the availability of some information the agent wants to know about.

For goals of type *maintain*, an agent keeps track of a desired state, and will continuously execute appropriate plans to re-establish this maintained state whenever needed. More details about goal representation and processing in Jadex can be found in [32].

Plans

Plans represent the behavioural elements of an agent and are composed of a head and a body part. The plan head specification is similar to other BDI systems and mainly specifies the circumstances under which a plan may be selected, e.g. by stating events or goals handled by the plan and preconditions for the execution of the plan. Additionally, in the plan head a context condition can be stated that must be true for the plan to continue executing. The plan body provides a predefined course of action, given in a procedural language. This course of action is to be executed by the agent, when the plan is selected for execution, and may contain actions provided by the system API, such as sending messages, manipulating beliefs, or creating subgoals.

Capabilities

Capabilities, introduced in [39], represent a grouping mechanism for the elements of a BDI agent, such as beliefs, goals, plans, and events. In this way, closely related elements can be put together into a reusable module, which encapsulates a certain functionality (e.g. for interaction with a FIPA directory facilitator). The enclosing capability of an element represents its scope, and an element only has access to elements of the same scope (e.g. a plan may only access beliefs or handle goals or events of the same capability). To connect different capabilities, flexible import / export mechanisms can be used that define the external interface of the capability (e.g. beliefs or goals visible to the outside).

6.2.3   Execution Model

This section shows the operation of the reaction and deliberation component, given the Jadex BDI concepts as described earlier. All of the required functionality is assigned to cleanly separated components, which will be explained in turn. Incoming messages are placed in the agent's global message queue by the underlying agent platform such as JADE (see chapter 5). Before the message can be forwarded to the system, it has to be assigned to a capability, which is able to handle the message. If the message belongs to an ongoing conversation, an event for the incoming message is created in the capability executing the conversation. Otherwise, a suitable capability has to be found, which is done by matching the message against event templates defined in

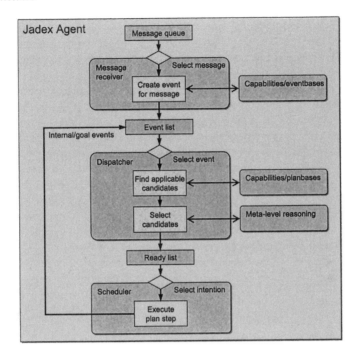

Figure 6.3. Jadex execution model

the eventbase of each capability. The best matching template is then used to create an appropriate event in the scope of the capability. In either case, the created event is subsequently added to the agent's global event list.

The dispatcher is responsible for selecting applicable plans for the events from the event list. This is done in two steps: First, a list of applicable plans is generated by matching the event against the plan heads as defined in the planbases of each capability, whereby only those capabilities have to be considered, where the event is visible. The second step is to select a subset of the applicable plans for execution. Regarding this step several important questions arise, such as if all of the applicable plans should be executed concurrently, or if the event is posted to another plan if the first plan fails [39]. The decision of which plan to execute is called meta-level reasoning and may be as simple as selecting the first plan from the list, or as complicated as finding and executing meta-plans for the decision. Jadex provides flexible settings to influence this event processing individually for event types and instances. As a default, messages are posted to only one single plan, while for goals, many plans are executed sequentially until the goal is reached or fi-

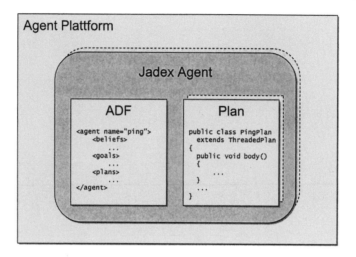

Figure 6.4. Jadex agent

nally failed, when no more plans are applicable. Internal events are posted to all plans at once, as they are considered only as a change notification and no return value is expected from executed plans. After plans have been selected, they are placed in the ready list, waiting for execution.

The execution of plans is performed by a scheduler, which selects the plans from the ready list. Plans are executed step-by-step, whereby (in contrast to other PRS-like systems) the length of plan step depends on the context, and not only on the plan itself. A plan is executed only until it waits explicitly or significantly affects the internal state of the agent (e.g. by creating or dropping a goal). Internal state changes can be caused directly or through side effects, e.g. when a belief change triggers the creation condition of a goal. After the plan waits or is interrupted, the state of the agent can be properly updated, e.g. a newly created goal might lead to other plans being scheduled.

6.3   Language

Jadex is neither based on a new agent programming language nor does it employ or revise an existing one. Instead, a hybrid approach is chosen, distinguishing explicitly between the language used for static agent type specification and the language for defining the dynamic agent behaviour. According to this distinction, a Jadex agent consists of two components: An agent definition file (ADF) for the specification of inter alia beliefs, goals and plans as well as their initial values and on the other hand procedural plan code (see Fig. 6.4). For defining ADFs, an XML language is used that follows the Jadex BDI metamodel specified in XML Schema. The XML structure specification is augmented by a declarative expression language, e.g. for specifying goal-conditions. The procedural part of plans (the plan bodies) are realized in an ordinary programming language (Java) and have access to the BDI facilities of an agent through an application program interface (API).

6.3.1   Specifications and Syntactical Aspects

The Jadex BDI metamodel defined in XML Schema is very extensive and hence cannot be presented completely in this paper (for a complete introduction see [170]). Generally, the corresponding language was specified with two design principles in mind. The first design objective is the support for strong typing and explicit representation of all kinds of elements, be it beliefs, goals or events. In consequence, this requires users to write detailed ADFs, but in return allows for more rigorous consistency checking of agent models. Additionally, at runtime certain kinds of failures can be discovered more easily, e.g. the attempt of storing a fact value in an undefined belief can be immediately reported.

The second design objective regards increasing the expressive power of the ADF for the following purposes: The arbitrary complex creation of objects (e.g. values within beliefs or parameters), the description of boolean conditions (e.g. when a certain goal should be dropped) and the construction of queries (e.g. for retrieving values from the beliefbase). To achieve this, an embedded expression language is used for specifying parts of the agent model, not easily represented in XML. Expressions are used throughout the XML ADF, whenever values have to be obtained for certain elements at runtime, e.g. values of beliefs, conditions of goals, etc. Expressions should be side effect free, because they are often evaluated internally by the system. The expression language has been designed to fully comply with the syntax of Java expressions (right hand side of assignments) extended with a subset of OQL (object query language) instructions [15]. The syntax of the OQL extension is depicted in Fig. 6.5 in EBNF notation. It allows for query statements being created in the well-known *select-from-where* form, whereby it can be additionally specified if exactly one (iota), the first satisfying (any) or all satisfying results are expected (line 1). In the *from* clause (lines 3–4) it is specified from which object set (line 4) or joined sets (line 3) results are generated. The identifiers define variables, which iterate over the object sets specified as arbitrary expressions. These iterated values are checked against the boolean *where* condition (line 6) and can possibly be ordered (line 7). The example query, corresponding to the example presented in section

```
01: select_expression ::= "SELECT" ("ALL" | "ANY" | "IOTA")?
02: (
03:   expression "FROM" ("$" identifier "IN" expression) ("," "$" identifier "IN" expression)*
04:   | "$" identifier "FROM" expression
05: )
06: ("WHERE" expression)?
07: ("ORDER" "BY" expression ("ASC" | "DESC")? )?


Example: SELECT $block FROM $beliefbase.blocks WHERE $block.isClear()
```

Figure 6.5.   OQL syntax in EBNF and query example

6.3.3, shows that it is possible to use Java method calls like isClear() in the expression language. While queries can be used in any expression, they are most useful for predefined views on subsets of the agent's beliefs, which can be evaluated at runtime (e.g. from within plans).

In the following the essential BDI concepts as presented in Section 6.2.2 will be taken on and their realization on language level will be detailed. These concepts are specified as part of an agent or capability description in the same manner. In Fig. 6.6 (left hand side) the allowed attributes and subtags of the agent tag are shown. Each agent type is identified by a name and package declaration and can be provided with a description text. In addition, the corresponding agent class and runtime properties can be set. For most cases, the default values are sufficient and need not be modified. It can be seen that besides the subtags for the core BDI concepts (beliefs, goals, plans and events which are explained below) several other elements can be declared. Most of these elements (languages, ontologies, servicedescriptions and agentdescriptions) are FIPA related and facilitate agent communication respectively the interaction with yellow page services. The remaining elements (imports, expressions, properties) are implementation details, serving for convenience (e.g. to avoid duplicate declarations) and agent configuration purposes, such as logging or debugging settings.

Beliefs

In Jadex, beliefs are represented in an object-oriented way allowing arbitrary Java objects being stored as facts. Like all elements of a capability, beliefs and belief sets can be supplied with a name, a description text and an exported flag. Exporting an element makes it accessible from the outer scope (respectively a capability or an agent) and is turned off by default. For beliefs and belief sets, the Java class for facts must be defined. Besides the type-relevant information, initial fact data can also be supplied for configur-

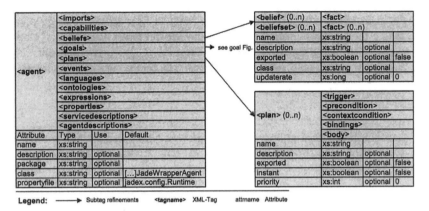

Figure 6.6.   Agent metamodel specification fragment (XML-schema)

ing an agent's mental state at creation time. The value of a fact has to be stated in the expression language and can be declared as static or dynamic, whereby dynamic facts are useful e.g. for representing values continuously sensed from an environment or time-relevant aspects. Re-calculation of such dynamic facts occurs on access and additionally in fixed time intervals (using the update rate). At runtime, beliefs and belief sets are accessible from within plans via operations on the beliefbase and additionally by issuing OQL-like queries.

Goals

As described earlier in Jadex four different goal types are distinguished (perform, achieve, maintain and query). All these goal types are based on the generic life cycle and hence exhibit many common properties that are summarized in an abstract base goal type (see Fig. 6.7). According to the lifecycle, creation, drop and context conditions can be specified as boolean expressions. Customization of goal types can be further achieved by defining named in-, out- and inout-parameters that are used to transfer information between a goal's originator and its processing plans. Additionally, binding parameters can be used for generating one goal instance for every possible binding. The runtime processing of goals can be refined using the various BDI-flags, which inter alia control if a goal is retried when a plan fails (retry), if meta-level reasoning is used (mlreasoning) and if applicable plans are tried sequentially or in parallel (posttoall). A complete explanation can be found in [170].

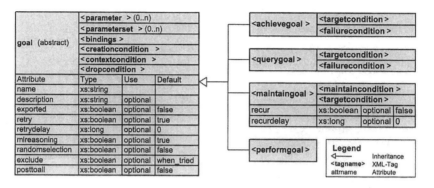

Figure 6.7. Goal metamodel specification (XML-schema)

From the abstract goal type, all concrete types are derived. The simplest one being the perform goal used for executing (possibly repeatedly) certain actions, which does not require extra specification data. An achieve goal extends this abstract goal type and adds support for the specification of a target and a failure condition. The target condition is used for describing the world state this goal seeks to bring about as a boolean expression. Similarly, a boolean failure condition has the purpose to abort goal processing in case its achievement has become impossible. The query goal provides the same kind of conditions, but exhibits a slightly different behaviour in that it is used for information retrieval purposes.

Most complex behaviour is exposed by the maintain goal type, which is used to monitor a specific world state (maintain condition) and automatically tries to reestablish this state whenever it becomes invalid. A boolean target condition can be used to refine the state that is tried to be restored. Maintain goals are not dropped when they are achieved once, but remain inactive until the monitored state is violated again. Moreover, a maintain goal can be configured to retry re-establishment in certain time intervals (recur and recurdelay), when it has failed for some reason. In addition to the specification of the four types of goals, possibly parametrized initial goals can be declared that will be created when the agent is born. At runtime, goal instances can be created from within plans by referring to their type name. Typically, some parameter values need to be supplied before a goal can be dispatched as top-level goal or as subgoal of the current plan.

Plans

The declaration of plans in Jadex is very similar to other PRS-like systems and requires the specification of the plan heads describing the circumstances under which a plan is applicable in the ADF. As plan trigger, internal events, messages, and goals, as well as a belief state condition (for data driven plans) can be provided. The pre- and context condition of a plan can be specified as boolean expressions. To facilitate goal achievement with plans, it is sometimes advantageous to create several different parametrized plan instances of a plan type and try them one after another until a plan succeeds. For this purpose, binding parameters can be specified and used for plan configuration. Furthermore, the selection of which plan is executed in response to an occurring trigger can be adjusted by setting a priority value. As part of the initial mental state of an agent, it can be further declared whether a plan is instantiated when the agent is created (using the instant flag).

The plan body needs to be supplied as expression for the creation of a suitable plan instance. Currently, two different types of plan bodies (standard and mobile) are supported, which both require a Java class to be implemented. Mobile plan bodies have several disadvantages compared to the standard versions, but nonetheless make sense in mobile scenarios as agent migration is provided. In Fig. 6.8 the skeleton of an application plan is depicted. Mandatory is only the extension of a corresponding framework class (Plan) and the implementation of the abstract body() method, in which the domain-specific plan behaviour can be placed. In addition to the body method, three other methods exist that optionally can be implemented. These methods are called when plan processing has finished according to the plans final state. The passed() method is called when the body method completes, whereas the failed() method is invoked when an uncatched exception is thrown within the body() method. Finally, the aborted() method is called, when plan processing was interrupted from outside. Two different abort cases can be distinguished, either when the corresponding goal succeeds before the plan is finished or when the plans root goal is dropped.

6.3.2 Software Engineering Issues

The overall goal of the Jadex project is to provide a sophisticated reasoning engine allowing to develop arbitrary complex intelligent agents. Therefore, while trying to be as easily useable as possible, the system does not sacrifice expressiveness for simplicity. Nonetheless, software engineering issues play an important role in the design of the system.

As stated earlier, a primary goal of the project is to facilitate a smooth transition from mainstream object-oriented software development to an agent-oriented approach. This is achieved by resorting to established techniques

```
01: /** Plan skeleton for an application plan. */
02: public class SomePlan extends jadex.runtime.Plan {
03:
04:   public void body() {
05:     // Plan code.
06:   }
07:
08:   public void passed() {
09:     // Optional cleanup code in case of a plan success.
10:   }
11:   public void failed() {
12:     // Optional cleanup code in case of a plan failure.
13:   }
14:   public void aborted() {
15:     // Optional cleanup code in case the plan is aborted.
16:   }
17: }
```

Figure 6.8.   Plan skeleton

wherever possible. E.g., the system builds on Java and XML, therefore the developer does not have to learn a new language. Another advantage is that the developer can continue to operate in a familiar environment. As the agent developer only has to create Java and XML files, existing development environments such as Eclipse[1] or IntelliJ IDEA[2] can be used to develop Jadex agents. In recent editions of these environments, features such as on-the-fly checking and auto-completion not only apply to Java coding but can also easily be adopted for XML ADF creation,[3] therefore offering extensive support for Jadex agent development.

Moreover, the system provides advanced software engineering features, such as reusability and consistency checking. The capability concept allows encapsulating agent functionality into a reusable module while maintaining the abstraction level of BDI elements. The explicit specification and strong typing of beliefs, goals, etc. facilitates consistency checks of ADFs to detect errors (e.g. spelling mistakes) as early as possible.

6.3.3   Example

To further explain the syntax and semantics of the Jadex agent languages, in this section a simple example is provided. The example does only cover a small subset of the features of Jadex. Another example covering all different types of goals can be found elsewhere [32]. The example presented

---

[1] http://www.eclipse.org/
[2] http://www.jetbrains.com/idea/
[3] In eclipse this can be realized by the XMLBuddy plug-in (see .http://xmlbuddy.com/).

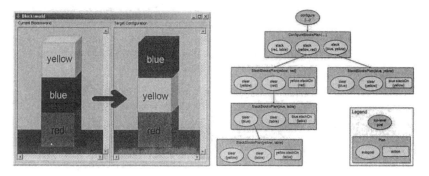

Figure 6.9. Blocksworld scenario (left) and goal/plan tree (right)

here is a fully functional agent, taken directly from the current Jadex distribution. The purpose of the agent is to establish given configurations in a blocksworld environment, where colored blocks are placed in stacks on top of a table. The example provides a graphical user interface, where the user can visually create custom block configurations (see Fig. 6.9, left hand side). The configurations have to be established by the agent by moving the blocks. As only clear blocks (without other blocks on top) can be moved, the agent has to perform some ad-hoc planning. The implemented solution is very simple, creating the stacks bottom-to-top. Fig. 6.9 (right hand side) shows the planning process. To achieve the target configuration, subgoals are created to stack the red block on the table, the yellow block on the red, and the blue block on the yellow (see ConfigureBlocksPlan). To stack two blocks on each other, a StackBlocksPlan clears both blocks and performs the stackOn action. To clear a block, all obstructing blocks are moved to the table.

The ADF of the agent is shown in Fig. 6.10, where tags (elements of the Jadex metamodel) are in boldface, and embedded expressions are in italics. The model starts with the declaration of the agent tag, specifying the name and package of the agent (line 1). The package is used as first place to resolve references to other files such as capabilities and Java classes. More packages and files can be explicitly specified in the imports section (lines 2-4). In this case the class java.awt.Color is imported, because it is used to represent the color of a block.

The beliefs of the agent are given in the beliefs section (lines 6-16). A belief "table" (lines 7-9) is used to represent the environment, which consists of a table on which blocks are located. As initial fact of the belief, an instance of the Table class (located in package jadex.examples.blocksworld) is created (line 8). The known blocks are collected in a belief set "blocks" (lines 10-15).

```
01: <agent name="Blocksworld" package="jadex.examples.blocksworld">
02:   <imports>
03:     <import>java.awt.Color</import>
04:   </imports>
05:
06:   <beliefs>
07:     <belief name="table" class="Table">
08:       <fact>new Table()</fact>
09:     </belief>
10:     <beliefset name="blocks" class="Block">
11:       <fact>new Block(new Color(240,16,16),$beliefbase.table)</fact>
12:       <fact>new Block(new Color(16,16,240),$beliefbase.table.allBlocks[0])</fact>
13:       <fact>new Block(new Color(240,240,16),$beliefbase.table.allBlocks[1])</fact>
14:       ...
15:     </beliefset>
16:   </beliefs>
17:
18:   <goals>
19:     <achievegoal name="clear">
20:       <parameter name="block" class="Block" />
21:       <targetcondition>$goal.block.isClear()</targetcondition>
22:     </achievegoal>
23:     <achievegoal name="stack">
24:       <parameter name="block" class="Block" />
25:       <parameter name="target" class="Block" />
26:       <targetcondition>$goal.block.lower==$goal.target</targetcondition>
27:     </achievegoal>
28:     <achievegoal name="configure">
29:       <parameter name="configuration" class="Table" />
30:       <targetcondition>
31:         $beliefbase.table.configurationEquals($goal.configuration)
32:       </targetcondition>
33:     </achievegoal>
34:   </goals>
35:
36:   <plans>
37:     <plan name="stack">
38:       <body>new StackBlocksPlan($event.goal.block, $event.goal.target)</body>
39:       <trigger><goal ref="stack"/></trigger>
40:     </plan>
41:     <plan name="configure">
42:       <body>new ConfigureBlocksPlan($event.goal.configuration)</body>
43:       <trigger><goal ref="configure"/></trigger>
44:     </plan>
45:     <plan name="clear">
46:       <bindings>
47:         <binding name="upper">
48:           select $upper from $beliefbase.blocks where $upper.lower==$event.goal.block
49:         </binding>
50:       </bindings>
51:       <body>new StackBlocksPlan($upper, $beliefbase.table)</body>
52:       <trigger><goal ref="clear"/></trigger>
53:     </plan>
54:   </plans>
55: </agent>
```

Figure 6.10. Blocksworld agent model

A number of blocks (class Block) with different colors is initially created given by single fact items (lines 11, 12, 13 ...). The first block is created on the table, while the other blocks are created on top of each other (referenced by table.allBlocks[]).

The agent has three achieve goals, each with a name, parameters and a corresponding target condition (lines 18-34). The "clear" goal (lines 19-22) represents the goal to clear (i.e. remove blocks located on top) a block given in a parameter (line 20). The target condition (line 21) refers directly to the isClear() method of this block. The "stack" goal (lines 23-27) aims at placing a given block (line 24) on a target block (line 25). Achieving this goal means that the block below the first block is now equal to the target block as stated by the target condition (line 26). To establish a complete configuration of blocks on the table, the "configure" goal (lines 28-31) is used. The desired configuration is given as a parameter of type Table (line 29). The target condition (line 30-32) refers to the configurationEquals() method implemented in the Table class. No initial instances of these three goal types are defined in the model. The agent starts idle, waiting for goals to appear, which are created by the user through a GUI.

The goals are handled by the plans of the agent (lines 36-54). In this example, there is one plan for each goal, although this kind of one to one mapping is not required. The plan head declarations of the first two plans "stack" (lines 37-40) and "configure" (lines 41-44) are straightforward. The trigger (lines 39 and 43) defines when the plan is applicable, in this case for goals of type "stack" and "configure", respectively. The body (lines 38, 42) defines how the plan body object is instantiated. In both cases, the creation expression refers to parameters of the triggering goal to supply the arguments for the Java constructor (cf. Figs. 6.11, 6.12). The "clear" plan definition is more complex, as the body of the "stack" plan is reused (see line 51) to move all blocks from the top of the block to be cleared to the table. To resolve the parameters used for body creation, a bindings declaration is used (lines 46-50). The variable $upper is assigned to all blocks located on top of the given block (select statement in line 48). For each of these variable assignments an instance of the plan is created, assuring that all blocks are removed from the given block.

The Java files of the two plan bodies are shown in Figs. 6.11 and 6.12, respectively. References to classes and methods provided by the Jadex engine are shown in boldface. Both plan classes define a constructor which takes the plan arguments and stores them in corresponding fields (lines 6-12 respectively 6-10) such that they are accessible from the body() methods, which will be described in turn.

The body() method of the StackBlocksPlan (Fig. 6.11, lines 14-24) first clears both blocks provided as arguments, and then moves the first block on

```
01: package jadex.examples.blocksworld;
02: import jadex.runtime.*;
03:
04: /** Plan to stack one block on top of another target block. */
05: public class StackBlocksPlan extends Plan {
06:   protected Block block;
07:   protected Block target;
08:
09:   public StackBlocksPlan(Block block, Block target) {
10:     this.block = block;
11:     this.target = target;
12:   }
13:
14:   public void body() {
15:     IGoal clear = createGoal("clear");
16:     clear.getParameter("block").setValue(block);
17:     dispatchSubgoalAndWait(clear);
18:
19:     clear = createGoal("clear");
20:     clear.getParameter("block").setValue(target);
21:     dispatchSubgoalAndWait(clear);
22:
23:     block.stackOn(target);
24:   }
25: }
```

Figure 6.11. Java code for StackBlocksPlan

top of the other. To clear the first block, a goal of type "clear" (cf. Fig. 6.10) is created (line 15) and the parameter is set to the block (line 16). The dispatchSubgoalAndWait() method (line 17) forces the agent to adopt the goal, and halts the execution of the plan until goal processing is finished. If the goal fails, an exception is thrown causing the whole plan to fail. Otherwise, the plan continues to clear the target block in a similar fashion (lines 19-21). Finally, the plan stacks the blocks on each other by calling the stackOn() method of the Block class (line 23).

In the ConfigureBlocksPlan (Fig. 6.12), the body() method (lines 12-25) consists of two loops through all stacks on the table, and all blocks of each stack, as returned by the getStacks() method of the Table class (line 13). This table object represents the desired target configuration. The agent now has to look up the corresponding blocks in its beliefbase, and then operate on these blocks such that they resemble the target configuration. The lookup is simple for the block itself, as the corresponding object can be obtained directly from the belief set (line 16). The lookup of the object below the block (lines 17-19) is somewhat more difficult, because the block could be located directly on the table (line 18) or on top of another block (line 19). To perform the actual changes to the retrieved objects, a "stack" goal is created

```
01: package jadex.examples.blocksworld;
02: import jadex.runtime.*;
03:
04: /** Plan to to establish a given configuration of blocks. */
05: public class ConfigureBlocksPlan extends Plan {
06:   protected Table table;
07:
08:   public ConfigureBlocksPlan(Table table) {
09:     this.table = table;
10:   }
11:
12:   public void body() {
13:     Block[][] stacks = table.getStacks();
14:     for(int i=0; i<stacks.length; i++) {
15:       for(int j=0; j<stacks[i].length; j++) {
16:         Block block=(Block)getBeliefbase().getBeliefSet("blocks").getFact(stacks[i][j]);
17:         Block target=stacks[i][j].getLower()==table
18:         ?(Table)getBeliefbase().getBelief("table").getFact()
19:         :(Block)getBeliefbase().getBeliefSet("blocks").getFact(stacks[i][j].getLower());
20:
21:         IGoal stack = createGoal("stack");
22:         stack.getParameter("block").setValue(block);
23:         stack.getParameter("target").setValue(target);
24:         dispatchSubgoalAndWait(stack);
25:       }
26:     }
27:   }
28: }
```

Figure 6.12. Java code for ConfigureBlocksPlan

and dispatched (lines 21-24). Because the loop processes the stacks bottom-to-top, the sequential execution of all "stack" goals ensures that the final configuration resembles the desired target configuration.

6.4 Platform

This section describes the realization of the Jadex reasoning engine, and its integration into the JADE platform. Figure 6.13 shows the essential components required for developing and executing a Jadex agent, and highlights the dependencies between those components. The components are distinguished in *core system components* (upper row) which realize the reasoning engine, *system interface components* (middle row) that provide and define the access points to the system, and *custom application components* (lower row) which have to be supplied by the agent developer. The links between the components can be categorized in *runtime* dependencies (i.e. between components in the first two columns from the left), dependencies that only apply during the *agent startup* phase (see third column components), and dependencies resolved at *design time* (right column).

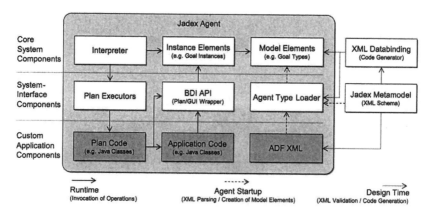

Figure 6.13. System realization

We will describe the components starting from the right. Jadex is based on a BDI *metamodel* defined in XML Schema (cf. Sect. 6.3.1). This schema is on the one hand used to validate the agent models specified in XML agent definition files (*ADF*). On the other hand, an *XML databinding* framework[4] is used to generate Java classes for the elements of the metamodel and for reading model elements from XML. When an agent is instantiated, the generated *agent type loader* reads the user supplied XML agent model and automatically creates the corresponding *model elements*.

From these model elements, instances are continuously created at runtime, represented by *instance elements*. The main *interpreter* operates on the current instance elements and executes plans to handle events and goals. *Plan executors* are used to hide the details of plan implementation types from the system. As a default, there is a plan executor for executing *plan code* written in Java. Plan code may access any other *application code* or third party libraries written in a suitable language. Both plan and application code has access to the reasoning engine through a *BDI API*. It is provided to plan and other application (e.g. GUI) code by wrappers that encapsulate the instance elements, and ensure proper synchronization and deadlock-avoidance when the API is called from the plans, or from external threads respectively.

For integration into JADE, the platform management tool (RMA) has been extended slightly to support launching of Jadex agents, by selecting the corresponding agent model with a file chooser. The Jadex interpreter itself is realized as a special type of JADE agent, which loads an agent model supplied

---

[4]JBind Java-XML Data Binding Framework, see http://jbind.sourceforge.net/

at startup, and creates its own instance of the reasoning engine according to the settings given in the model (e.g. initial beliefs, goals, and plans). The functionalities corresponding to the execution model components (message receiver, dispatcher, scheduler, cf. section 6.2.3), are implemented as cyclic behaviours (cf. chapter 5), always running inside the agent. These behaviours call the reasoning engine to process incoming messages, and perform internal reasoning. In each JADE agent cycle, the reasoning engine is called to process one event and execute one plan step. Using a reference to the JADE agent object, Jadex plans have direct access to all operations of the JADE API as well (e.g. for handling of FIPA ACL messages).

6.4.1 Available tools and documentation

The system distribution contains complete documentation materials for quick start and reference purposes. An introductory tutorial made up of several exercises shows the usage of basic system features in a step-by-step manner. Moreover, the distribution provides several example applications including their commented source code. A user guide provides a systematic overview of all features and also serves as a reference manual. In addition, Javadocs of the plan programming API and a reference to the metamodel defined in XML Schema are provided. The available tools are covered in a separate guide. Apart from the documentation material included in the distribution, there are publicly available online tools kindly hosted by Source-Forge.net, such as web forums for discussion and support requests, a database for bug-reports and feature requests, and a general mailing list with online archives.

As a Jadex agent is still a JADE agent, all runtime tools provided by the JADE platform such as Sniffer and Dummy agent can also be used with Jadex agents. To enable a comfortable testing of the internals of Jadex agents additional tool agents have been developed. In Fig. 6.14 an example application (marsworld) is depicted together with the logger and introspector tools in a typical debugging session. The BDI introspector (Fig.6.14 bottom left and right hand side) serves two purposes. First, it supports the visualization and modification of the internal BDI concepts thus allowing inspection and reconfiguration of an agent at runtime. Secondly, it simplifies debugging through a facility for the stepwise agent execution. In the step mode, it is possible to observe and control each event processing and plan execution step having detailed control over the dispatcher and scheduler. Hence it can be easily figured out what plans are selected for a given event or goal.

With the help of the logger (see Fig.6.14 on the top right) the agent's outputs can be directed to a single point of responsibility at runtime. In contrast to simple console outputs, the logger agent preserves additional information

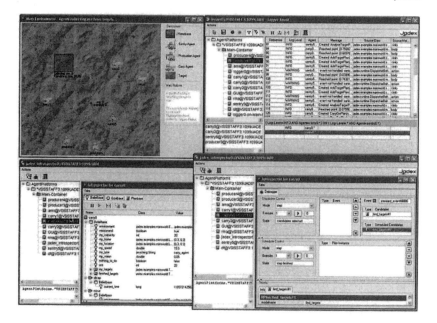

Figure 6.14. BDI introspector and logger screenshots

about the output such as its time stamp and its source (the agent and method). Using these artifacts the logger agent offers facilities for filtering and sorting messages by various criteria allowing a personalized view to be created.

Moreover, a tracer tool for on-line visualization of agent execution based on ideas from [132] is provided. It generates a unified view of multi-agent and internal agent behaviour, relating message-based communication and internal agent processes. The Jadexdoc tool allows generating documentation of agent applications similar to Javadoc. In addition to these tools already included in the latest release, a tool for multi-agent application deployment is currently in development (see [29]).

6.4.2   Standards compliance, interoperability and portability

One driving factor for the development of Jadex was the need for a FIPA-compliant platform supporting advanced BDI reasoning capabilities. FIPA-compliance is achieved through the JADE platform, which provides sophisticated implementations of all important FIPA specifications. The Jadex reasoning engine, realized on top of the JADE platform, in itself only supports

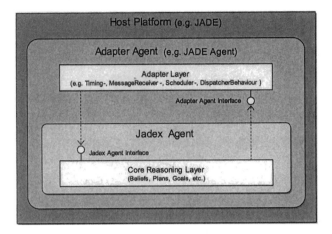

Figure 6.15. Platform integration

homogeneous (i.e. BDI) agents, but provides interoperability with agents based on other models. Agents realized using the conventional JADE programming techniques can be executed directly together with Jadex agents running on the same platform. Interoperability with other kinds of agents is straightforward as long as those agents adhere to the FIPA standard. E.g. in an example application, Jadex agents have been successfully connected to agents running on the CAPA platform [76], which provides a petri-net based computation model for agents.

The reasoning engine has been realized as a separate component, intentionally limiting the dependencies to the underlying platform. To use the reasoning engine on top of other platforms, an adapter has to be realized (see Fig. 6.15). This adapter has to implement a handful of methods used by the Jadex engine (e.g. to send messages) and has to call the engine when it is expected to do the reasoning. Therefore, although the current implementation is designed to be used with JADE, the reasoning engine can be easily integrated with other FIPA-compliant agent platforms such as CAPA [76] or ADK[5], given that they provide a similar interface for message handling. It is also possible to use the system in conjunction with other middleware environments such as J2EE or .NET, when FIPA-compliance is not needed. Currently, in addition to the JADE integration, we have developed experimental adapters for the DIET agent platform [147] and for running a set of Jadex agents as a standalone Java application.

---

[5]http://www.tryllian.com/

The engine was realized in Java 1.4 and includes the third party packages JBind for XML data binding and Apache Velocity[6] for generating the content of some tool dialogs. To support mobile devices, a port of the engine is also available in a reduced version based on J2ME / CDC. Moreover, all kinds of tools and libraries with a Java API can easily be used to provide additional features. For example, in a larger project the Cayenne database mapping framework[7] was used to connect agents to a relational database.

6.5   Applications supported by the language and/or the platform

Jadex is a general-purpose development environment for creating multi-agent system applications, allowing to build agents with reactive (event-based) and deliberative (goal-driven) behaviour. It is not bound to a specific target domain, but has been used to realize applications in different domains such as simulation, scheduling, and mobile computation. Jadex originated in the MedPAge ("Medical Path Agents") project [166, 167], which is part of the German priority research programme 1083 *Intelligent Agents in Real-World Business Applications* funded by the Deutsche Forschungsgemeinschaft (DFG). In cooperation with the business management department of the University of Mannheim, the project investigates the advantages of using agent technology in the context of hospital logistics. In this project Jadex is used to realize a multi-agent application for market-based negotiation of treatment schedules [167], as well as for the simulation of a hospital model to test the negotiation mechanism [31]. In other contexts, Jadex was used to realize portable PDA-based applications. A personal mobile task planner was developed, to test the Jadex J2ME port and to prove the usefulness of BDI agents on mobile devices [104]. Elsewhere, in the PITA ("Personal Intelligent Travel Assistant") project at the Delft University of Technology, Jadex was used to realize a prototype of a mobile personal travel assistant application [9].

Besides building specific agent applications, Jadex has also been used for teaching and research regarding agent oriented software development in general. Due to its simple language based on well-known technologies such as Java and XML, and the extensive documentation material and illustrative example applications, Jadex is well suited for teaching purposes. It has been successfully applied in several courses at the University of Hamburg, and is also evaluated by other institutes. Regarding research in agent systems, the project is also designed as a means for researchers to further investigate

---

[6] http://jakarta.apache.org/velocity/
[7] http://objectstyle.org/cayenne/

which mentalistic concepts are appropriate in the design and implementation of agent systems. The combination of XML Schema with Java databinding techniques allows the Jadex metamodel to be flexibly adapted and extended for experimentation purposes. While investigating different representations for beliefs, goals and plans, the system has been applied to several well-known AI problem domains (blocksworld, cleanerworld, mars robots, hunter-prey). These applications are also included in the distribution. Moreover, the Technical University of Karlsruhe has used Jadex to implement an experimental system for representing norms in multi-agent systems [204].

6.6   Final Remarks

In this chapter, the Jadex BDI reasoning engine has been presented. The realization of the system is motivated mainly by three factors. Firstly, the system aims to combine the benefits of agent middleware and internal agent reasoning processes. Secondly, it intends to enhance the state-of-the-art BDI architecture by addressing some shortcomings of current BDI agent platforms such as implicit goal representation and thirdly, the system targets on making agent technology more easily usable by exploiting current software engineering techniques such as XML, Java and OQL.

The architecture of Jadex is in principle similar to traditional PRS systems, when event and goal processing is considered. Nevertheless, conceptual differences exist mainly concerning the representation of BDI core concepts and as well on language level. According to the usability requirement, beliefs are expressed in an object-oriented way instead of using logical formulae or relational models. Moreover, goals are represented as explicit durable entities instead of relying on events. On language level, Jadex differentiates between the description of an agent's behaviour and its static structure. Therefore, for each of these purposes different languages are employed. The static agent structure is declared in an XML-dialect following the Jadex BDI metamodel specified in XML-schema, whereas ordinary Java is used for plan realization. BDI-specific facilities are made accessible from within plan through an application program interface.

Ongoing work currently focuses on two aspects of the system: Extensions to internal concepts and additional tool support. On the conceptual level extensions to the basic BDI-mechanisms are developed, such as support for planning, teams, and goal deliberation. It is planned to utilize the explicit representation of goals by improving the BDI architecture with a generic facility for goal deliberation, which alleviates the necessity for designing agents with a consistent goal set. Additionally the explicit representation allows investigating task delegation by considering goals at the inter-agent level. Work on tools mainly addresses the usability of agent technology as a mainstream software engineering paradigm. The tool support of Jadex currently focuses on the implementation and testing phase supplying tools like the debugger and logger agent. To achieve a higher degree of usability it is planned to support the design phase as well with a graphical modeling tool based on the MDA-approach [8]. Additionally, a tools for deployment of multi-agent applications is being developed [29].

The current version is Jadex 0.931, which can be freely downloaded under LGPL license from the project homepage http://jadex.sourceforge.net/. It is termed a beta stage release, and has reached considerable stability and maturity to be used in experimental and practical settings.

Acknowledgments

This work is partially funded by the German priority research programme 1083 *Intelligent Agents in Real-World Business Applications*.

Chapter 7

JACK™ INTELLIGENT AGENTS: AN INDUSTRIAL STRENGTH PLATFORM

Michael Winikoff

RMIT University
GPO Box 2476V
Melbourne, 3001, AUSTRALIA
winikoff@cs.rmit.edu.au

Abstract   Software agents offer a range of benefits to the development of complex software systems. However, before these benefits can be realised by the computing industry there is a need for an agent platform that can be accepted by industry. In this paper we describe the JACK agent platform: a mature and robust commercial product. We argue that JACK meets requirements such as familiarity, scalability and integratibility which make it suitable for adoption by industry. We also describe interesting features of JACK such as the use of capabilities for structuring agents, and JACK's approach to teamwork which allows hierarchical team structures.

Keywords: Agent Oriented Programming Language, Belief-Desire-Intention, Agent Platform.

7.1   Motivation

Software agents offer a range of potential benefits to the development and deployment of complex software systems, such as increased flexibility and adaptability, and more natural models of complex "nearly decomposable" systems [122, 123, 141, 142]. These benefits stem from the combination of features that are generally considered to be associated with intelligent software agents: being *autonomous*, *proactive*, *reactive* and *social*. Some argue that because agents are autonomous they reduce coupling [123, 161]. Some focus on the use of plans and goals in Belief-Desire-Intention (BDI) agents (and similar platforms), arguing that the resulting number of ways in which a goal can be achieved gives agents flexibility in dealing with situations, and robustness in recovering from various types of failure (e.g., [164, Section 2.5]). Others argue that aspects of agents (e.g., autonomy, flexibility) are already being adopted by mainstream software engineering, and that this is evidence that these aspects are useful to modern software systems [243].

However, in order for these benefits to be realisable by the computing industry, a number of key technological pieces are required. One of the key pieces is a *methodology* (including concepts, notations, a process and techniques) that guides practitioners in designing agent systems. We do not focus on this here, but note that a number of methodologies have been developed including Gaia [242], Tropos [33], MaSE [57], Prometheus [164], ROADMAP [125] and others [13, 105]. Some of these methodologies have also been evaluated and compared in various ways [44, 50, 208, 210].

A second key piece of technology is an *agent platform* which can be used to create agent systems. Like the term "methodology", the meaning of the term "agent platform" is somewhat debatable. We believe that an agent platform needs to contain at least the following components:

- An agent-oriented programming language that allows agents to be written directly using agent concepts (e.g., plans, goals, beliefs), rather than encoded in non-agent-oriented languages.

- A library or framework providing facilities for inter-agent communication including facilities for transmitting and receiving messages, and for locating agents (e.g., a name server).

JACK™ *Intelligent Agents* (referred to as "JACK" in the remainder of this chapter) [40] is an agent platform that includes these components and more. JACK includes an agent-oriented programming language; a platform for executing agents with infrastructure such as message marshalling and a name server; and development tools including a design tool, a graphical plan editor and a number of debugging views. Additionally, JACK includes a number of additional functionalities such as the ability to construct hierarchical *teams* of agents [121].

Looking at the history of object-oriented technologies, it is interesting to note that object-oriented programming languages such as Simula (developed in the 1960s) and Smalltalk (developed in the 1970s) significantly pre-dated work on object-oriented analysis and design (in the 1980s and 1990s). By analogy with this history one could argue that the availability of a widely accepted "standard" agent-oriented programming language is more crucial to the success of agents as a technology than the development of a widely accepted methodology. To be widely accepted an agent platform must be accepted by industry, and so it is natural to ask what an industry-acceptable agent platform might look like.

We believe that to be acceptable to industry an agent platform must be:

- Familiar: presented as an extension of objects, rather than as a revolutionary new paradigm [161]. In particular, this means that the programming language should be easily learned by programmers who are used to currently popular languages (e.g., Java). In particular, this rules out languages that are based on alternative, less mainstream, paradigms such as logic programming.

- Integratable: the platform must allow agents to communicate and integrate not just with existing software including objects written in Java or C++, but also with databases, web servers, graphical user interfaces, etc. In particular, in order to flexibly integrate with a wide range of existing systems, the agent platform must be agnostic (or at least flexible) with respect to communication infrastructure. Supporting a single approach only, such as FIPA[1], is not desirable as there are many communication and integration approaches in current use (e.g., Web Services, CORBA, Java RMI, HLA).

- Scalable: the language must support good software engineering practice, including the provision of suitable facilities for structuring large systems.

- Industrial Strength (Robust, Stable, Efficient): the implementation must be robust and reliable, and it must be able to support large numbers of agents efficiently.

- Documented and Supported: when using a technology that is not (yet) widely-known, it is vital to have good documentation and support.

Additionally, it is important for the agent platform to provide development tools (such as an integrated development environment and design tools), and debugging tools.

It is clear that, in today's computing environment, developing an agent platform built on top of the Java platform is highly attractive: it provides for portability across computing platforms and access to a rich collection of libraries. One approach to using the Java platform as a basis is to use the Java language as the programming language and provide a library of agent features. This approach has the benefit of familiarity – the programming language used is Java itself – but has the drawback that the language's semantics is fixed and cannot be changed. This approach is taken by the Jadex[2] system

---

[1] Foundation for Intelligent Physical Agents, http://www.fipa.org.
[2] http://vsys1.informatik.uni-hamburg.de/projects/jadex/

(see Chapter 6), and one consequence is that when a plan has a sub-goal, the programmer must write code to check whether the sub-goal has succeeded, and if not fail the plan. This check cannot be done automatically in Jadex (as it should be) without changing Java's execution semantics. An alternative approach to using the Java platform as a basis is to create a new language and implement it using Java, either by compiling it to Java or writing an interpreter for the new language in Java. The new language can be quite different to Java (e.g., JAM [114] or Jason (see Chapter 1)) or, as in JACK, a conservative extension of Java.

Although there are clear benefits to using Java as a basis and there are good reasons to conservatively extend Java's syntax, this does have the drawback of yielding a programming language that is relatively verbose. To some degree, JACK addresses this issue by using development tools that generate code skeletons by interaction with a GUI.

In the following section we briefly describe the JACK agent language and its features. In section 7.3 we discuss the JACK agent platform, and in section 7.4 we present applications developed with JACK. Although JACK is a commercial platform which caters for industrial usage, one of JACK's major design goals was "to enable further applied research" [113], and so we briefly discuss research that has extended or built on JACK in section 7.5.

7.2   Language

The JACK programming language extends Java in a number of ways, both syntactic and semantic. The JACK language is a superset of the Java programming language, so all of Java's libraries and facilities are easily accessible.

In the following sections we briefly describe the JACK programming language and its execution.

7.2.1   Specifications and Syntactical Aspects

Syntactically, JACK extends Java in three ways:

1. JACK adds new top-level declaration types which are used to declare agents, beliefsets, views, events, plans and capabilities.

2. Each of the top-level types is defined using various # declarations which define the properties of the entity and relationships between entities.

3. Within plan bodies JACK defines a range of @ statements such as posting an event (e.g., @post) or waiting for a condition (@wait_for). Some of the @ statements defined by JACK are listed in figure 7.1.

- @post, @subtask – simple event posting within an agent. @post is asynchronous, whereas @subtask waits for the event processing to finish before continuing.

- @send, @reply – inter-agent communication.

- @achieve, @insist – post a (goal) event under certain conditions. @achieve(condition,goal_event) checks whether the condition holds, and posts the event if it doesn't. @insist(condition,goal_event) is similar, but also checks whether the condition holds after the processing triggered by the event has finished. If not, the event is posted again.

- @maintain – checks for condition while handling event. @maintain(condition,event) will subtask the event, but will monitor the condition while the event processing runs. If the condition becomes false the plans that handled the event are aborted.

- @sleep, @wait_for – do nothing for a certain amount of time (@sleep) or until a certain condition is true (@wait_for).

Figure 7.1. Some statements provided by JACK

Figure 7.2 shows how these three syntactic extensions are used to define a (very simple) plan called ProcessRequest which is triggered by a message (declared with the #handles declaration), and replies to it with a response. The top-level entities that JACK defines are:

Agent: An agent is an obvious basic entity for an agent-oriented programming language! In JACK, agents are specified by defining the events they handle and send, the data (including beliefsets) they have, and the plans and capabilities they use.

Beliefset: A beliefset is effectively a (small) relational database that is stored in memory, rather than on disk. JACK makes it easy to define these and to define queries on beliefsets. Beliefsets can also post events in certain situations (e.g., whenever the beliefset is modified).

View: Views are "virtual" beliefsets that are computed from other beliefsets.

Event: An event is an occurrence in time that represents some sort of change that requires a response. Events are used in JACK (and in other BDI architectures) to model messages being received, new goals being adopted, and information being received from the environment.

```
public plan ProcessRequest extends Plan {
  #handles event Request req;
  #sends event Response resp;

  context() {
    req.isValid;
  }

  #reasoning method body() {
    // Can contain Java code as well
    // as JACK @-statements
    ...
    @reply(req,resp.response(...));
  }
}
```

Figure 7.2. A (very simple) Plan

Plan: A plan is a "recipe" for dealing with a given event type. Plans include
an indication of which event they handle, a *context condition* which
describes in which situations the plan can be used, and a plan body.
The plan body, which can include Java code as well as JACK code, is
what is actually executed as the system runs.

Capability: A capability is a modularisation construct. We discuss capabilities in section 7.2.3.

The execution of JACK is fairly typical for a BDI architecture. Events
(which include messages from other agents) trigger plans. Each event will
normally have a number of plans that handle that event, these are the *relevant*
plans. Of the relevant plans, some will be *applicable* to the agent's current
situation. This is determined by evaluating the plan's context condition[3]. If
there are no (more) applicable plans the event has failed, and failure handling
is triggered. Otherwise, one of the applicable plans is selected and its body
is executed. This is summarised in figure 7.3.

The execution of a plan's body is fairly straightforward: the statements in
the plan body are executed in sequence. However, there is one key difference
between executing Java code and executing JACK code: each statement can

---

[3] If the context condition has multiple solutions this will lead to multiple plan instances being considered
as applicable.

1. Event posted.

2. Determine the set of relevant plans.

3. Determine the applicable plans.

4. Select an applicable plan and run it.

5. If plan fails, go to step 4 (select an applicable plan).

Figure 7.3. Event handling in BDI architectures

fail, and if it does the rest of the plan is not executed and failure handling is triggered instead.

When a plan fails the event that triggered it is considered to have not been handled, and alternative plans for handling it are considered. This process looks for another applicable plan to try. If there is another applicable plan, it is tried. If all applicable plans have failed the event cannot be handled. If the event was posted from a plan (events can also be posted from Java code) that plan fails and its triggering event is re-posted in an attempt to find an alternative applicable plan for it.

This execution cycle of events triggering plans is common to a whole family of BDI architectures (e.g., dMARS [59], JAM [114], PRS [97, 118], UM-PRS [134]). However, there are some details of the cycle that are specific to JACK and distinguish it from other platforms. Firstly, by default[4] JACK re-computes the applicable set when considering alternative plans due to failure. This means that when a plan fails and alternatives are considered, the applicability of these alternatives is evaluated in the current situation, not the situation when the event was first posted. Some other BDI architectures (such as JAM) do not re-compute the applicable plan set, and thus select plans based on out-of-date information when failure occurs.

Another detail that is specific to JACK is that the context condition is actually split into two parts: a context condition and a relevance condition. The relevance condition is a Boolean condition that is only evaluated once (eagerly) and can only access the details of the event, not any other data. The relevance condition is used to exclude plans based on the details of the event (which do not change). For example, if the event is a request for credit which specifies the amount and there are separate plans depending on the amount requested, the selection of plans can be done using a relevance condition

---

[4]This behaviour, and other aspects of event handling, can be customised on a per-event-type basis.

---

1. Event posted.

2. Find plans that #handle it.

3. Determine the set of relevant plans using relevant() method (Relevant method can only access event, not beliefs).

4. Determine applicable plans using context().

5. Select a plan and run its body(). (meta-reasoning can be used to make the selection).

6. If plan fails, go to step 4 (recompute applicable plan set).

Figure 7.4. Event handling in JACK

rather than a context condition. The JACK execution cycle is summarised in figure 7.4.

When there are multiple applicable plans that can be used, the question arises of which one an agent should select (step 5 in figure 7.4). JACK provides a number of mechanisms that allow the programmer to specify how a plan should be selected. One mechanism is that plans will (by default) be selected in the order in which they are listed in the agent. Another mechanism runs another plan (a "meta-plan") to decide which plan to select.

It is worth mentioning that JACK actually provides a variety of event types which behave differently. For example, message events do not trigger failure handling if their handling plan fails.

7.2.2   Semantics and Verification

Although JACK is quite well documented, its semantics have not been formally specified. Since JACK is a superset of Java, formally defining JACK's semantics would require a formal definition of Java's semantics, something that is still an active area of research[5] [3].

However, although JACK itself has not been formally specified, the event-plan execution cycle which JACK shares with other BDI platforms has been formalised in various ways by various researchers. Anand Rao's work on AgentSpeak(L) [180] aims to bridge the "BDI gap" between theories and implementations by defining a language capturing the essence of BDI platforms whilst having precisely defined semantics. Although the formal semantics

---

[5]For example, the formalisation described at http://www-sop.inria.fr/oasis/java/java_sem.html is for a subset of Java.

given by Rao is incomplete, the work has inspired a number of implementations of the language such as AgentTalk[6], an implementation based on SIM_AGENT [143], an implementation in Java that is designed to run on hand-held devices [178], and the Java-based Jason[7] (see Chapter 1).

Since Rao introduced AgentSpeak(L), a number of authors have published complete formal semantics for the language. The specification language Z ("Zed") was used to formally specify the essential execution cycle of AgentSpeak [60], and an operational semantics for AgentSpeak was given by Bordini and Moreira [24]. However, neither of these formalisations included the failure handling mechanism. A precise operational semantics including failure handling was given by Winikoff *et al.* [236] for a language (called "CAN") which is a superset of AgentSpeak.

Since JACK's semantics has not been formalised, JACK programs cannot be formally verified. However, verification of entire implemented systems is not currently realistic. Research into model checking of agent programs is still quite young [19], and is not yet applicable to large agent programs. Consequently, we believe that presently formal techniques are best applied to verifying *aspects* of systems, such as key algorithms or interaction patterns.

7.2.3 Software Engineering Issues

One of JACK's strengths is its support for modern software engineering practices. In addition to the features provided by Java (objects, packages), JACK adds a number of features that can be used to structure an agent system.

One new feature is that a plan's body can be broken down into a number of separate *reasoning methods*, rather than being a single monolithic block of JACK code. This allows a single plan to be structured internally.

Another feature that was introduced by JACK (and subsequently adopted by Jadex) is *capabilities* [39]. A capability is the agent-oriented equivalent of a module, corresponding to a coherent ability that an agent has. Capabilities contain plans and beliefs, and specify which events they handle and post. In addition, capabilities can also contain sub-capabilities which allow hierarchical module structures to be specified as appropriate.

Another Software Engineering practice is *consistency checking*. JACK checks that the various declarations of which events are posted and handled by which entities (agents, capabilities and plans) are consistent. Additionally, the JACK agent programming language is, as an extension of Java, strongly

---

[6]http://www.cs.rmit.edu.au/~winikoff/agenttalk
[7]http://jason.sourceforge.net/

and statically typed, and the type checking done at compile-time can catch a range of mistakes made by the programmer.

As JACK is a superset of Java, integrating with existing Java code is straightforward. An example of this is the work of [55] which integrated JACK with the JSHOP planner (which is written in Java). JACK can also be integrated with existing C++ code using JACOB (see section 7.3.2). JACK has also been successfully integrated with systems in Fortran, C, and Ada.

7.2.4   Other features of the language

In addition to the features discussed above, the JACK agent language includes a number of other significant features. Perhaps the most significant is its support for "team-oriented" programming.

JACK's support for teams is an optional extension which adds two new concepts (teams and roles) and extends Plans to TeamPlans [121]. A team is an entity which, like an agent, can contain plans, capabilities, data, etc. but, unlike agents, a team can also have *sub-teams*, enabling natural modelling of hierarchical organisational structures. It is important to realise that a team is an active entity that can have beliefs and execute (team) plans; it is not merely a collection of agents. Indeed, when the team extension is enabled, an individual agent is modelled simply as a team that has no sub-teams!

For each team type, roles are used to specify the interface (in terms of events received and sent) that must be fulfilled by its sub-teams.

The team extension also extends Plans to TeamPlans by adding the ability to delegate tasks to sub-teams, and to perform steps in parallel. Team plans also differ from plans in that they have an `establish()` reasoning method which assembles the sub-teams that will be involved in the plan (the "task team"). Each TeamPlan that is run by a team can have a different assignment of sub-teams. For example, given a team of soccer-playing robots, one TeamPlan may require two attackers, whereas another TeamPlan may require both a defender and a goal keeper.

Figure 7.5 shows a simple example TeamPlan. This TeamPlan specifies that feeding a baby requires two sub-teams, both playing the role of a parent. One parent prepares the food at the same time as the other parent calms the baby. Once this is done, the baby is fed.

JACK's teams support also includes other features, such as being able to automatically repair teams, and being able to automatically propagate beliefs from a team to its sub-teams and vice versa.

JACK's approach to teamwork is different to standard approaches that regard teams as a collection of agents having certain patterns of mental attitudes (e.g., joint intentions), existing approaches to teamwork [47, 216] do not consider teams to be entities in their own right, and do not support hi-

```
teamplan FeedBaby extends TeamPlan {
   #handles event BabyHungry pfv;
   #uses role Parent parents as p1;
   #uses role Parent parents as p2;

   //establish the task team.
   #reasoning method establish() { ... }

   body() {
      @parallel(ParallelFSM.ALL,false,null) {
         @team_achieve(p1, p1.prepareFood.pf());
         @team_achieve(p2, p2.calmBaby.cb());
      };
      @team_achieve(p2,p2,feedBaby.fb());
   } // body
} // FeedBaby team plan
```

Figure 7.5. A simple TeamPlan

erarchical team structures. Comparisons of JACK's approach to teamwork with other approaches to teamwork can be found in [109, 117].

Another feature of JACK is an event type called InferenceGoal. Whereas other event types are handled by finding an applicable plan and executing it, with alternative plans being considered (for some event types) only if plan execution fails, an InferenceGoal event is handled by executing *all* applicable plans in sequence. This behaviour is useful for performing certain types of reasoning such as emulating rule firing in expert systems.

Finally, the JACK compiler is modular, and the JACK language can be extended using plugins, but this aspect is not currently well documented, and extending the JACK language in this way is difficult without extensive support from Agent Oriented Software.

7.3   Platform

In this section, we briefly discuss features and properties of the JACK platform including tool support for design, programming and debugging, as well as support for various forms of communication and integration.

7.3.1   Available tools and documentation

According to a recent survey of agent researchers, the areas that were seen as most desirable to be supported by third party tools were "Integrated Development Environments, Debugging tools, and parsers/language tools" [235]. JACK addresses the first two areas by providing an integrated development environment, and a range of debugging tools.

The JACK Development Environment (JDE) (see figure 7.6) allows the developer to create agents, events, plans, beliefsets etc. by dragging and dropping, rather than typing # declarations. The JACK skeleton code for the entities is automatically generated. The JDE also provides a Graphical Plan Editor (on the right side of figure 7.6) which allows the bodies of plans to be specified using a graphical notation, rather than textual code.

The JDE also includes a Design Tool (middle of figure 7.6) which allows overview diagrams in the style of Prometheus [164] to be drawn. This can be used to create the system's structure by placing entities onto the canvas and linking them together. It can also be used to create an overview of an existing system by adding entities to a canvas, in which case the links between entities are automatically added. The JDE maintains consistency between the design diagrams and the underlying model, and therefore with the generated code.

JACK provides a number of debugging tools. The simplest is a textual trace of processing steps which is enabled from the command line. This can be configured to show various types of steps: changes to beliefsets, events being posted and processed, messages being sent and received, and steps in plans. Although this information is easy to obtain, it is obtained from a single run-time instance of the JACK platform, and is therefore less useful for debugging distributed systems of agents.

For debugging distributed agents *interaction diagrams* are more useful. An interaction diagram graphically displays messages sent between agents. A single interaction diagram can collect and display messages from agents across a distributed system.

Interaction diagrams depict the messages between agents. However, when debugging, it is also useful to be able to trace the internal execution of agents. JACK provides graphical plan tracing, which traces the execution of plans that have been specified using the Graphical Plan Editor. When a plan begins executing its graph is shown, and as the plan executes the currently executing node is highlighted. The graph also shows the values of the plan's variables and parameters. The execution of the agent can be controlled: it can be run as normal, single-stepped, or stepped with a delay in between steps.

The newest version of JACK also provides an additional debugging tool: a browser that allows the state of agents (including their beliefs and active tasks) to be inspected.

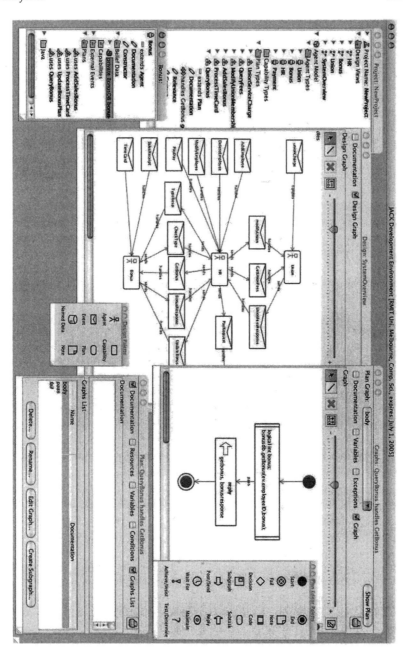

Figure 7.6. The JACK Development Environment (JDE)

All of these development, design and debugging tools – as well as the JACK language, and other facilities such as JACK's support for teamwork, the Webbot interface to JSP, and JACOB (see next section) – have clear and extensive documentation. Additionally, JACK's documentation package also includes "practicals": a tutorial sequence introducing JACK.

7.3.2   Standards compliance, interoperability and portability

There are many approaches to communication and integration, such as CORBA, HLA, Java RMI and FIPA. Consequently, JACK's approach to communications is agnostic. While a lightweight communications infrastructure is provided, and can be used out-of-the-box, it is also possible to extend and/or replace JACK's communications infrastructure.

We begin by discussing JACK's lightweight communications infrastructure including a discussion of JACOB. We then look at an example of extending JACK to make it FIPA-compliant. Note that this extension is not part of the JACK distribution: JACK is a commercial product, and since most agent systems today are not open and are not FIPA-compliant, there is limited demand by customers of Agent Oriented Software to make JACK FIPA-compliant. Rather, it is more important to be able to integrate JACK code with existing code in Java and C++ (which is supported by JACOB), and with existing applications such as databases (supported by JACOB using JDBC), web servers (supported by Webbot using JSP), and graphical user interfaces (provided by Java libraries such as AWT or Swing).

JACK's lightweight communications mechanism supports sending messages between agents. These messages can contain Java objects which are serialised by the sender and "reconstituted" by the recipient of the message. JACK provides a number of mechanisms for serialising objects: Java's serialisation can be used, but this tends to produce large messages, and only supports communication with other Java software. Alternatively, JACOB provides more compact serialisations, and allows objects to be "reconstituted" by Java or C++ programs. JACOB provides a number of serialisation formats: a plain ASCII format that is compact yet human readable, a binary format which is more compact, an XML format, and a JDBC format.

When the recipient of a message is in the same Java process as the sender, then the message is addressed simply using the name of recipient agent. However, JACK supports flexible distribution of agents: it is possible to have multiple agents per Java process, to have agents distributed in different Java processes (which can be on different machines), or to flexibly mix these. This flexible distribution requires a slightly more sophisticated addressing scheme than simply using agent names, and JACK introduces the concept of a *portal*.

Roughly speaking, a portal can be thought of as a handle on a Java process, and sending a message to an agent at another portal is done by addressing the agent as *agentname@portalname*. Each portal acts as a name server for other portals, i.e., each portal keeps track of the addresses of other portals.

Thus, JACK's provided communication infrastructure supports communication amongst flexibly distributed agents, as well as between agents and existing software written in Java or C++.

We now briefly describe a third-party extension to JACK which supports building FIPA-compliant JACK agents. The FIPA JACK plugin[8] [241] was developed at RMIT University and was used as the basis for its AgentCities platform. The plugin provides FIPA compliant services, specifically an Agent Management System (AMS), Directory Facilitator (DF) and Message Transport Service (MTS). The plugin also provides a new agent base class (FIPAAgent). Agents which extend this class automatically register with the AMS, and are able to send and receive FIPA-compliant messages. The FIPA JACK plugin also includes a GUI for examining the agents that are registered with the AMS and for sending messages for testing purposes.

7.3.3 Other features of the platform

JACK is efficient: it allows flexible distribution of agents, with multiple agents sharing a Java process. It also allows for many agents to run on a single machine, while still supporting distributed agent systems across machines. Benchmarking[9] on an average PC running Linux shows that over 1000 agents can be created per second, and that 100,000 messages can be sent per second (within the same Java process).

These benchmarks are supported by a recent paper [231] which compared and benchmarked a number of agent platforms, including JACK (version 3.51), JADE, FIPA-OS and Zeus. It found JACK to be by far the fastest platform. JACK was also found to have the lowest memory requirement per-agent when creating 100 agents.

JACK is compact enough to be run on limited hardware. It has been demonstrated on a Psion 5mx and, for a recent demonstration involving an Unmanned Aerial Vehicle, JACK was run on a Hewlett-Packard iPAQ PDA.

---

[8] Available from `http://www.cs.rmit.edu.au/agents/protocols/`
[9] `http://www.agent-software.com/shared/products/faq.html`

7.4   Applications supported by the language and/or the platform

Application areas for JACK can be loosely categorised as:

- *Autonomous systems* which operate independently (or mostly independently) from humans. For example, Unmanned Air Vehicles [139] and Holonic manufacturing [85, 90].

- *Modelling human-like decision making.* This takes advantage of the basis of the Belief-Desire-Intention model in human folk psychology [28]. Typically, this application category involves simulation of humans [91, 112, 159].

- *Decision support* applications where the system assists humans in making decisions. For example the Collection Plan Management System (CPMS) [140] provides human decision makers with a number of possible plans.

- *Architectural "glue"* where a system is structured as a collection of autonomous agents in order to obtain the reduced coupling and improved maintainability associated with this architectural style. For example, the weather alerting system developed for the Australian Bureau of Meteorology [85, 149].

These are just some areas where JACK has been used. Other applications of agents where JACK could be used as an implementation platform include electronic commerce, business process modelling, and entertainment.

We now describe a number of applications developed in JACK. We have chosen to describe applications that illustrate different ways in which JACK has been used, and which have been described in the literature.

Many of JACK's applications are military: usually associated with logistics (planning) and simulation, rather than with battlefield use. One such application is the Collection Plan Management System (CPMS) (see [140] and [113, Section 6.1]), which assists human in planning the deployment of surveillance and reconnaissance resources. The system comprises a database with information on the terrain, the available resources, and the tasks to be carried out; a visualisation module; and a planning system written in JACK. The planning system presents a number of possible plans for assessment by the human experts. The JACK planner is structured as a collection of agents mirroring the existing command and control (C2) structure, i.e., there is an agent for each entity (brigade, company, platoon, etc.) that constructs plans for the resources that it controls. Another application written in JACK, which concerns planning the deployment of military resources, in this case aircraft, is described by Marc *et al.* [145].

Another area where JACK has been used is as architectural "glue" to connect together components of a system. By structuring a system as a collection of agents, one obtains a system that is more loosely coupled, and that is easier to modify and extend. One example of this application of JACK is the alerting system developed for the Australian Bureau of Meteorology (see [149] and [85, Section 5]). The system receives information from a range of sources including storm predictions, current observations from automated weather stations, predictions issued for the area around airports and information about bush fires. Various conditions, such as discrepancies between forecasts and observations, are checked for and alerts are generated. The system is structured as a multi-agent system where agents subscribe to information providers. Experiences with extending this system have been positive, for example extending the system to deal with a new type of information source only took a number of days.

A basic property of agents is that they are autonomous, and so a natural application area for JACK is developing software that operates autonomously. One example is the recent use of JACK on an Unmanned Aerial Vehicle (UAV) [139]. The role of JACK is not to control the vehicle directly, but rather to provide higher-level decision-making about what to do next, e.g., where should the UAV fly to? JACK's ability to deal with failure and to flexibly achieve goals is crucial in providing the UAV with a decision making capability that allows it to be independent and robust. In addition, JACK's support for teams can be used to allow multiple vehicles to cooperate in achieving their goals; for example, one UAV might act as a decoy allowing another UAV with a video camera to approach undetected. A feasibility demonstration of JACK onboard a UAV has been done[10] and development of team-based UAV control is ongoing, with flight testing scheduled for early 2005.

Finally, *Holonic manufacturing* is another application area where JACK has been used to develop autonomous software. In this case, the software controls a manufacturing cell [85, 90]. The challenges in agent-based manufacturing are to support more flexible manufacturing — for example to allow custom orders and changes to orders — and to be robust, i.e., to deal appropriately with a range of issues such as shortage of parts and failure of manufacturing equipment.

---

[10]http://www.agent-software.com/shared/resources/pressReleases/
Avatar-JACK-F040706USb.pdf

7.5   JACK: A Platform for Research

In addition to being aimed at industrial application development, JACK
has also been found to be suitable as a basis for research. We describe this here
for two reasons, firstly because one the goals of JACK is to "enable further
applied research" [113], and secondly because this research has, in some cases,
involved extending JACK, and so it shows that JACK can be easily extended.

One area of research concerns making BDI agents more intelligent, or at
the very least more rational. One issue that is shared by BDI platforms is
that although a BDI agent may have multiple goals that are being pursued at
a given time, no reasoning is done about the interaction between the goals.
In a sequence of papers, Thangarajah *et al.* [219–222] described an extended
BDI execution cycle which incorporates reasoning about the interactions,
both negative and positive, between concurrent goals. This extended BDI
cycle was implemented in JACK [218].

Another strand of research that has focused on JACK's execution model
is the work in [157–159] which looks at (i) making the decision making
of JACK agents more "human-like" by adding selection of plans based on
recognition of situations, and learning from mistakes [157]; and (ii) adding
psychologically-plausible variability in decision making by incorporating
factors such as fatigue, time-of-day and human perception processes (how
human vision tracks objects) [158, 159]. The latter work is being applied to
simulate changes of behaviour in military personnel [91].

JACK has also been extended with look-ahead planning [55] by integrating
with JSHOP, an HTN (Hierarchical Task Network) planner written in Java.

Finally, work by Poutakidis *et al.* [173, 174] has proposed and implemented on top of JACK a debugger that automatically detects errors by monitoring messages between agents and raising an alert if the messages do not
conform to the interaction protocol that is meant to be followed.

7.6   Final Remarks

We have presented the JACK language and platform, including the unique
features of the JACK language, such as teamwork, and the tool support that
is provided by JACK.

At RMIT University we have taught an undergraduate course on agent-
oriented programming and design for a few years[11]. The course, which
runs in a single 12 week semester, covers an introduction to agents, the
Prometheus agent-oriented software engineering methodology, and JACK[12].
During the course, the students complete a design and implement an agent

---

[11]The course was first taught in 2001, and has been taught subsequently in 2002, 2003 and 2004.
[12]JACK is covered in four lectures.

system, working in teams of 1-3 students. Typical projects have included a group calendar system, a library management system, and a stock trader simulation. Our experience has been that the vast majority of the students manage to learn JACK and that the students use JACK effectively by the end of the course, i.e., that their code is agent-oriented, not just object-oriented code wrapped in plans.

Acknowledgments

I would like to thank Leanne Veitch (of Agent Oriented Software) for proof-reading a draft of this paper, Nick Howden (of Agent Oriented Software) for comments on a draft of this paper, and Ralph Rönnquist (of Agent Oriented Software) for writing the summary appendix. I would like to acknowledge the support of Agent Oriented Software and of the Australian Research Council under grant LP0453486 ("Advanced Software Engineering Support for Intelligent Agent Systems"). Finally, I would like to thank the people who have taught the course on Agent Oriented Programming and Design at RMIT: Lin Padgham, Wei Liu, and David Poutakidis.

III

INDUSTRIAL-STRENGTH APPLICATIONS

Chapter 8

THE DEFACTO SYSTEM: COORDINATING HUMAN-AGENT TEAMS FOR THE FUTURE OF DISASTER RESPONSE*

N. Schurr[1], J.Marecki[1], J.P. Lewis[1], M. Tambe[1], and P. Scerri[2]

[1] *University of Southern California*
Powell Hall of Engineering,
3737 Watt Way, Los Angeles, CA 90089-0781
{ schurr, marecki, tambe } @usc.edu, zilla@computer.org

[2] *Carnegie Mellon University,*
5000 Forbes Avenue
Pittsburgh, PA 15213
pscerri@cs.cmu.edu

Abstract   Enabling effective interactions between agent teams and humans for disaster response is a critical area of research, with encouraging progress in the past few years. However, previous work suffers from two key limitations: (i) limited human situational awareness, reducing human effectiveness in directing agent teams and (ii) the agent team's rigid interaction strategies that limit team performance. This paper presents a software prototype called DEFACTO (Demonstrating Effective Flexible Agent Coordination of Teams through Omnipresence). DEFACTO is based on a software proxy architecture and 3D visualization system, which addresses the two limitations described above. First, the 3D visualization interface enables human virtual omnipresence in the environment, improving human situational awareness and ability to assist agents. Second, generalizing past work on adjustable autonomy, the agent team chooses among a variety of "team-level" interaction strategies, even excluding humans from the loop in extreme circumstances.

*This research was supported by the United States Department of Homeland Security through the Center for Risk and Economic Analysis of Terrorism Events (CREATE). However, any opinions, findings, and conclusions or recommendations in this document are those of the author and do not necessarily reflect views of the U.S. Department of Homeland Security.

Keywords: Multiagent Systems, Adjustable Autonomy, Teamwork, Disaster Response.

8.1   Introduction

We envision future disaster response to be performed with a mixture of humans performing high level decision-making, intelligent agents coordinating the response and humans and robots performing key physical tasks. These heterogeneous teams of robots, agents, and people [203] will provide the safest and most effective means for quickly responding to a disaster, such as a terrorist attack. A key aspect of such a response will be agent-assisted vehicles working together. Specifically, agents will assist the vehicles in planning routes, determining resources to use and even determining which fire to fight. However, despite advances in agent technologies, human involvement will be crucial. Allowing humans to make critical decisions within a team of intelligent agents or robots is prerequisite for allowing such teams to be used in domains where they can cause physical, financial or psychological harm. These critical decisions include not only the decisions that, for moral or political reasons, humans must be allowed to make, but also coordination decisions that humans are better at making due to access to important global knowledge, general information or support tools.

Already, human interaction with agent teams is critical in a large number of current and future applications [38, 49, 92, 203]. For example, current efforts emphasize humans collaboration with robot teams in space explorations, humans teaming with robots and agents for disaster rescue, as well as humans collaborating with multiple software agents for training [73, 106].

This paper focuses on the challenge of improving the effectiveness of applications of human collaboration with agent teams. Previous work has reported encouraging progress in this arena, e.g., via proxy-based integration architectures[176], adjustable autonomy[73, 202] and agent-human dialogue [2]. Despite this encouraging progress, previous work suffers from two key limitations. First, when interacting with agent teams acting remotely, human effectiveness is hampered by interfaces that limit their ability to apply decision-making skills in a fast and accurate manner. Techniques that provide telepresence via video are helpful [92], but cannot provide the global situation awareness. Second, agent teams have been equipped with adjustable autonomy (AA) [203] but not the flexibility critical in such AA. Indeed, the appropriate AA method varies from situation to situation. In some cases the human user should make most of the decisions. However, in other cases human involvement may need to be restricted. Such flexible AA techniques have been developed in domains where humans interact with individual agents [202], but whether they apply to situations where humans interact with agent teams is unknown.

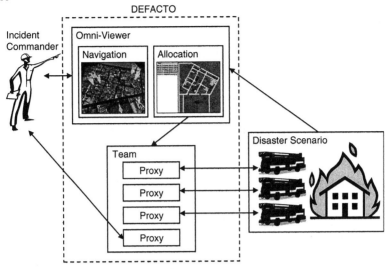

Figure 8.1. DEFACTO system applied to a disaster rescue.

The structure of this chapter is follows: we first intruduce DAFACTO and its key components followed by the extended characteristics of its agents. Next we explain the nature of the DEFACTO multi agent coordination platform and provide a description of the system execution platform. Finally we demonstrate the impact of DEFACTO adjustable autonomy strategies through experiments in the disaster rescue domain.

8.2 Application Domain

We report on a software prototype system, DEFACTO (Demonstrating Effective Flexible Agent Coordination of Teams through Omnipresence), that enables agent-human collaboration and addresses the issues of enhanced user interface and flexible adjustable autonomy outlined in the previous section. The user interface (which we refer to as Omni-Viewer) and proxy-based teamwork (called *Machinetta*) are incorporated in DEFACTO in a way depicted in Figure 8.1.

The Omni-Viewer is an advanced human interface for interacting with an agent-assisted response effort. The Omni-Viewer provides for both global and local views of an unfolding situation, allowing a human decision-maker to precisely assess the information required for a particular decision. A team of completely distributed proxies, where each proxy encapsulates advanced coordination reasoning based on the theory of teamwork, controls and coordinates agents in a simulated environment. The use of the proxy-based team brings realistic coordination complexity to the prototype and allows more realistic assessment of the interactions between humans and agent-assisted response. Currently, we have applied DEFACTO to a disaster rescue domain. The incident commander of the disaster acts as the *human user* of DEFACTO. This disaster can either be "man made" (terrorism) or "natural" (earthquake). We focus on two urban areas: a square block that is densely covered with buildings (we use one from Kobe, Japan) and the University of Southern California (USC) campus, which is more sparsely covered with buildings. In our scenario, several buildings are initially on fire, and these fires spread to adjacent buildings if they are not quickly contained. The goal is to have a human interact with the team of fire engines in order to save the most buildings. While designed for real world situations, DEFACTO can also be used as a training tool for incident commanders when hooked up to a simulated disaster scenario.

To provide flexible AA, we generalize the notion of *strategies* from single-agent single-human context [202]. In our work, agents may flexibly choose among team strategies for adjustable autonomy instead of only individual strategies; thus, depending on the situation, the agent team has the flexibility to limit human interaction, and may in extreme cases exclude humans from the loop.

Finally, we present results from detailed experiments with DEFACTO in Robocup Rescue domain, which reveal two major surprises. First, contrary to previous results [203], human involvement is not always beneficial to an agent team— despite their best efforts, humans may sometimes end up hurting an agent team's performance. Second, increasing the number of agents in an agent-human team may also degrade the team performance, even though increasing the number of agents in a pure agent team under identical circumstances improves team performance. Fortunately, in both the surprising instances above, DEFACTO's flexible AA strategies alleviate such problematic situations.

DEFACTO is currently instantiated as a prototype of a future disaster response system. DEFACTO has been repeatedly demonstrated to key police and fire department personnel in Los Angeles area, with very positive feedback.

8.2.1   Omni-Viewer

Our goal of allowing fluid human interaction with agents requires a visualization system that provides the human with a global view of agent activity as well as showing the local view of a particular agent when needed. Hence, we have developed an omnipresent viewer, or Omni-Viewer, which will al-

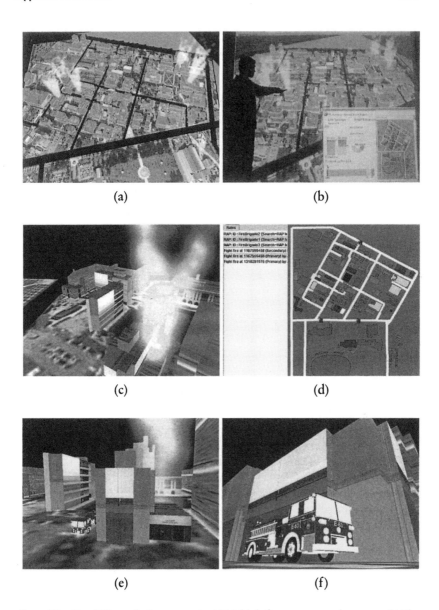

Figure 8.2. Omni-Viewer during a scenario: (a) Multiple fires start across the campus (b) The Incident Commander uses the Navigation mode to quickly grasp the situation (c) Navigation mode shows a closer look at one of the fires (d) Allocation mode is used to assign a fire engine to the fire (e) The fire engine has arrived at the fire (f) The fire has been extinguished.

low the human user diverse interaction with remote agent teams. While a global view is obtainable from a two-dimensional map, a local perspective is best obtained from a 3D viewer, since the 3D view incorporates the perspective and occlusion effects generated by a particular viewpoint. The literature on 2D- versus 3D-viewers is ambiguous. For example, spatial learning of environments from virtual navigation has been found to be impaired relative to studying simple maps of the same environments [184]. On the other hand, the problem may be that many virtual environments are relatively bland and featureless. Ruddle points out that navigating virtual environments can be successful if rich, distinguishable landmarks are present [185].

To address our discrepant goals, the Omni-Viewer incorporates both a conventional map-like 2D view, Allocation Mode (Figure 8.2-d) and a detailed 3D viewer, Navigation Mode (Figure 8.2-a). The Allocation mode shows the global overview as events are progressing and provides a list of tasks that the agents have transfered to the human. The Navigation mode shows the same dynamic world view, but allows for more freedom to move to desired locations and views. In particular, the user can drop to the virtual ground level, thereby obtaining the world view (local perspective) of a particular agent. At this level, the user can "walk" freely around the scene, observing the local logistics involved as various entities are performing their duties. This can be helpful in evaluating the physical ground circumstances and altering the team's behavior accordingly. It also allows the user to feel immersed in the scene where various factors (psychological, etc.) may come into effect.

In order to prevent communication bandwidth issues, we assume that a high resolution 3D model has already been created and the only data that is transfered during the disaster are important changes to the world. Generating this suitable 3D model environment for the Navigation mode can require months or even years of manual modeling effort, as is commonly seen in the development of commercial video-games. However, to avoid this level of effort we make use of the work of You et. al. [214] in rapid, minimally assisted construction of polygonal models from LiDAR (Light Detection and Ranging) data. Given the raw LiDAR point data, we can automatically segment buildings from ground and create the high resolution model that the Navigation mode utilizes. The construction of the USC campus and surrounding area required only two days using this approach. LiDAR is an effective way for any new geographic area to be easily inserted into the Omni-Viewer.

We use the JME game engine to perform the actual rendering due to its cross-platform capabilities. JME is an extensible library built on LWJGL (Light Weight Java Game Library), which interfaces with OpenGL and OpenAL. This environment easily provides real-time rendering of the textured campus environment on mid-range commodity PCs. JME utilizes a scene graph to order the rendering of geometric entities. It provides some important features such as OBJ format model loading (which allows us to author the model and textures in a tool like Maya and load it in JME) and also various assorted effects such as particle systems for fires.

8.2.2   Proxy-based teamwork

Taking into account the uncertainty and communication problems that often arise in disaster rescue domains robust multi agent teams are more likely to perform better that centralized approaches. To this end, DEFACTO is build on the state-of-the-art multi agent infrastructure called *Machinetta*. The modular structure of Machinetta main components and the fact that it provides coordiantion algorithms rather than fixed multi-agent infrastructure ensures its versatility which contributes to the reusability of DEFACTO for different domains. The robustness of Machinetta is achieved through decentralized role allocation, communication and coordination algorithms which use the concept of moving agents instead of fixed messages. Details on Machinetta are explained in section 8.4.

A key hypothesis in this work is that intelligent distributed agents will be a key element of a future disaster response. Taking advantage of emerging robust, high bandwidth communication infrastructure we believe that a critical role of these intelligent agents will be to manage coordination between all members of the response team. Specifically, we are using coordination algorithms inspired by theories of teamwork to manage the distributed response[215].

The general coordination algorithms are encapsulated in *proxies* with each proxy representing one team member in the team. Machinetta Proxies, which extend the successful Teamcore proxies [176] are implemented in Java and are freely available on the web.

Notice that the concept of a reusable proxy differs from many other "multiagent toolkits" in that it provides the coordination *algorithms*, e.g., algorithms for allocating tasks, as opposed to the *infrastructure*, e.g., APIs for reliable communication.

8.3   Agents

Currently, DEFACTO is applied to a Robocup Rescue domain which incorporates detailed disaster simulator as well as templates for three types of agents: Fire Engines, Ambulances and Police Cars. At this stage of the system development we focus on Fire Engines and simulate only the fire spread and building damage. Thus, agents in our simulation are Fire Engines taking on new Fight Fire requests and reporting the status of buildings.

Main aspects of these agents are:

- Pro-activeness: each agent stores a list of plans it is able to perform and whenever plan preconditions are met, roles associated with plans are immediately triggered. On the other hand, agents pro-activness can be varied through adjustable autonomy strategies resulting in the increased performance of the whole team.

- Reactivness: each agent moves around the environment, scans it for emerging fires and reports the status of the buildings on fire. In case of an environment change agent's first task is to comunicate the news to other team members and consequently establish the basis for a new *Fight Fire* plan.

- Mobility: agent movement affects its sensing of the environment and choice of which fire to fight first; Priority is given to the closest burning building. In addition, agents are sucseptible to road congestion generated in real time by the traffic simulator.

- Configurability: agents can have flexible level of intelligence depending on the contents of their declarative configuration files which store agent beliefs, plans, adjustable autonomy strategies etc.

- Flexible architecture: The modular structure of Machinetta Proxies allows them to be reused for different domains with interchangable coordination algorithms.

8.3.1   Adjustable Autonomy

In this paper, we focus on a key aspect of the proxy-based coordination: Adjustable Autonomy. Adjustable autonomy refers to an agent's ability to dynamically change its own autonomy, possibly to transfer control over a decision to a human. Previous work on adjustable autonomy could be categorized as either involving a single person interacting with a single agent (the agent itself may interact with others) or a single person directly interacting with a team. In the single-agent single-human category, the concept of flexible transfer-of-control strategy has shown promise [202]. A transfer-of-control strategy is a preplanned sequence of actions to transfer control over a decision among multiple entities, for example, an AH_1H_2 strategy implies that an agent (A) attempts a decision and if the agent fails in the decision then the control over the decision is passed to a human H_1, and then if H_1 cannot reach a decision, then the control is passed to H_2. Since previous work focused on single-agent single-human interaction, strategies were individual agent strategies where only a single agent acted at a time.

An optimal transfer-of-control strategy optimally balances the risks of not getting a high quality decision against the risk of costs incurred due to a delay in getting that decision. Flexibility in such strategies implies that an agent dynamically chooses the one that is optimal, based on the situation, among multiple such strategies ($H_1 A$, AH_1, $AH_1 A$, etc.) rather than always rigidly choosing one strategy. The notion of flexible strategies, however, has not been applied in the context of humans interacting with agent-teams. Thus, a key question is whether such flexible transfer of control strategies are relevant in agent-teams, particularly in a large-scale application such as ours.

DEFACTO aims to answer this question by implementing transfer-of-control strategies in the context of agent teams. One key advance in DE-FACTO, however, is that the strategies are not limited to individual agent strategies, but also enables team-level strategies. For example, rather than transferring control from a human to a single agent, a team-level strategy could transfer control from a human to an agent-team. Concretely, each proxy is provided with all strategy options; the key is to select the right strategy given the situation. An example of a team level strategy would combine A_T Strategy and H Strategy in order to make $A_T H$ Strategy. The default team strategy, A_T, keeps control over a decision with the agent team for the entire duration of the decision. The H strategy always immediately transfers control to the human. $A_T H$ strategy is the conjunction of team level A_T strategy with H strategy. This strategy aims to significantly reduce the burden on the user by allowing the decision to first pass through all agents before finally going to the user, if the agent team fails to reach a decision.

8.4 Multi-Agent System

The Machinetta software consists of five main modules, three are domain independent and two are tailored for specific domains (Figure 8.3. The three domain independent modules are for coordination reasoning, maintaining local beliefs (state) and adjustable autonomy. The domain specific modules are for communication between proxies and communication between a proxy and a team member. The modules interact with each other only via the local state with a blackboard design and are designed to be "plug and play", thus, e.g., new adjustable autonomy algorithms can be used with existing coordination algorithms. The coordination reasoning is responsible for reasoning about interactions with other proxies, thus implementing the coordination algorithms. The adjustable autonomy algorithms reason about the interaction with the team member, providing the possibility for the team member to make any coordination decision instead of the proxy. For example, the adjustable autonomy module can reason that a decision to accept a role to rescue a civilian from a burning building should be made by the human who will go into the building rather than the proxy. In practice, the

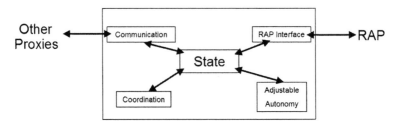

Figure 8.3. Proxy Architecture

overwhelming majority of coordination decisions are made by the proxy, with only key decisions referred to team members.

Communication: communication with other proxies

Coordination: reasoning about team plans and communication

State: the working memory of the proxy

Adjustable Autonomy: reasoning about whether to act autonomously or pass control to the team member

RAP Interface: communication with the team member

Description of Machinetta Proxy components

Teams of proxies implement *team oriented plans* (TOPs) which describe joint activities to be performed in terms of the individual *roles* to be performed and any constraints between those roles. Typically, TOPs are instantiated dynamically from TOP templates at runtime when preconditions associated with the templates are filled. Typically, a large team will be simultaneously executing many TOPs. For example, a disaster response team might be executing multiple fight fire TOPs. Such fight fire TOPs might specify a breakdown of fighting a fire into activities such as checking for civilians, ensuring power and gas is turned off and spraying water. Constraints between these roles will specify interactions such as required execution ordering and whether one role can be performed if another is not currently being performed. Notice that TOPs do not specify the coordination or communication required to execute a plan, the proxy determines the coordination that should be performed.

8.4.1   Organisation

The proxy based approach to coordination is completely distributed, with each proxy working closely with the team member it represents in the environment. Since the underlying algorithms are based on an operationalization of the theory of teamwork[215], coordination requires that joint intentions and mutual beliefs are formed in a distributed manner before the team begins executing a task. Recent changes to Machinetta have relaxed the requirements on mutual beliefs and joint intentions to allow bigger teams to function effectively without infeasible communication overhead[203] Specifically, agents are only required to form joint intentions and mutual beliefs with other team members with whom they are directly collaborating on a sub-goal, rather than with the whole team. This leads to the possibility of the team performing duplicate or conflicting tasks, hence additional conflict resolution algorithms are required to remove these conflicts.

Underlying the conflict resolution mechanism, and in fact several key algorithms in Machinetta, is a static, logical network involving all the members of the team[203] This network is referred to as the *associates network*. As well as maintaining mutual beliefs and joint intentions between direct collaborators, team members share critical information with their neighbors in the associates network. By ensuring that the associates network has a *small worlds* property [232], there is very high probability that at least one agent will get to know of any conflict and can initiate a resolution process[137]. Team members collaborating on a sub-plan form a sort of sub-team with their neighbors in the associates network by virtue of their joint intention and mutual beliefs. While the associates network remains static the members of a sub-team, and indeed the sub-plans, can change over time, resulting in an emergent organizational structure consisting of dynamically changing, overlapping sub-teams. (If needs be, I have a figure for this.) Notice that no hierarchy or centralized control of any type is present in Machinetta.

The algorithms in Machinetta are designed to be very scalable, allowing large teams to be deployed to achieve complex tasks. Fully distributed simulations involving up to 500 team members have been successfully demonstrated and key algorithms have been shown to work efficiently with up to 10,000 team members. While no Machinetta algorithms require the associates network to be fixed when the team is initiated or for the whole team to be known, to date all uses of Machinetta have involved domains where the entire team is known in advance. However, by leveraging the underlying associates network and some careful algorithm design there is no need for yellow pages type services, because team members need only interact with neighbors in the network. Provided new team members can integrate themselves successfully into the network, maintaining the network's small worlds property, Machinetta can support dynamic addition of new team members.

8.4.2   Interaction

When developing large teams, protocol and software robustness is critically important. When hundreds or thousands of distributed team members asynchronously coordinate to simultaneously achieve hundreds of sub-plans over a period of time, any "bugs" in the interaction code will be inevitable found[1] Since developing completely bug free code is extremely difficult even for professional software developers, we developed a novel way of implementing interaction that is particularly robust and relatively easy to debug. Rather than sending messages between proxies and, thus, having distributed state that is prone to difficult to locate bugs, we are exploring the use of mobile agents that transfer both coordination state and a message as they move between proxies.

One hypothesis we are exploring is that the use of mobile agents for coordination leads to high degrees of robustness in at least two key ways. First, it is easier to develop reliable means to know whether messages are "lost", since the agent itself can ensure its own movement around the team. Second, coordination algorithms are simpler to implement because they are entirely encapsulated within the code of a single mobile agent (rather than being spread across proxies.) Thus, management of interaction state and handling of coordination failures, etc., is greatly simplified.

The use of mobile agents as a means for implementing coordination protocols means that the proxies can be thought of as a type of mobile agent platform. However, unlike traditional mobile agent platforms, the proxies are active in providing information to the mobile agents and even, when the adjustable autonomy decides a human should make a decision, making decisions on the mobile agents behalf. Since the proxies are connected in a small worlds network, it is possible to think of the coordination as being implemented by mobile agents moving around a small worlds network of active mobile agent platforms.

8.4.3   MAS Environment

Machinetta is designed to be both domain independant and to work with highly heterogeneous teams. As such, it has been possible to demonstrate Machinetta in several simulation environments. In addition to DEFACTO, Machinetta has also been used for coordination of high fidelity simulations of search and rescue robots. The most stringent tests of Machinetta's coor-

---

[1]Murphy's Law meets the Law of Large Numbers.

dination capabilities will come in late 2005 when it is used for an Air Force flight test involving three simulated unmanned aerial vehicles (UAVs) and one real UAV. Initial testing has shown Machinetta can effectively coordinate large numbers of UAVs to efficiently execute a wide area search and destroy mission with sufficiently low communication bandwidth to be feasible in a military domain[201].

The domains in which Machinetta have been used, though varied, share some common traits. Specifically, the domains have typically allowed complex tasks to be broken down into smaller subtasks with most of the required coordination being for specific subtasks rather than across subtasks. Machinetta has been required to deal with dynamics in all the domains in which it have been used, but, although some domains have contained hostile forces, explicit adversarial reasoning has not been performed.

8.5 Experiments

We have conducted experiments with the DEFACTO system connected to the Robocup Rescue simulation environment. All the simulation components were running on one desktop with two AMD 1.8 GHz processors and 4GB of ram. The following processes were simulated on the desktop:

- All the Machinetta proxies and their communication server

- Robocup rescue kernel including traffic, blocade, fire and building collapse simulators

- Allocation viewer.

8.5.1 Evaluation

DEFACTO was evaluated in two key ways, focusing on key individual components of the system. First, we performed detailed experiments comparing the effectiveness of Adjustable Autonomy (AA) strategies over multiple users. In order to provide DEFACTO with a dynamic rescue domain we chose to connect it to a simulator. We chose the previously developed RoboCup Rescue simulation environment [128]. In this simulator, fire engine agents can search the city and attempt to extinguish any fires that have started in the city. To interface with DEFACTO, each fire engine is controlled by a proxy in order to handle the coordination and execution of AA strategies. Consequently, the proxies can try to allocate fire engines to fires in a distributed manner, but can also transfer control to the more expert user. The user can then use the Omni-Viewer in Allocation mode to allocate engines to the fires that he has control over. In order to focus on the AA strategies (transferring the control of task allocation) and not have the users

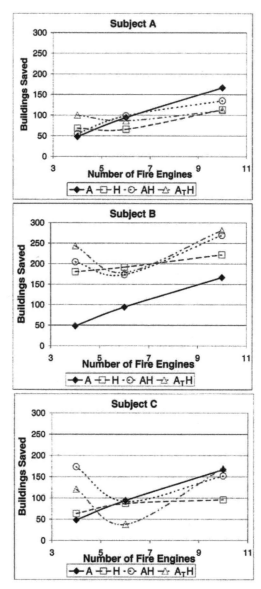

Figure 8.4. Performance of subjects 1, 2, and 3.

ability to navigate interfere with results, the Navigation mode was not used during this first set of experiments.

The results of our experiments are shown in Figure 8.4, which shows the results of subjects 1, 2, and 3. Each subject was confronted with the task of aiding fire engines in saving a city hit by a disaster. For each subject, we tested three strategies, specifically, H, AH and $A_T H$; their performance was compared with the completely autonomous A_T strategy. AH is an individual agent strategy, tested for comparison with $A_T H$, where agents act individually, and pass those tasks to a human user that they cannot immediately perform. Each experiment was conducted with the same initial locations of fires and building damage. For each strategy we tested, varied the number of fire engines between 4, 6 and 10. Each chart in Figure 8.4 shows the varying number of fire engines on the x-axis, and the team performance in terms of numbers of building saved on the y-axis. For instance, strategy A_T saves 50 building with 4 agents. Each data point on the graph is an average of three runs. Each run itself took 15 minutes, and each user was required to participate in 27 experiments, which together with 2 hours of getting oriented with the system, equates to about 9 hours of experiments per volunteer.

Figure 8.4 enables us to conclude the following:

- *Human involvement with agent teams does not necessarily lead to improvement in team performance.* Contrary to expectations and prior results, human involvement does not uniformly improve team performance, as seen by human-involving strategies performing worse than the A_T strategy in some instances. For instance, for subject 3, human involving strategies such as AH provide a somewhat higher quality than A_T for 4 agents, yet at higher numbers of agents, the strategy performance is lower than A_T.

- *Providing more agents at a human's command does not necessarily improve the agent team performance* As seen for subject 2 and subject 3, increasing agents from 4 to 6 given AH and $A_T H$ strategies is seen to degrade performance. In contrast, for the A_T strategy, the performance of the fully autonomous agent team continues to improve with additions of agents, thus indicating that the reduction in AH and $A_T H$ performance is due to human involvement. As the number of agents increase to 10, the agent team does recover.

- *No strategy dominates through all the experiments given varying numbers of agents.* For instance, at 4 agents, human-involving strategies dominate the A_T strategy. However, at 10 agents, the A_T strategy outperforms all possible strategies for subjects 1 and 3.

Strategy	H			AH			$A_T H$		
# of agents	4	6	10	4	6	10	4	6	10
Subject 1	91	92	154	118	128	132	104	83	64
Subject 2	138	129	180	146	144	72	109	120	38
Subject 3	117	132	152	133	136	97	116	58	57

Table 8.1. Total amount of allocations given.

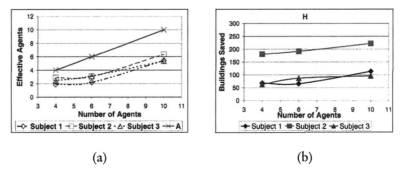

(a) (b)

Figure 8.5. (a) AG_H and (b) H performance

- *Complex team-level strategies are helpful in practice*: $A_T H$ leads to improvement over H with 4 agents for all subjects, although surprising domination of AH over $A_T H$ in some cases indicates that AH may also a useful strategy to have available in a team setting.

Note that the phenomena described range over multiple users, multiple runs, and multiple strategies. The most important conclusion from these figures is that *flexibility is necessary to allow for the optimal AA strategy to be applied*. The key question is then how to select the appropriate strategy for a team involving a human whose expected decision quality is EQ_H. In fact, by estimating the EQ_H of a subject by checking the "H" strategy for small number of agents (say 4), and comparing to A strategy, we may begin to select the appropriate strategy for teams involving more agents. In general, higher EQ_H lets us still choose strategies involving humans for a more numerous team. For large teams however, the number of agents AG_H effectively controlled by the human does not grow linearly thus A_T strategy becomes dominant.

Unfortunately, the strategies including the humans and agents (AH and $A_T H$) for 6 agents show a noticeable decrease in performance for subjects 2 and 3 (see Figure 8.4). It would be useful to understand which factors contributed to this phenomena.

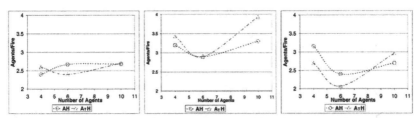

Figure 8.6.   Amount of agents per fire assigned by subjects 1, 2, and 3

Our crucial predictions were that while numbers of agents increase, AG_H steadily increases and EQ_H remains constant. Thus, the dip at 6 agents is essentially affected by either AG_H or EQ_H. We first tested AG_H in our domain. The amount of effective agents, AG_H, is calculated by dividing how many total allocations each subject made by how many the A_T strategy made per agent, assuming A_T strategy effectively uses all agents. Figure 8.5-(a) shows the number of agents on the x-axis and the number of agents effective used, AG_H, on the y-axis; the A_T strategy, which is using all available agents, is also shown as a reference. However, the amount of effective agents is actually about the same in 4 and 6 agents. This would not account for the sharp drop we see in the performance. We then shifted our attention to the EQ_H of each subject. One reduction in EQ_H could be because subjects simply did not send as many allocations totally over the course of the experiments. This, however is not the case as can be seen in Table 8.1 where for 6 agents, the total amount of allocations given is comparable to that of 4 agents. To investigate further, we checked if the quality of human allocation had degraded. For our domain, the more fire engines that fight the same fire, the more likely it is to be extinguished and in less time. For this reason, the amount of agents that were tasked to each fire is a good indicator of the quality of allocations that the subject makes 8.5-(b). Figure 8.6 shows the number agents on the x-axis and the average amount of fire engines allocated to each fire on the y-axis. AH and A_TH for 6 agents result in significantly less average fire engines per task (fire) and therefore less average EQ_H.

The second aspect of our evaluation was to explore the benefits of the Navigation mode (3D) in the Omni-Viewer over solely an Allocation mode (2D). We performed 2 tests on 20 subjects. All subjects were familiar with the USC university campus. Test 1 showed Navigation and Allocation mode screenshots of the university campus to subjects. Subjects were asked to identify a unique building on campus, while timing each response. The average time for a subject to find the building in 2D was 29.3 seconds, whereas the

3D allowed them to find the same building in an average of 17.1 seconds. Test 2 again displayed Navigation and Allocation mode screenshots of two buildings on campus that had just caught fire. In Test 2, subjects were asked first asked to allocate fire engines to the buildings using only the Allocation mode. Then subjects were shown the Navigation mode of the same scene. 90 percent of the subjects actually chose to change their initial allocation, given the extra information that the Navigation mode provided.

8.6   Related Work and Summary

We have discussed related work throughout this paper, however, we now provide comparisons with key previous agent software prototypes and research. Among the current tools aimed at simulating rescue environments it is important to mention products like TerraSim, JCATS and EPICS. Terra-Tools is a complete simulation database construction system for automated and rapid generation of high-fidelity 3D simulation databases from cartographic source materials. Developed by TerraSim, Inc. TerraTools provides the set of integrated tools aimed at generating various terrains, however, it cannot simulate rescue operations not it has any notion of intelligence. JCATS represents a self-contained, high-resolution joint simulation in use for entity-level training in open, urban and subterranean environments. Developed by Lawrence Livermore National Laboratory, JCATS gives users the capability to detail the replication of small group and individual activities during a simulated operation. Although it provides a great human training environment, JCATS does not allow to simulate intelligent agents. Finally, EPICS is a computer-based, scenario-driven, high-resolution simulation. It is used by emergency response agencies to train for emergency situations that require multi-echelon and/or inter-agency communication and coordination. Developed by the U.S. Army Training and Doctrine Command Analysis Center, EPICS is also used for exercising communications and command and control procedures at multiple levels. Similar to JCATS however, intelligent agents and agent-human interaction cannot be simulated.

Given our application domains, work of Scerri et. al. on robot-agent-person (RAP) teams for disaster rescue is likely the most closely related to DEFACTO [203]. Our work takes a significant step forward in comparison. First, the omni-viewer enables navigational capabilities improving human situational awareness not present in previous work. Second, we provide team-level strategies, which we experimentally verify, absent in that work. Third, we provide extensive experimentation, and illustrate that some of the conclusions reached in [203] were indeed preliminary, e.g., they conclude that human involvement is always beneficial to agent team performance, while our more extensive results indicate that sometimes agent teams are better off excluding humans from the loop. Human interactions in agent teams is also investigated in [38, 214], and there is significant research on human interactions with robot-teams [92, 49]. However they do not use flexible AA strategies and/or team-level AA strategies. Furthermore, our experimental results may assist these researchers in recognizing the potential for harm that humans may cause to agent or robot team performance. Significant attention has been paid in the context of adjustable autonomy and mixed-initiative in single-agent single-human interactions [111, 2]. However, this paper focuses on new phenomena that arise in human interactions with agent teams.

This paper presents a large-scale prototype, DEFACTO, that is based on a software proxy architecture and 3D visualization system and provides two key advances over previous work. First, DEFACTO's Omni-Viewer enables the human to both improve situational awareness and assist agents, by providing a navigable 3D view along with a 2D global allocation view. Second, DEFACTO incorporates flexible AA strategies, even excluding humans from the loop in extreme circumstances. We performed detailed experiments using DEFACTO, leading to some surprising results. These results illustrate that an agent team must be equipped with flexible strategies for adjustable autonomy so that the appropriate strategy can be selected. Exciting feedback from DEFACTO's ultimate consumers illustrates its promise and potential for real-world application.

Chapter 9

ARTIMIS RATIONAL DIALOGUE AGENT TECHNOLOGY: AN OVERVIEW

David Sadek

France Télécom · Division R & D
2, avenue Pierre-Marzin
22307 Lannion Cedex · France
david.sadek@francetelecom.com

Abstract   ARTIMIS is an effective intelligent agent technology designed and developed by France Telecom. It provides a generic framework to instantiate dialogue agents that are able to engage in rich interactions with human users (with no restriction on the communication media) as well as with other software agents. Several operational ARTIMIS-based applications have been developed, and commercial services have begun to be deployed. ARTIMIS relies on the principle that a system's ability to carry on a natural dialogue with a human user must result from the system's inherent intelligence. Consequently, an intelligent dialogue system needs to be first conceived and designed as an intelligent system. ARTIMIS provides a generic framework for the development of intelligent agents whose behaviour is wholly driven by explicit cognitive principles, such as rationality, communication and cooperation. ARTIMIS agents can also be components of multi-agent systems. In this case, to interact with other agents, they use the FIPA ACL standard (Agent Communication Language), whose formalism and semantics come from ARCOL, the ARTIMIS Communication Language.

Keywords: Rational agent technology, natural human-computer dialogue, multi-agent context, inter-agent communication language, effective applications.

9.1   Introduction

ARTIMIS is a rational agent technology designed and developed by France Telecom [195]. It provides a generic framework to instantiate dialogue agents that are able to engage in rich interactions with human users (with no restriction on the communication media) as well as with other software agents.

The foundational work underlying ARTIMIS technology handles communication as a special case of intelligent behaviour: an intelligent dialogue system has to be first an intelligent system. The necessity of machine intelligence obviously appears in contexts that require, at the same time, a complex and user-friendly interaction with a human being. This is overtly illustrated in natural human-computer dialogue. It is not anodyne that the Turing test requires a dialogue situation. The capabilities underlying dialogue phenomenon (perception, reasoning, learning, etc.) are required by other so-called intelligent behaviours, namely behaviours that display problem solving capacities. Therefore, the ability to engage into a dialogue relies on a common ground that endows it with a non-primitive character. Rational behaviour appears as the most consensual manifestation of intelligence [156, 186][1]. Roughly speaking, to behave rationally is to be driven by principles that select in an optimal way the actions leading to futures compliant with a given set of motivations and goals.

The approach underlying ARTIMIS technology right away targets real systems. It has therefore the ambition to cover at the theoretical level the different components of rational, communicative, and social behaviours of an agent. In an original way, it unifies under the same point of view the problem of designing dialogue systems and that of designing intelligent artificial agents. This approach points out the paradigm of rational dialogue agent as the one that has to ground the construction of intelligent systems. Moreover, by virtue of the genericity of its principles, it is intended to provide the robustness required from an intelligent system, namely to adequately react to complex situations or incompletely specified ones when the system is designed.

In section 9.2, the range of ARTIMIS technology applications is briefly overviewed. In section 9.3, the formal theory that underlies ARTIMIS is introduced and the agent architecture is presented, along with a description of the different components of the technology. Section 9.4 focuses on one of the multi-agent capabilities of ARTIMIS, namely the inter-agent communication language. Concrete application cases are then exemplified in section 9.5. Some remarks conclude the chapter.

9.2   Application domain

Primarily designed to support advanced interactive services and to offer user-friendly cooperative intelligent interfaces to information bases, AR-

---

[1]See also [75] for different considerations on economic rationality.

TIMIS intelligent agent technology de facto strongly relates to end-user applications.

When instantiated in a human-agent interaction context, ARTIMIS allows for implementing interactive services that enable natural dialogue with human users, whatever the communication media is. The resulting dialogue agents display advanced functionalities, such as natural language, mixed-initiative interaction, request and response negotiation, cooperative reactions, etc. [192, 199].

ARTIMIS can also be used in multi-agent environments, namely contexts involving several interacting software agents (but also web services, databases, etc.). Along these lines, its use field is extended to mediation applications, in which an ARTIMIS agent can manage, in a unified and cooperative way, the relationship between a user and regular information sources [148]. In this context, the main offered functionalities are: identification of proposals that best fit the user's request, construction of proposals possibly combining information coming from different sources (*e.g.* travels combining trains and flights, obtained from web sites providing information about a single transportation mode), suggestion of alternative solutions, etc.

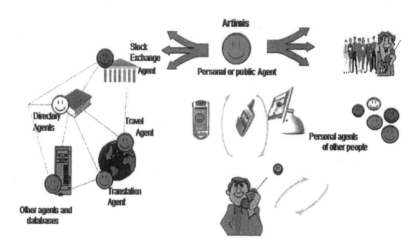

Figure 9.1. ARTIMIS: a wide range of applications

Thanks to its genericity, ARTIMIS range of potential applications is very wide[2]. It encompasses various application domains: personal or public assistants, information and transaction services, telecommunication services (hotlines, portals,...), directories (yellow pages, tourist guides,...), banking and financial services (stocks, account management,...), e-commerce, e-learning and education, intelligent interfaces for Internet search engines, games (intelligent communicating clones and avatars), etc.

9.3   ARTIMIS as an autonomous agent

9.3.1   Formal rational interaction theory

The ARTIMIS approach of rational interaction is governed by two main ideas. The first one is that, for an agent, engaging and following up a dialogue with a human interlocutor or with another agent can be totally justified by rational behaviour principles. Therefore, it is not necessary for an agent to have a structural dialogue model or a communication protocol, since the instances of such a model or a protocol are dynamically retrieved by rational behaviour. The second idea is that a single formal theory can account for the different aspects of an agent's cognitive and communicative behaviour.

The early theoretical work that formally investigated the idea of rationality as the basis of communication is that of [45, 46][3]. This pioneer work introduced a robust, fine-grained, methodological framework to express formal theories of intention and to study intentional action and certain aspects of communication. However, strictly speaking, it did not directly formalise "operational" principles of rational behaviour, neither the mechanisms that underlie cooperation. In other respects, its theoretical aim did not disclose a direct implementation into real systems.

The ARTIMIS model is a formal theory of rational interaction expressed in a homogeneous logical framework [188][4]. The basic concepts of this framework are mental attitudes and actions. The theory shows how advanced behaviours result from the application of primitive principles and from their combination. It is expressed within a unique formal model (a quantified modal logic, with a well-defined semantics) and modularly constructed in different components, as briefly presented below.

---

[2]Examples of ARTIMIS-based applications are presented in section 9.5.
[3]Other works come within a similar approach. See, *e.g.*, [179, 240, 237].
[4]See also [34, 138] for presentations and analysis of different aspects of the theory, and for extensions.

Basic formal concepts

The first component of the theoretical framework corresponds to the formalisation of the basic concepts that enable to express the notions of mental state and behaviour. The formal account is expressed in a first order modal language with identity. For the sake of brevity, only the aspects of the formalism used in this chapter are introduced in the following. Symbols $\neg, \wedge, \vee, \Rightarrow$, and $\Leftrightarrow$ represent classical connectives of negation, conjunction, disjunction, logical implication and equivalence. $\forall$ and $\exists$ are respectively the universal and existential quantifiers. x, y, and z are symbols for individual variables. a, a_1, and a_2 are variable schemata denoting action expressions (see below). p and p' are taken to be closed formulae (denoting propositions), ϕ, ψ and δ formula schemata, and i, j and h variable schemata denoting agents. Notation $\models \phi$ means that formula ϕ is valid.

The concept of action (or event) and the basic mental attitudes of belief, uncertainty and choice (or, to some extent, goal) are modelled. These mental attitudes are respectively formalised by the modal operators B, U and C. Formulae as $B_i p$, $U_i p$ and $C_i p$ can be respectively read "i (implicitly) believes (that) p", "i thinks that p is more likely than $\neg p$", and "i desires that p currently holds". The logical rules that express their inherent properties and relationships are formalised. The resulting agents are fully introspective and have consistent beliefs [5]. An agent's uncertainties are not closed under logical consequence. Intention is defined as a complex combination of belief and choice [189] in a relatively similar way as [45], although with some fundamental differences. It is formalised by the modal operator I. Formula as $I_i p$ can be read "i brings about p". The definition of intention entails that it necessarily generates a planning process. It also imposes that an agent cannot bring about a situation if the agent believes that the situation already holds:

$$\models I_i \phi \Rightarrow B_i \neg \phi$$

As far as *action* is concerned, complex action expressions are recursively built over the set of primitive actions (or events) using a sequence operator $(a_1; a_2)$, a nondeterministic choice operator $(a_1 \mid a_2)$, and an iteration operator $(a*)$. A sequence can be formed with a single agent that may be the *void* event. The *introspection action*, noted $\langle i, \phi? \rangle$, is a particular event that can be performed if and only if agent i explicitly believes ϕ. It enables the agent to handle conditional steps within plans. In order to reason about action,

---

[5] For an agent i, the logical model for operator B_i is a KD45 possible-worlds-semantics Kripke structure (see, *e.g.*, [103]) with the fixed domain principle (see, *e.g.*, [94]). This structure is also the framework for the interpretation of uncertainty, the set of possible worlds being viewed as a probability space. The concept of choice is also interpreted in terms of possible worlds, characterised by a specific accessibility relation.

two modal operators are introduced, a being an action expression and ϕ a formula: $Feasible(a, \phi)$ means that a can take place and if it does, ϕ will be true after that, and $Done(a, \phi)$ means that a has just taken place and ϕ was true before that. $Agent(i, a)$ means that i denotes the only agent of the events (or actions) appearing in a[6].

The following abbreviations are used, *True* being the propositional constant always true:

$$
\begin{array}{rcl}
Feasible(a) & \equiv & Feasible(a, True) \\
Done(a) & \equiv & Done(a, True) \\
Bif_i\phi & \equiv & B_i\phi \vee B_i\neg\phi \\
Bref_i\delta(x) & \equiv & (\exists y)B_i(\iota x\delta(x) = y) \\
Uif_i\phi & \equiv & U_i\phi \vee U_i\neg\phi \\
Uref_i\delta(x) & \equiv & (\exists y)U_i(\iota x\delta(x) = y) \\
AB_{n,i,j}\phi & \equiv & B_iB_jB_i...\phi
\end{array}
$$

In the forth and sixth abbreviations, ι is the operator for definite description, defined as a term producer as follows:

$$
\phi(\iota x\delta(x)) \quad \equiv \quad \exists y\phi(y) \wedge \delta(y) \wedge \forall z(\delta(z) \Rightarrow z = y)
$$

$\iota x\delta(x)$ is read "the (x which is) δ". $Bref_i\delta(x)$ means that agent i (thinks that she/he/it) knows the (x which is) δ[7]. $Uif_i\phi$ means that either agent i is uncertain about ϕ (in the sense defined above) or that he is uncertain about $\neg\phi$. $Uref_i\delta(x)$ has the same meaning as $Bref_i\delta(x)$, except that agent i has an uncertainty attitude with respect to $\delta(x)$ instead of a belief attitude. In the last abbreviation, which introduces the concept of *alternate beliefs*, n is a positive integer representing the number of B operators alternating between i and j.

There is no restriction on the possibility of embedding mental attitude or action operators. For example, formula $U_iB_jI_jDone(a, B_ip)$ informally means that agent i believes that, probably, agent j thinks that i has the intention that action a be done before which i has to believe p.

A fundamental property of the proposed logic is that the modelled agents are perfectly in agreement with their own mental attitudes. Formally, the following property holds:

$$
\models \phi(i) \Leftrightarrow B_i\phi
$$

---

[6]The semantics of operators *Feasible* and *Done* is defined in terms of accessibility relations on possible worlds, specifying a model with a branching future and a linear past. For the detailed semantics, see [188, 189].

[7]Formula $Bref_i\delta(x)$ can be used for $(\exists x)B_i\delta(x)$. In such a case, the operator ι produces an *indefinite description*, meaning that the uniqueness constraint, corresponding to the component $\forall z(\delta(z) \Rightarrow z = y)$ in the definition of $\phi(\iota x\delta(x))$, is abandoned.

where $\phi(i)$ is a formula governed by a modal operator formalising a mental attitude of agent i.

Rationality principles

The second component of the theory deals with the properties that relate an agent's intentions with the actions enabling it to achieve them [190]. It formally establishes the axioms that ground an agent's rational behaviour, namely the rationality principles. These principles enable an agent to generate intentional action.

The components of an action model, in particular, of a communicative act (CA) model that are involved in a planning process characterise both the reason for which the action is selected and the conditions that have to be satisfied for the action to be planned. For a given action, the former is referred to as the *rational effect* (RE)[8], and the latter as the *feasibility preconditions* (FP), or the qualifications of the action.

Two rationality principles relate an agent's intention to its plans and actions. The planning process is driven by their alternate use. The first principle gives an agent the capability of planning an act whenever the agent intends to achieve its RE. It states that an agent's intention to achieve a given goal generates its intention that be done one of the acts (1) known to the agent, (2) whose RE corresponds to the agent's goal, and (3) that the agent has no reason for not doing them. The second principle imposes on an agent, whenever it selects an action (by virtue of the first rationality principle), to seek the satisfiability of its FPs[9]. It states that an agent having the intention that some action be done, adopts the intention that the action be feasible, unless it believes that it is already feasible. Formally, the two rationality principles are stated as follows:

$$\models I_i p \Rightarrow I_i Done(a_1 \mid ... \mid a_n)$$

where a_k (k ranging form 1 to n) are all the actions such that: (1) agent i knows action a_k, (2) p is the rational effect of a_k (*i.e.*, the reason for which a_k is planned), and (3) $\neg I_i \neg Done(a_k)$

$$\models I_i Done(a) \Rightarrow B_i Feasible(a) \vee I_i B_i Feasible(a)$$

Importantly, unlike in classical plan-based approach, in this framework, the rationality principles just introduced intrinsically specify a planning algorithm — with no need for any external plan calculus mechanisms — that

---

[8]This effect is also referred to as the perlocutionary effect in some of our previous work [192, 193], in analogy with the use of the term in Speech Acts Theory, yet with the same meaning as the rational effect used here.

[9]See [193] for a generalised version of this property.

deductively generates action plans, through the inference of causal chains of intentions.

Communicative act models

The third component of the theory underlying ARTIMIS gives a fine-grained account of a set of primitive communicative acts[10], by precisely determining the preconditions and effects that characterise each one of them and endow it with its semantics[11]. In this approach, communicative acts are viewed as ordinary actions, handled by the rationality principles in a regular way.

A model of rational action should specify the feasibility preconditions and the rationale of the action. The expression of such a model is, in general, complex for two main reasons. The first one is that the set of action qualifications is potentially infinite (see [193] for the case of communicative acts). The second reason is that the effect of an action on the world is strongly context-dependent and cannot be formulated in general terms [168]; furthermore, "summarising" what an action should leave unchanged is a difficult problem.

A solution that goes round the problem of effect specification is directly related to the expression of the rationality principles. In fact, if it is not possible to specify the actual effects of an action, it is yet possible to state (in a logically valid way) what is expected from an action, that is, what are the reasons for which the action has been selected. This is exactly what is expressed by the first rationality principle. This semantics for action effect, within the framework of a model of rational behaviour, allows one to overcome the problem of effect unpredictability.

The set of feasibility preconditions for a CA can be split into two subsets: the *ability preconditions* and the *context-relevance preconditions*. The ability preconditions characterise the intrinsic ability of an agent to perform a given CA. For instance, to *sincerely assert* some proposition p, an agent has to believe that p. The context-relevance preconditions characterise the relevance of the act with respect to the context in which it is to be performed. For instance, an agent can be intrinsically able to make a promise while believing that the promised action is not needed by the addressee.

The specification of an action's feasibility preconditions and rational effect is axiomatised within the logical theory through the two following properties:

---

[10]See [7, 205] for the foundational work on Speech Act theory and the concept of performatives, which underlies the notion of communicative acts used in our framework.
[11]This specification is at the basis of the FIPA ACL standard.

$$B_i(Feasible(a) \Leftrightarrow FP(a))$$
$$B_i(Done(a) \Rightarrow RE(a))$$

As an example, below is a simplified model (as far as the expression of the preconditions is concerned) of the communicative act of *informing* about the truth of a proposition[12]:

$$\langle i, Inform(j, \phi) \rangle$$
$$FP : B_i\phi \wedge \neg B_iB_j\phi$$
$$RE : B_j\phi$$

This model is directly axiomatised within the logical theory through the above mentioned rationality principles and the following schema:

$$B_h(Feasible(\langle i, Inform(j, \phi) \rangle)) \Leftrightarrow B_i\phi \wedge \neg B_iB_j\phi$$
$$B_h(Done(\langle i, Inform(j, \phi) \rangle)) \Rightarrow B_j\phi)$$

It is worth noting that, unlike in classical plan-based approaches, actions are not handled as data structures by a planning process, but have a logical semantics within the theory itself.

Belief reconstruction

The fourth component of the theory deals with the evolution of agent's beliefs, in particular as a consequence of observing communicative actions. It formalises the *belief reconstruction* process (after each event or action) and mainly deals with the converse process of CA planning, namely the CA *consummation* process. Our approach of belief reconstruction relies on a so-called *observation principle*, which accounts for a distinction between what an agent observes (from the actions of other agents or, more generally, from what is occurring in the world) and the actions (or the events) that actually take place (such as the actions that are really performed by other agents). On this basis, importantly, an agent comes to the conclusion that an action (or an event) it has just observed has really occurred, only under certain *admission* conditions. Roughly speaking, an agent considers that an action a realised by what it has just observed has occurred, only if what the agent believed before the occurrence of a is consistent with the fact that a was feasible, otherwise the agent rejects a or puts into question the admissibility of

---

[12]In fact, this version of the *Inform* act model is the operationalised version. The complete theoretical version (regarding the FPs, yet not including the components due to mutual exclusiveness with acts *Confirm* and *Disconfirm*; see section 9.4) is the following:

$$\langle i, Inform(j, \phi) \rangle$$
$$FP : B_i\phi \wedge \bigwedge_{n>1} \neg AB_{n,i,j}\neg B_i\phi \wedge \neg B_iB_j\phi \wedge \bigwedge_{n>2} \neg AB_{n,i,j}Bj\phi$$
$$RE : B_j\phi$$

where $AB_{n,i,j}\phi$ is an abbreviation for $B_iB_jB_i\ldots$, n being a positive integer representing the number of B operators alternated between i and j.

the previous event(s) that make(s) *a* unfeasible. In addition to the properties underlying action admission and consumption, our specification of the belief reconstruction process also involves an account on how a *memory* of beliefs is formed after the occurrence of an action (or an event), and also on belief *persistence* (and *revision* related to action consumption). We will not go into the details of such a process here (one can see [191, 188] for a detailed presentation of belief reconstruction in our theory). Let us just mention two basic properties.

After an observation, *whenever an agent admits an action (or an event) corresponding to the observation, and only in this case,* it is necessarily committed to believe that its effects and persistent qualifications hold.

As far as CAs are concerned, the agent has to come to believe that the act's performer has the intention (to make public her/his/its intention) to achieve the rational effect of the act[13]. This is captured by the following property:

$$B_i(Done(a) \wedge Agent(j,a) \Rightarrow I_j B_i I_j RE(a))$$

The persistent FPs of a CA are those that do not refer to time (more specifically to action sequencing). Let us call them PFPs. The following property holds:

$$B_i(Done(a) \Rightarrow PFP(a))$$

Social context

The last component of the theory is relative to the properties enabling an agent to evolve in a social environment, typically a multi-agent context. It determines and formalises the basic principles of belief and intention transfer, and those of cooperative behaviour, together with a set of cognitive properties endowing an agent with the motivations to harmoniously react to its environment solicitations. Such properties are optional in the sense that they may be adopted or not adopted depending on the intended behaviour of the modelled agent (see [188, 34, 199] for more details).

A minimal cooperation is required for communication to be possible. For example, suppose that an agent *i* asks an agent *j* if proposition *p* is true; if both agents respect the semantics of the communication language, *j* knows that *i* intends to know if *p* is true. But, without a minimal cooperation, *j* is in no way constrained to react to *i*'s request.

Informally, the *minimal principle of cooperation* states that agents must not only react when they are addressed but, more than that, they must adopt the interlocutor's intention whenever they recognise it, and if they have no objection to adopt it. In other words, *if an agent i believes that an agent j*

---

[13]This kind of act effect is called the *intentional effect.*

intends to achieve property p, and that itself does not have an opposite intention, then i will adopt the intention that j will (eventually) come to believe p. Such a principle is formalised by the validity of the following property:

$$B_i I_j \phi \wedge \neg I_i \neg \phi \Rightarrow I_i B_j \phi$$

In particular, if an agent i thinks that an agent j is expecting something from it (and i has no objections for doing it), then i adopts the intention that j will come to believe that i has done what was expected. Thus, from j's point of view, agent i is cooperating.

It is worth noting that the minimal principle of cooperation has a far range in application: it may lead to cooperative behaviours that are much more complex than merely answering questions, such as making an agent forward a request to a competent agent if it cannot answer the request by itself.

The previous property does not ensure that agent i really believes what it will make j believe. Sincerity is an integral part of cooperation commitments, yet still optional in the specification of an agent in general. In terms of mental attitudes, sincerity can be expressed as follows: *An agent i cannot have the intention that an agent j comes to believe that a proposition p is true without itself believing p or without having the intention to come to believe p.* This property translates into the validity of the following schema:

$$I_i B_j \phi \Rightarrow B_i \phi \vee I_i B_i \phi$$

This property taken together with the previous one ensures that an agent will act sincerely, and therefore will cooperate. They account for the fact that whenever an agent i is aware of the objectives of an agent j, then, as far as possible, i will help j to achieve them.

A corrective answer is produced with the intention of correcting a belief that is considered wrong. Such a belief is usually a presupposition inferred (by implicature [102]) from the recognised communicative act. A corrective intention arises in an agent when its belief of a proposition, about which it is competent is in contradiction with that of its interlocutor. Formally, this property is expressed by the validity of the following schema:

$$B_i(\phi \wedge B_j \neg \phi \wedge Comp(i, \phi)) \Rightarrow I_i B_j \phi$$

where competence is defined as follows:

$$Comp(i, \phi) \equiv (B_i \phi \Rightarrow \phi) \wedge (B_i \neg \phi \Rightarrow \neg \phi)$$

9.3.2   ARTIMIS agent architecture and implementation

Global functional architecture

ARTIMIS agents are driven by rationality, communication and cooperation principles formalised in a rational interaction theory, and directly coded
into the technology kernel. An ARTIMIS agent involves a set of generic
properties, which embodies its innate potential. This potential is independent of its specific use in a given application domain.

The technology kernel relies on a central module called the **rational unit**,
which implements the cognitive capacities of a rational agent through inference procedures automating the axiomatic theory. The kernel also involves a
knowledge management component, and a **language processing component** (understanding and generation of "high level" languages, such as natural
language) that enable an ARTIMIS agent to interact with humans. Moreover,
the technology comprises a **media processing layer** that allows for easily
connecting it to external interfaces, such as speech processing systems, animated faces, graphic avatars (to build embodied conversational agents), etc.,
or enabling it to use language FIPA ACL [89] when interacting with other
agents.

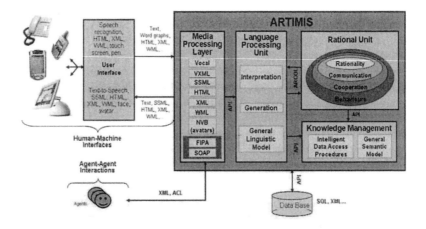

Figure 9.2.   ARTIMIS functional architecture

Rational unit

The rational unit is the decision kernel of the agent. It endows the agent with the capability to reason about knowledge and action. It performs cooperative rational reaction calculus producing motivated plans of actions, such as plans of (or including) communicative acts. The communication "protocols" are dynamic and flexible: there are no pre-defined inter-agent dialogue patterns.

By itself the rational unit is an intelligent communicating agent. It can be used as a regular communicating agent in a multi-agent infrastructure. In the context of human-agent interaction, the user is viewed as a particular agent; no assumption is made about the interlocutor's type. To be used in such a context, the rational unit requires natural language processing components [198, 165] that bridge the gap between the human language and the internal semantic knowledge representation in terms of communicative acts with semantic contents expressed in a powerful language (a first-order modal language): ARCOL (see section 9.4).

From the dialogue management point of view, the rational unit can be viewed as a "dialogue manager". Using its generic reasoning capabilities, it calculates the system's reaction to the user's requests and responses. To produce its reactions, it may also require the Knowledge Management component (see below).

The rational unit faithfully implements the kernel of the rational interaction theory. It is operated by an inference engine [34, 35] based on a "syntactic" approach of deductive reasoning in first order modal logic (namely, extended modal resolution with schema instantiation and sub-formula unification)[14]. The axiom schemata, of a very general scope, already pre-defined by the interaction theory, are part of an ARTIMIS agent's rational unit. However, the "programmer" can define specialised schemata for a given application. The set of schemata drives the rational unit reasoning process and, therefore, its reaction to its environment solicitations.

Environment solicitations such as requests from the user or from other software agents are conveyed to the rational unit as logical sentences of the rational interaction theory. The inference engine calculates the consequences of these sentences and, in particular, responses or requests for precision to send to the interlocutor (a human user or a software agent), as well as non-communicative actions.

Concretely, for a given formula, the inference engine looks up if there is any behaviour principle that applies to this formula in order to deduce logical consequences. This procedure is then applied to the new derived con-

---

[14]One can see [86, 130] for related aspects to this automated inference method.

sequences, until ending all the possibilities: such a procedure is a so-called *saturation-based inference algorithm*. Among all the consequences, the inference engine selects those referring to the actions (including communicative acts) to be performed by the agent, which form the agent's reactions.

EXAMPLE 9.1 *Assume that after utterance analysis/interpretation the recognised communicative act is that the user or another agent wants to inform AR-TIMIS that she/he/it wants to know if p (e.g., if there is any agent technology researcher at Lannion). On the basis of the rationality principles, the system infers the intention of the user to know if p. The cooperation principles allow the system to adopt the intention that the user eventually comes to know if p. Again, based on the rationality principles, the system adopts the intention of informing the user that p or informing her/him/it that not p. The system then selects the one of these two actions that is currently feasible (for example, if the system believes p, the action selected is that of informing the user that p) and transmits it (i.e., communicative act) to the natural language generator. Note that in the case of a negative answer, ARTIMIS will produce, as far as possible, a suggestive response, such as names of information technology researchers at Lannion.*

Knowledge management unit

This component supplies two main functionalities:

- Constraint restriction and relaxation calculus mechanisms.

- Standard interfaces (ODBC, Oracle, XML, etc.) to external information systems (for example, to get information in real time).

The reasoning process carried out by the rational unit partially relies on specific application data. For example, if an ARTIMIS Agent is intended to provide a train schedule, it needs to have data about the train stations, the connections between them and about temporal notions. Theses data are organised in a KL-One-like semantic network implemented as a set of facts.

The semantic network allows for expressing notions of class, sub-class, and instances. It also defines a notion of relation between classes, which applies to the different class instances. For example, for a Directory application the semantic network involves the following classes: *People* (whose instances are the set of people known in the directory) and *Job* (whose instances are the people jobs). These two classes are related by the relation *JobOf*. To indicate that John is a lawyer, the semantic network involves the fact *JobOf(John, Lawyer)*.

The rational unit can access the semantic network at any time of its inference procedure when the derived consequences depend on the nature of the data. In the Directory application, if the user asks for the job of John, the answer of ARTIMIS will depend on its query to the semantic network.

The semantic network also involves semantic proximity notions, which are particularly useful to produce the cooperative reactions of an ARTIMIS agent. For example, *Lawyer* will be considered as semantically closer (according to a certain metrics) to *Attorney* than to *Medical Doctor*. This construction enables to achieve two symmetric operations: constraint relaxation and constraint restriction.

Constraint relaxation consists in providing a close answer to what has been requested when the "exact" response does not exist. The rational unit has access to the database through a procedural attachment engine that seeks satisfactory "approximate" solutions when no "exact" solution to the user's request is found. This is implemented by "compiling" the semantic network into a product metric space where the dimensions are the application relations (such as the relation *JobOf* introduced in the example above). A distance function $d(a, b)$ is assigned to each dimension in order to quantify the approximation made when relaxing a into b. Constraint relaxation is viewed as the operation of finding the nearest neighbours in the metric space.

EXAMPLE 9.2 *If we ask the Directory application to provide the list of the product managers, and it does not exist any, the inference procedure can trigger a constraint relaxation process in order to suggest, for example, the list of project managers.*

Conversely, the restriction process consists in finding a way to reduce a too wide set of solutions, by introducing additional constraints when the request is too "weak". According to the current context, the constraint to be instantiated (by the user) could be, for example, the one corresponding to the dimension with the longest diameter.

EXAMPLE 9.3 *If there are fifty project managers in the Directory, restriction will provide the most discriminating dimension (for example, the department they work for), in order to pose a relevant question to better qualify the user's request.*

Language processing unit

At the input side, this component relies on semantic and linguistic models to contextually interpret the user's (spoken or written) natural language utterances, possibly combined with other communication media (such as direct manipulation), and builds up a logical representation directly usable by the rational unit. At the output side, it achieves the converse function, that of generation, in order to express in a "high level language" (*e.g.*, multimodal natural language) the system responses.

Language understanding

The goal of the understanding process is to reconstruct, as far as possible, in a logical form, the dialogue acts realised by the input utterances. The utterance analysis is based on detecting "small" syntactic structures (typically words) that are going to activate one or more notions mainly coming from the semantic network.

The relation between the user's input vocabulary and the semantic network is therefore done by means of a concept activation mechanism. The concepts correspond to the semantic notions conveyed by the word sequences of the vocabulary. These activated notions partially depend on the application, but they also represent more general concepts such as user's intentions and beliefs, negation, existential and universal quantification, cardinalities, etc.

Therefore, the interpretation module has at its disposal a set of activated concepts (which can be a list of possibilities in the case of non-determinism due to syntactic overlapping). It transforms them, through a semantic completion process, into a well-formed logical sentence that represents the semantic content of the dialogue act. This process relies on the assumption of semantic connectivity of user's utterance, that is to say that the concepts mentioned by the user have necessarily something to do with each others. It assumes that the utterance corresponds to a path in the semantic network. The semantic completion process aims at connecting to each others activated concepts through relations existing in the semantic network, even by adding, if necessary, concepts that were not explicitly mentioned. In some sense, this process determines the understood notions in the utterance.

The interpretation module has also to take into account the context of the user's utterance. To do that, it disposes of the concepts previously evoked both by the user and the ARTIMIS agent. Thus, a part of theses concepts can be used by the completion process.

It is worth noting that the analysis method (namely a *semantic-island driven analysis*) and the semantic completion ensure certain robustness to the analysis/interpretation process, particularly required in the context of spontaneous speech. In other respects, note also that the only part that depends on user's language is the link between the used vocabulary and the semantic network concepts. Indeed, the semantic data of the network represent language-independent notions. This makes particularly easy the application transfer from a (natural) language to another one.

EXAMPLE 9.4 *Consider utterance:* "I'd like to know the phone number of a project manager in agent technology located at Lannion", *recognised by the speech recognition system as* "I'd like X project manager agent technology X Lannion"), *which in turn, activates the concepts of user's intention, project manager, and Lannion. The inferred semantic complements are that the request deals with a telephone number of an individual, whose position is project manager, on a topic that is agent technology, and whose location is Lannion. Formally, this leads to the construction of the following dialogue act:*

$$\langle u, Inform(s, I_u Bref_u \iota x(phone - number(x) \wedge \exists y \ individual(y)$$
$$\wedge position(y, project - manager) \wedge topic(y, agent - technology)$$
$$\wedge location(y, lannion) \wedge phone - number(x, y)))\rangle$$

meaning that the user (u) informs the system (s) that she/he wants (I_u ...) to know (Bref_u ...) the telephone number of a project manager in agent technology at Lannion.

Language generation

The generation module achieves the converse task of the interpretation one. It must transcribe a sequence of communicative acts produced by the rational unit into an output (such as a natural language utterance) understandable by the user.

The generation process proceeds in two phases [165]. The first one determines the surface acts (specifying, in particular, the utterances modes: declarative, imperative, interrogative) and reference acts (specifying, in particular, the designation modes: nominal groups, pronouns, proper nouns, etc.), that achieve the dialogue act(s) to be sent to the user. In the second phase, the best formulation of the acts specified in the first phase is found, depending on the linguistic resources actually available (*e.g.*, language, lexicon, grammatical structures) and on the current linguistic context (dialogue history, vocabulary and syntax used by the user in the previous dialogue turn, preferences of the user, etc.).

As for the language understanding process, using intermediary representation levels for the information to verbalise makes easier the portability to a new application and language.

EXAMPLE 9.5 *If the system wants to inform the user that there is a relation of type "department" between "the agent technology project manager" and "information technology", it would send the following message to the generator:*

$$\langle s, Inform(u, department(\iota y(individual(y)$$
$$\wedge position(y, project - manager) \wedge topic(y, agent - technology)$$
$$\wedge location(y, lannion), information - technology))\rangle$$

According to the dialogue context, the generator will produce a declarative sentence with a proper noun and a nominal group, or a positive answer with a pronoun and a proper noun, or an elliptic sentence with a proper noun, etc.:

"The department of the project manager on agent technology located at Lan-

nion is information technology".
"Yes, she/he belongs to the information technology department".
"information technology department".
etc.

Media processing layer

This component allows for input and output formatting according to the targeted media. Thus, it is possible to connect an ARTIMIS-based application to any interface type, with almost no new code development. AR-TIMIS agents already have interfaces to handle VXML and SSML (for voice platforms), HTML (to be operated behind an HTTP server), ACL (to interoperate with other FIPA compliant agents), XML, and also the possibility of direct TCP/IP connection.

For example, in an end-user application over the telephone, in order to have a voice interaction with an ARTIMIS agent, it is required to connect it to speech recognition and synthesis systems.

Some implementation features

ARTIMIS is based on an explicit first-order modal reasoning process. Its communicative and cooperative behaviour is specified declaratively, in terms of logical properties, which are implemented as such. To change its behaviour only requires modifying this set of logical properties. No translation from logics to another language is needed.

ARTIMIS technology is available on Solaris, Windows, and Linux platforms. A classical machine configuration (PC, 1 GHz, 256 MO Ram) is sufficient to simultaneously run about 30 ARTIMIS agents in real time. Also, the ARTIMIS operational platform is compliant with Patrol-like supervising software.

9.4   ARTIMIS agents in multi-agent systems

As constituents of ARTIMIS technology, communicative acts and cooperation principles (see section 9.3) enable ARTIMIS agents to be naturally part of multi-agent systems.

To interact with other agents, ARTIMIS uses the FIPA ACL (Agent Communication Language) standard, and its associated content language, SL (Semantic Language). In fact, both of these languages come from ARCOL, the ARTIMIS communication language [196].

ARCOL is a performative-based language, with a non-ambiguous, fine-grained semantics. Basically, an ARCOL message is specified as a CA type applied to a semantic content. The semantic contents of CAs may be of three different types: propositions, individuals, and actions (including CAs).

ARCOL introduces a set of primitive CAs and provides the formal mechanisms (namely, rationality principles and combination operators with their semantics specified in terms of feasibility preconditions and rational effects) that enable to build macro-acts and complex interaction protocols.

Below are the definitions of simplified models of ARCOL primitive acts[15]:

$\langle i, INFORM(j, \phi) \rangle$
meaning: agent i informs agent j that proposition ϕ is true
$\quad FP : B_i \phi \wedge \neg B_i(Bif_j\phi \vee Uif_j\phi)$
$\quad RE : B_j\phi$

$\langle i, REQUEST(j, a) \rangle$
meaning: agent i requests agent j to perform action (*e.g.*, CA) a
$\quad FP : FP(a)[i \setminus j] \wedge B_i Agent(j, a) \wedge \neg B_i I_j Done(a)$
$\quad RE : Done(a)$

$FP(a)$ being the feasibility preconditions of a, and $FP(a)[i \setminus j]$ the part of the FPs of a that are mental attitudes of i.

$\langle i, CONFIRM(j, \phi) \rangle$
meaning: agent i confirms to agent j that proposition ϕ is true
$\quad FP : B_i \phi \wedge B_i U_j \phi$
$\quad RE : B_j \phi$

$\langle i, DISCONFIRM(j, \phi) \rangle$
meaning: agent i disconfirms to agent j that proposition ϕ is true
$\quad FP : B_i \neg\phi \wedge B_i(U_j\phi \vee B_j\phi)$
$\quad RE : B_j \neg\phi$

Some macro-acts result from the planning of a nondeterministic choice. They are selected by an agent when it intends to achieve the rational effect of one of the acts composing the choice, no matter which one it is. To do that, one of the feasibility preconditions of the acts must be satisfied, no matter which one it is. Macro-acts cannot be achieved as such but are required to abstract, for example, an *Inform* within the scope of a *Request*, to form a yn-question or a wh-question. In the case of *Inform* acts, such macro-acts are defined as follows:

$\langle i, INFORMIF(j, \phi) \rangle$
$\quad \equiv \langle i, INFORM(j, \phi) \rangle \mid \langle i, INFORM(j, \neg\phi) \rangle$

---

[15]The preconditions of act *Inform* are revisited according to the models of acts *Confirm* and *Disconfirm*, introduced below, in such a way that only one act be context-relevant at a given time (*i.e.*, in such a way that the preconditions of the three act models be mutually exclusive).

meaning: agent i informs agent j that proposition ϕ is true or that it is false
$$FP : Bif_i\phi \wedge \neg B_i(Bif_j\phi \vee Uif_j\phi)$$
$$RE : Bif_j\phi$$

$\langle i, INFORMREF(j, \iota x\delta(x))\rangle$
$\equiv \langle i, INFORMREF(j, \iota x\delta(x) = r_1)\rangle \mid \dots \mid$
$\langle i, INFORMREF(j, \iota x\delta(x) = r_k)\rangle$
meaning: agent i informs agent j of the value of the referent x denoted by $\delta(x)$
$$FP : Bref_i\delta(x)) \wedge \neg B_i(Bref_j\delta(x) \vee Uref_j\delta(x))$$
$$RE : Bref_j\delta(x)$$

where $\iota x\delta(x)$ is a definite description and r_k identifying referring expressions (*e.g.*, standard names or definite descriptions) [187].

On this basis, using the rationality principles, a set of *dialogue acts*, that are, in fact, inter-agent communicative plans (such as FIPA ACL *Query-ref* and *Query-if*), are specified. For example, the following model for a *direct strict yes-no-question plan* can be build up:

$\langle i, YN - QUESTION(j, \phi)\rangle$
$$FP : B_iBif_j\phi \wedge \neg Bif_i\phi \wedge \neg Uif_i\phi \wedge B_i\neg B_j(Bif_i\phi \vee Uif_i\phi)$$
$$RE : Bif_i\phi$$

Actually, such an act encapsulates (in terms of feasibility preconditions and rational effect) the following two-act plan:

$\langle i, REQUEST(j, \langle j, INFORMIF(i, \phi)\rangle)\rangle; \langle j, INFORMIF(i, \phi)\rangle$

Along these lines, FIPA ACL perfomatives and complex interaction protocols have been defined, using ARCOL's formalism and semantics.

Let us call SL the first-order modal language in which the rational interaction theory underlying ARTIMIS is couched, and SCL the semantic content language of communicative acts. If it is taken to be SL itself, SCL happens to be a very expressive language but may turn out to be complex to use as such if an ARTIMIS-like agent technology is not available to process it. For "simpler" agents and for implementation reasons, the content language may be taken to be a less-expressive formalism, *e.g.*, a subset of SL.

Suppose that one want to simplify SCL, for example by restricting it to a first-order predicate logic language. Let us call this simplified version SCL1. In this case, ARCOL is accordingly restricted to a language ARCOL1. Yet, we would like to enable the agents to communicate their mental attitudes (beliefs, intentions, etc.). One solution is to augment the set of ARCOL1's communicative acts with complex acts (typically, macro-acts) that intrinsically integrate in their semantics relevant mental attitudes. For example, the act of agent *i informing* agent *j* that it (*i.e.*, *i*) has a given intention, has the following semantics in ARCOL:

$$\langle i, INFORM(j, I_i p)\rangle:$$
$$FP : I_i p \wedge \neg B_i(Bif_j I_i p \vee Uif_j I_i p)$$
$$ER : B_j I_i p$$

This act can be defined in ARCOL1 as follows[16]:

$$\langle i, INFORM\text{-}I(j, p')\rangle:$$
$$FP : I_i p' \wedge \neg B_i(Bif_j I_i p' \vee Uif_j I_i p')$$
$$ER : B_j I_i p'$$

Of course, this ARCOL1's new act $\langle i, INFORM\text{-}I(j, p')\rangle$ is only an abbreviated form of $\langle i, INFORM(j, I_i p)\rangle$ from ARCOL since propositions p and p' are expressed in SCL and SCL1, respectively.

The major downside of this solution is that it requires the definition of an additional communicative act each time the semantic content cannot be expressed in the first-order modal language.

In any case, since agents are intended to express communicative acts that refer to mental attitudes, the corresponding technology must enable the manipulation of such notions. Subsequently, if agents have these notions explicitly represented in their own kernels, there is no *a priori* reason not to include them into the agent communication language.

For more details about ARCOL (and about cooperation protocols adopted by FIPA with an informative status), see [196]. One can also see [193] for comprehensive details about ARCOL basis and semantics.

9.5 Cases of ARTIMIS-based applications

9.5.1 ARTIMIS as a natural human-computer dialogue agent

ARTIMIS has been demonstrated on several service prototypes displaying a natural dialogue with a human user, and on different interaction media (including multimodal devices) and languages. It has also been experimented in the context of different field trials in various application domains: directories, tourist guides, banking and stock exchange, travel, Internet portals, etc.

More recently, ARTIMIS has been commercially deployed by France Telecom in a FAQ-like application, namely the help of Wanadoo instant messag-

---

[16]Note that, while the ARCOL's act $\langle i, INFORM(j, I_i p)\rangle$ is (by construction) an *assertive* (of an intention that intrinsically includes a commitment), the ARCOL1's act $\langle i, INFORM\text{-}I(j, I_i p)\rangle$ can be viewed as a *commissive*.

ing service, *Le Messager*. This application, called *Assistant Messager*, consists in a conversational buddy that assists the user in using the instant messaging.

In such applications, ARTIMIS is able to manage an intelligent cooperative dialogue in natural language. As examples, here are sample dialogues from some of the applications just mentioned (S standing for the system and U for the user).

ARTIMIS Plan Resto : Paris restaurant guide

ARTIMIS *Plan Resto* has been experimented by end-users on different communication media: speech over the telephone, typed natural language on Internet, multimodal interaction combining speech and direct manipulation on a PDA. The following example presents a sample spoken dialogue collected over the telephone:

S: Welcome to PlanResto, Paris restaurant guide with direct connection. The general user guide can be activated at any time by saying general user guide. If you are not a regular user please say I am not a regular user. May I help you?
U: I'm not a regular user.
S: PlanResto is a Paris restaurant guide. As with a human operator, converse with it in a natural way. Do not hesitate to correct it in case of misunderstanding. Feel free to interrupt it. Speak loud enough and distinctly, with no pausing and no excessive articulating. Avoid noisy surrounding. Can I help you formulating your request?
U: I'd like a vegetarian restaurant close to the Picasso Museum.
S: There isn't any vegetarian restaurant close to the Musée Picasso. However, there are vegetarian restaurants close to the Musée Cognacq-Jay, close to Filles du Calvaire and close to Hôtel Carnavelet. Which suggestion are you interested in?
U: I'd like the last solution.
S: I found two vegetarian restaurants close to the Hôtel Carnavalet. The first reference is the restaurant Le Loir dans la Théière. Do you want to have more information, hear about the next restaurant or make a new request?
U: What's its address?
S: The restaurant Le Loir dans la Théière is located 3 rue des Rosiers. Do you want more information, to be connected to this restaurant or make a new request?
U: Finally, I would prefer a Canadian restaurant.
S: There isn't any Canadian restaurant close to Hôtel Carnavalet. However, there are Canadian restaurants close to the Cloître des Billettes. Does this suggestion suit you?
U: Yes please.
S: You want a Canadian restaurant close to the Cloître des Billettes. I've found one called Equinox. Do you want more information, to be connected with this

restaurant or make another request?
U: Could you give me the phone number of this restaurant?
S: The phone number of Equinox restaurant is 01 42 71 92 41.
U: It's OK. Goodbye.
S: Do you really want to leave Plan Resto?
U: Yes.
S: Thanks for calling Plan Resto. Goodbye for now!

ARTIMIS help buddy for the Wanadoo instant messaging: L'Assistant Messager

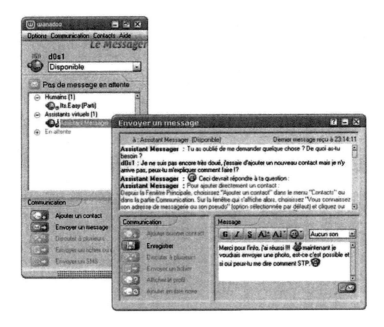

Figure 9.3. Chat with a virtual contact: Wanadoo "Assistant Messager"

Example translated from French.

S: Welcome Droopy! I hope you're well. I'm L'Assistant-Messager. I'm here to explain to you how to use Le-Messager-Wanadoo. You can converse with me. I'll try to help you. What can I do for you?
U: Hi, it's the first time I am using Le-Messager. Could you tell me what is it and what availability means?
S: Ok, so you want information about "instant messaging" and "availability". I

need more precisions. I can suggest some help:
1) to discover Le-Messager-Wanadoo
2) to know what an availability state is
Which suggestion are you interested in?
U: Give me 1.
S: Here is the answer I found:
Le-Messager Wanadoo is an Internet real time communication tool. The connection state of each subscriber is memorised in a central server. Thus, at any time, it is possible to know if your contacts are connected and available to communicate. To use it, you need an email address and a password. The pseudo can only be created on the Wanadoo portal.
I can give you additional information, if this answer is not sufficient for you. Do you want it?
U: No thank you, it's ok for now.

[Later...]

S: So, you're back! Do you realise that it's more than 1 day that we haven't talked. Do you have any new question on Le-Messager-Wanadoo? I'm always available to help you. What can I do for you?
U: Could you tell me how to delete a contact?
S: I've got the answer to your question: To take off a person from your contacts, select your addressee list, then you have two ways to delete the contact:
· Using the contextual menu: right-click and choose "Delete".
· Using the menu "Contacts": choose entry "Contacts" then select entry "Delete a contact or a file".
What can I do for you now?
U: What's your name?
S: My name is HelpWare, L'Assistant-Messager. I'm just here to give you any information you need about Le-Messager-Wanadoo. What do you want to know?
U: Do you know any joke?
S: I've 3 heads, 3 legs, 1 arm and 6 fingers, who am I?
A liar!
U: Very funny, how old are you? :-)
S: Right now I am precisely 10 months, 25 days, 8 hours, 29 minutes and 40 seconds!
U: Are you a genius or a machine!?
S: A human or a machine, no matter what I am :-) I'm here to help you use Le-Messager-Wanadoo. How can I help you?
U: It's ok, thanks! See you.
S: If you don't need me anymore, you can just close my dialogue window!

9.5.2 ARTIMIS as mediation agent

In this class of applications, ARTIMIS is virtually located between a human user and domain-specific agents. By interacting with such agents, it acquires from them pieces of information that it aggregates and organises before delivering them as a global solution to the user in a high level language and a user-friendly and cooperative format.

For instance, ARTIMIS has played this role as a Travel Assistant, in particular in the context of the *Agentcities* IST European project [1, 148]. In this application, it delivers to the user information on travelling between the main European cities. It gets such information by interacting with train and flight schedule information agents (*i.e.*, FIPA-agentified web sites). In this context, ARTIMIS displays an added-value as a mediation agent on several aspects:

- Offering a global trip by aggregating the different responses from the information agents.

- Suggesting the most interesting journey according to different criteria (duration, earliest arrival, latest departure, etc.).

- Suggesting alternative travels when the one targeted by the user does not exist.

- Interacting with the user in natural dialogue.

- etc.

In the Travel Assistant application, ARTIMIS uses a *FIPA-Query* standard protocol to interact with the domain-specific agents. In this protocol, the first communicative act sent by ARTIMIS to the information agents is a *Query-ref* or a *Query-if*. Each addressee responds either by sending a *Refuse*, or by sending an *Inform* conveying the information found out[17]. The mediation agent then organises the obtained information according to the user's request.

It is worth noting that although ARTIMIS can use a FIPA standard protocol to interact with simpler agents, it is also able to process "free-style" requests coming from the user or from another agent, which do not fit a specific protocol. For instance, to identify flights according to some criteria, the interlocutor could ask ARTIMIS for the sought information using a *Query-ref* act ("What are the flights that are so and so?"), or an *Inform* act of the intention to know such flights ("I want to know the flights that are

---

[17]The *Inform* may be optionally preceded by an *Agree*.

so and so."). In the second case, the semantic content of the act expresses an intention of the interlocutor. ARTIMIS handles such a content and, on the basis of its cooperation principles comes to the same behaviour as for a regular *Query-ref.*

Below is a sample dialogue with ARTIMIS as a Travel Assistant:

S: Welcome on ARTIMIS-Voyage. How can I help you?
U: I'd like to go to Nice on tomorrow.
S: A trip to Nice on Friday, April 1st, 2005. What's your departure city?
U: I'd like to leave from Brest in the afternoon and arrive before 6pm.
S: A trip from Brest to Nice on Friday, April 1st, 2005, leaving after 12am and arriving before 6pm. How do you want to travel, by train or by plane?
U: I don't care.
S: A trip by train or by plane from Brest to Nice on Friday, April 1st, 2005 leaving after 12am and arriving before 6pm. Do you want to wait for the response, to receive it by email, or to be called back?
U: I am waiting.
S: Thank you for waiting. I am going to consult the travel sites.

[...]

There is a flight leaving from Brest on Friday, April 1st, 2005 at 2:15pm and arriving at Nice at 5:35pm. Would you like the details of this journey, the alternative solutions, or any other information?
U: Give me the details.
S: There are two steps. First step: departure from Brest by plane on Friday, April 1st, 2005 at 2:15pm; arrival at Paris Orly-West at 3:30pm. Second step: departure from Paris Orly-West by plane at 4:10pm; arrival at Nice at 5:35pm. Would you like the alternative solutions?
U: Yes, the alternatives please.
S: The quickest trip by plane is: departure from Brest on Friday, April 1st, 2005 at 5:40pm, arrival at Nice at 8:50pm. Would you like to know the steps of this journey?
U: And by train?
S: I don't know any trip by train from Brest to Nice on Friday, April 1st, 2005 leaving after 12pm and arriving before 6pm. However, there is a train departing from Brest on Friday the 1st of April 2005 at 8:49am, and arriving at Nice at 10:51pm. Would you like to know the steps of this journey or an alternative solution?
U: I'd like to have the details.
S: There are 3 steps. First step: Departure from Brest by train on Friday, April 1st, 2005 at 8:49am; arrival at Paris Montparnasse at 1:30pm. Second step: departure from Paris Gare de Lyon by train at 2:21pm; arrival at Toulon at 7:34pm. Third step: departure from Toulon at 9:11pm; arrival at Nice on at 10:51pm.

Would you like any other information?
U: No, thank you.
S: Do you really want to leave ARTIMIS-Voyage?
U: Yes please.
S: Thanks for calling ARTIMIS-Voyage. Goodbye for now!

9.6   Conclusion

The agent paradigm aims at introducing the required intelligence both into automatic handling of knowledge and into human-machine interaction. One of the objectives is to produce a changeover from software providing functions to software offering interoperating services [197]. In other respects, multi-agent technology constitutes a relevant framework to instantiate the concept of *semantic web services*.

ARTIMIS technology bridges the gap, in a "clean" way, between basic research and real (end-user) applications. It also opens new scientific and technological perspectives for the study and development of effective "intelligent" interactive agents. So far, it appears as the unique operational implementation of a generic cognitive agent technology that allows both for natural dialogue with a human user (whatever the communication media is) and advanced interactions with other software agents.

ARTIMIS offers several advantages. Its specifications, *i.e.*, the theory of rational interaction, are *semantically well-defined*. Interestingly, it can be guaranteed that ARTIMIS *follows its specifications* soundly (*e.g.*, keeps its commitments). ARTIMIS can be *easily maintained, adapted, and customised*.

ARTIMIS technology is customer-oriented. It has been developed to support advanced services, mainly those requiring cooperative dialogue with human users. There are tremendous obvious commercial interests in ARTIMIS-like technology, in particular for specifically designed "high-quality" user-friendly interactive services [194], and for intelligent application development tools.

More generally, associated with a permanent multimedia connectivity, "semantics technology" will, in the coming years, contribute to offer a seamless and coherent inter-service and inter-media continuum. As soon as the market begins to witness *generic* agent technologies along with standards for widely shared communication languages, ontologies and knowledge representation, this will mark the real technological leap forward introducing a deep change, notably in telecommunication use and market. The present scientific, technical and industrial landscape holds every indication that these fundamental changes will take place progressively over the very next years.

SUMMARIES FOR QUICK REFERENCE AND COMPARISON

The appendices of this book provide summaries of the main features of the programming languages presented in the book. Appendix A shows a list of questions that the editors posed to the contributing authors about their language and its platform. The following seven appendices provide the answers given by the authors of the respective chapters.

Appendix A: Comparison Criteria

1. **Agent-Oriented Programming Language**

   (a) **Functionality**

   Does the language support various agent concepts such as, mental attitudes, deliberation, adaptation, social abilities, and reactive as well as cognitive-based behaviour?

   (b) **Communication**

   Does the language provide high-level (i.e., speech-act based) primitives for communication (as well as general addressing mechanism such as broadcast and multi-cast)?

   (c) **Underlying Computational Model**

   Does the language support the design of mobile agents, and if so, which kind of mobility (weak and/or strong)?

   (d) **Simplicity**

   How easy it is to use and understand the language?

   (e) **Preciseness**

   Does the language have clear and precise semantics? How has it been formalised?

   (f) **Expressiveness**

   Is the language suitable for the implementation of a variety of agent-oriented programs and applications or is it purpose-specific?

   (g) **Extensiveness**

   Does the language allow the definition of new language components from the basic constructs in a systematic way?

   (h) **Verification**

   Does your approach provide a clear path for the (formal) verification of programs written in this language?

   (i) **Software Engineering Principles**

   Have Software Engineering and Programming Language principles, such as abstraction, inheritance, modularity, overloading, information hiding, error handling, generic programming, etc., been considered or adopted within design of this language?

   (j) **Language Integration**

   i. Does your approach deal with the possibility of integrating the language with existing (well-known) programming language (e.g., Java)?

    ii. Can the language be interfaced with other programming languages, or does it allow the invocation of methods/programs built using other (classical) programming languages?

2. Platform

(a) Deployment and Portability

    i. Does the platform provide material, such as documentation, tutorials or training of any kind, installation and deployment guidelines, to help users in deploying their systems?

    ii. Does the platform require a specific computing environment (computer architecture, operating system, libraries, etc.) to be used / deployed?

(b) Standards Compliance

To what extent does the platform adhere to the standards (FIPA, MASIF, etc.) with respects to: general architecture, naming service, white- and yellow-page services, mobility services, agent-life cycle management, etc.?

(c) Platform Extensibility

Can the platform be extended with additional functionality, for example through Open Source collaboration?

(d) Available Tools

    i. What tools are provided by the platform for the management, monitoring, logging and debugging of applications?

    ii. What documentation for on-line help, and manuals for the platform's installation, use, and maintenance are available?

    iii. Are there tools for administration, management, and configuration of the platform? Is an IDE provided?

(e) Tool Integration

In existing applications, what tools (e.g., JESS, web services, JSP) have been integrated or are known to work well with applications running on this platform ?

(f) Technical Interoperability

Is an application aimed at running on this platform tied to a specific programming language, specific architectures (e.g., .NET, J2EE), or are there special operating system requirements?

(g) Performance Issues

    i. What number of agents can be expected to run efficiently within a single instance of the platform, what scale of number of messages can be handled by the platform, etc.?

ii. What is the current state of the platform (simple prototype, available as a commercial product, stable Open Source distribution, etc.)?

(h) **Multi-Agent Systems Features**

   i. Does the platform support open multi-agent systems and heterogeneous agents?

   ii. Does the platform provide centralised or distributed control, and hierarchical structure of agents?

   iii. Does the platform offer libraries for programming multi-agent systems (libraries of interaction protocols, agent or group templates, reusable agent or organisation components, etc.)?

3. **Applications Supported by the Language and Platform**

(a) **Typical Examples**

What types of application have already been developed with this platform (toy problems, real-world applications, industrial applications)? What are the most prominent examples?

(b) **Targeted Domains**

Is any particular domain of application (e.g., simulation, resource allocation, mobile computation) targeted by your approach?

Appendix B: *Jason* Summary

1(a) *Jason* is based on a BDI logic-programming language and therefore fully supports all these concepts; it does not as yet support agent organisations, but there is ongoing work to support that in the future.

1(b) Speech-act based communication is available in *Jason*, based on KQML performatives and some extra ones that are used for exchanging plans (rather than beliefs).

1(c) SACI supports strong mobility, but we have not as yet provided mobility within *Jason*; however, given that this is already available through SACI, it is straightforward to provide a standard internal action allowing AgentSpeak programmers to use mobility (this should be available in *Jason*'s next release).

1(d) The core of *Jason* is an AgentSpeak interpreter, which is, in our opinion, the most simple and elegant, yet quite expressive, agent-oriented programming language that appears in the literature.

1(e) There is formal semantics for AgentSpeak with the main extensions available in *Jason*; the semantics was given using Plotkin's structural approach to operational semantics.

1(f) *Jason* should be suitable for any application for which BDI agents are suitable (varied applications of such agents have appeared in the literature).

1(g) The "internal action" construct allows for some form of extensibility, and there are various customisation mechanisms available in *Jason*.

1(h) Model checking techniques that apply directly on (a restricted version of) AgentSpeak are being developed by Bordini, Fisher, Wisser, and Wooldridge. To our knowledge, this is the only agent programming language for which work on model checking techniques has been published.

1(i) Very little has been considered in this area as yet; however, methodologies suitable for BDI-like agents, such as Prometheus (by Padgham and Winikoff), should be suitable for implementation with *Jason*.

1(j).i The same "internal action" construct mentioned above allows for a high-level approach to integration with Java (the agent code itself remains a clear logical description of the agent's reasoning, as Java or legacy code is simply referenced in the high-level internal actions).

1(j).ii This can be achieved by the use of JNI (Java Native Interface) and the internal action mechanism mentioned above.

2(a).i *Jason* has sufficient documentation, and further tutorials are under preparation; when agents are not situated in some real-world environment, deployment in a networked system is trivial with *Jason* (through the use of SACI).

2(a).ii No, it runs on any platform for which Java is available.

2(b) *Jason* provides these services through SACI, which is KQML compliant; however, the distribution infrastructure can be customised, so a different infrastructure (e.g., one that is FIPA compliant) can be used if necessary.

2(c) *Jason* is available *Open Source* and in most extensions attempted so far it has proven very easy to extend (because of the customisation mechanisms, this often means that not change in the interpreter itself is required); there are a number of extensions planned for the near future.

2(d).i *Jason* has a debugging mode in which the system can be run step by step and a "mind inspector" which allows the user to check the mental attitudes of agents running across a network.

2(d).ii There is documentation which is partly a tutorial on AgentSpeak and partly a manual for using the platform; improvements on this documentation and further tutorials are expected.

2(d).iii *Jason* comes with an IDE which is very simple to use.

2(e) Applications developed with *Jason* have not made use of integrated tools, but in principle any tool that integrates satisfactorily with Java should integrate with *Jason* as well.

2(f) Applications require a Java Virtual Machine to run, but there are no operating system requirements.

2(g).i *Jason* has changed significantly in the last year, and we have not yet updated such statistics, but we plan to include such figures in the manual in future releases.

2(g).ii We have recently released version 0.6 (open source, as usual); although there are stable versions, various significant changes have been made from each version to the next (*Jason* is very much work on progress).

2(h).i Again through the use of SACI, open multi-agent systems are easily supported; although heterogeneity is in principle possible, various features (e.g., plan exchange) still consider that the all agents are developed in AgentSpeak.

2(h).ii Both centralised and distributed execution is available; social structures are still not currently supported, but this is ongoing work.

2(h).iii This is not as yet available, but certainly planned for the future.

3(a) So far, apart from academic coursework, *Jason* has only been used for social simulation and autonomous characters for computer animation.

3(b) BDI agents are suitable for a variety of domains; we are particularly interested in Semantic Web and Grid-based applications; specifically, we plan to develop Grid-based social simulations in the near future.

Appendix C: 3APL Summary

1(a) The language supports the implementation of mental attitudes (beliefs, goals, plans, and reasoning rules), the implementation of a deliberation cycle, and reactive as well as deliberative behavior.

1(b) The language provides a speech-act based programming construct (the Send operator) for communication.

1(c) The language does not support the design of mobile agents.

1(d) The general ideas of the language can be understood relatively easily, especially for someone familiar with the idea of cognitive agents, as a limited number of language constructs is available. The details of the formal semantics will take some more time to comprehend.

1(e) The language has a clear and formal semantics, for the most part defined by means of a transition system.

1(f) The applications that can be developed using the 3APL platform and the 3APL programming language are those that are best understood in terms of cognitive and social concepts like beliefs, goals, plans, actions, norms, organizational structures, resources and services that are part of the multi-agent environment.

1(g) The mental and external actions enable two forms of extensibility. Also, the possibility to program the deliberation process in Java allows the programmer to define new language components.

1(h) The formal semantics of the language provides the basis for the formal verification of 3APL programs, both for theorem proving and model-checking approaches.

1(i) Limited forms of abstraction, modularity and reusability are supported. Also, since the deliberation cycle and the shared environment are programmable as separate modules, the principle of separation of concern is respected.

1(j) The 3APL platform and interpreter are programmed in Java. By means of external actions, Java can be called from the 3APL program. Further, a Java implementation of Prolog is used to implement the belief base of agents.

2(a).i There is a user guide that explains the use of the 3APL platform and the 3APL programming language through examples that are also available with the distribution. This user guide is under constant development.

2(a).ii The 3APL platform can be run on Windows, Linux and Unix (Solaris) machines on which Java 2 SDK 1.4 is installed.

2(b) The 3APL platform supports limited naming and yellow page services.

2(c) The 3APL platform is not open source yet, but the source is available on request.

2(d).i The platform provides a simple editor to write and modify individual agent programs. It also provide different execution modes such as single and multi-agent systems, either in a step-by-step or continuous fashion. Finally, it provides debugging tools such as different windows to observe the internal state of individual agents and a sniffer tool that visualizes the communication between agents.

2(d).ii The only available documentation is the user guide. An online tutorial will be available soon.

2(d).iii The 3APL platform provides a simple form of an IDE.

2(e) Since the 3APL platform is written in Java, any tools that can be integrated with Java can be integrated with the 3APL platform as well.

2(f) The applications run on the 3APL platform should be programmed in terms of individual agents that are programmed in the 3APL language.

2(g).i Applications with a maximum of 5 agents can be run efficiently within a single instance of the platform.

2(g).ii The 3APL platform is an advanced prototype platform.

2(h).i The current platform does not support open and heterogeneous multi-agent systems.

2(h).ii The platform provides only distributed control of agents.

2(h).iii The 3APL platform does not offer libraries yet.

3(a) Typical implemented examples are auctions, applications using Contract-Net protocols, cooperative systems, Axelrod's tournament and simple logistic applications.

3(b) Resource allocation, social simulation and all kinds of applications that can be described by BDI agents are target applications.

Appendix D: IMPACT Summary

1(a) Yes, our language supports reasoning with beliefs, time, probabilities and various other concepts (not all of them are yet implemented). Deliberation is realised through computing (feasible) status sets and is related to computing stable models.

1(b) Yes, speech-act primitives are available, although only very basic message passing capabilities are realised in the base language.

1(c) Yes, *IMPACT* supports weak mobility.

1(d) We have run several classroom labs with students. They did not have to go through the technical semantics, but were given several examples and learned by analogy. They were able to implement a non-trivial application involving 6 agents (each of them developed independently) and successfully putting them together (*Gofish post office*, [62]).

1(e) Yes, the semantics is clearly defined and uses technical machinery developed in the last three decades in logic programming.

1(f) The language is suitable for arbitrary agent applications. It is not specific for a restricted class of applications.

1(g) Yes, the language allows not only the definition of macros of basic constructs, but also the introduction of completely new features. This is due to annotations of programs, an area which has been well investigated in the last two decades.

1(h) Yes, as our semantics is based on rigourous formal methods and first attempts to verify *IMPACT* agents are on their way.

1(j).i The *Code Call Condition* mechanism provides a way to integrate any software program written in any programming languages.

1(j).ii This can be achieved by the *IMPACT* implementation and the *Code Call Condition* mechanism.

2(a).i The *IMPACT* project homepage (http://www.cs.umd.edu/projects/impact/) provides extensive documentations to help users develop and deploy systems.

2(a).ii No, it runs on any platform where Java is available.

2(b) While *IMPACT* is not FIPA compliant, it should not be too difficult to achieve this. We concentrated on extending our framework and not on compliance to certain standards.

2(c) *IMPACT* can be easily extended by new functionalities. Although it is not open source yet, any collaboration is welcome.

2(d).i It is provided by *IMPACT AgentDE*, *IMPACT* Server, Agent Roost, and Agent Log.

2(d).ii The software user documentation is available at `http://www.cs.umd.edu/projects/impact/Docs`.

2(d).iii *IMPACT* provides a network accessible, easy-to-use IDE.

2(e) We have shown that the *IMPACT* project has built a lot of applications integrating many tools.

2(f) Applications require loading Java runtime library on the target platform, but no specific operating system is required.

2(g).i We have not undertaken such statistics yet. In our experiments there were around 10-15 agents with quite a number of messages sent among them.

2(g).ii The current version is stable and available for academic purposes only. It is licensed by the University of Maryland.

2(h).i Yes, *IMPACT* supports open multi-agent systems and heterogeneous agents.

2(h).ii *IMPACT* provides both centralised and distributed control. The hierarchical structuring of agents has not yet been supported within *IMPACT*.

2(h).iii Yes, they are provided in *IMPACT AgentDE* during the development and deployment of agents.

3(a) Besides smaller classroom examples (6 agents developed by 4-7 students) several real applications such as Aerospace applications, US Army Logistics Integration Agency's "Virtual Operations Centre", and US Army STRICOM's JANUS project where *IMPACT* technology is used to analyse massive amounts of simulation data.

3(b) There is no specific targeted domain for *IMPACT*. It is a general system dealing with heterogenous, distributed information sources and available legacy code.

Appendix E: CLAIM Summary

1(a) The CLAIM language is suitable to design stationary or mobile intelligent agents, having a powerful mental state containing knowledge, goals and capabilities, allowing an autonomous, reactive or goal-oriented behavior.

1(b) CLAIM supports unicast, multicast or broadcast communication between agents. It offers a set of predefined messages inspired from the speech-acts theory but also leaves the possibility to the designer to define his own messages.

1(c) The CLAIM language offers support for the agents' migration as a main feature. The CLAIM agents are both intelligent and mobile. There is a strong mobility at the agents' processes level and a week mobility for the invoked Java methods (see section 1.3.1).

1(d) The facility in developing several simple or complex applications proved that CLAIM is easy to use.

1(e) CLAIM has a formal operational semantics consisting in a set of reduction rules between states of programs.

1(f) The variety of implemented applications proved the expressiveness of CLAIM.

1(g) The language offers to the developer the possibility to define his own ontology for agents' knowledge and his own messages and goals for agents.

1(h) The language's operational semantics is a first important step towards the programs' verifications. Our current work tackles this aspect.

1(i) The notion of generic class is central in CLAIM.

1(j).i The agents in CLAIM can invoke Java methods or Web Services for computational purposes. We intend to give the agents the possibility to invoke methods implemented in other programming languages.

1(j).ii See 1(j).i

2(a).i The platform contains installation and deployment guidelines. The documentation is represented by several published articles, concerning the language as well as the platform. A tutorial and a documentation of the API will be soon available.

2(a).ii The platform is implemented in Java, is portable and can be installed on every computer supporting *Java Virtual Machine*. So the platform is platform-independent. We have already tested it on Windows, Unix-based and Macintosh systems.

2(b) SyMPA is compliant with the specifications of the MASIF standard from the OMG.

2(c) The platform is extensible.

2(d).i The platform offers management and monitoring functions at the central system and at the agent system level. For every running agent there is a graphical interface for visualizing the agent's behavior, communication and migration. Momentary, there are no debugging tools.

2(d).ii See 2(a).i

2(d).iii Each agent system offers an editor for defining agents and classes of agents, a compiler for verifying the definitions' syntax and an execution engine for deploying agents.

2(e) The CLAIM agents can invoke Web Services. There is also an extension of SyMPA allowing to heterogeneous agents to interact using the Web Services features.

2(f) There are no specific operating system requirements. Being implemented in Java, the platform only requires the *JRE*.

2(g).i Until now, we performed tests with up to 30 communicating and mobile agents on a computer (including their graphical interfaces) and we deployed the platform on 10 connected computers. We intend to test the platform on a larger-scale environment.

2(g).ii The platform is a prototype that served for developing several complex applications by different people.

2(h).i The platform supports open multi-agent systems. Agents are dynamically created and removed. Without any add-on, the platform supports only CLAIM agents. Nevertheless, we developed an interoperability environment that allows to heterogenous agents to interact using a Web Services based approach.

2(h).ii The agents in CLAIM are hierarchically represented. An agent has a parent and can have several sub-agents. In this version there is a centralized management but different management solutions will be available in the future.

2(h).iii Classes of agents can be defined in CLAIM that can be parameterized and reused later.

3(a) Our agent-oriented environment has already been used to develop several applications. One can easily design applications focused on the reasoning abilities of an agent, but the main purpose of CLAIM is to develop distributed applications that takes advantage of the agents' mobility and adaptability allowed by the language's features. The most prominent applications were those of electronic commerce and distributed libraries.

3(b) CLAIM can be used to develop a wide area of agent-based applications (see section 4.4).

Appendix F: JADE Summary

1(a) JADE provides a very general but primitive agent model offering both reactive and social abilities. This model can serve as a useful basis to implement more sophisticated agent architectures.

1(b) JADE provides high level communication through FIPA ACL messages. Moreover, it uses different low level communication mechanisms to improve performance.

1(c) JADE supports mobile agents through a sort of enhanced weak mobility that allows an agent to move from a node to another node only when its execution reaches a stable state.

1(d) This criteria is not appropriate, because JADE does not offer an own language, but software libraries that allow the development of multi-agent systems through the use of Java.

1(e) This criteria is not appropriate for the same reason expressed in 1(d).

1(f) JADE has been developed and used to realize systems for different application domains.

1(g) This criteria is not appropriate for the same reason expressed in 1(d).

1(h) The current implementation of JADE does not offer any support for the formal verification of programs developed by using the JADE software libraries.

1(i) JADE offers the same software engineering and programming language principles offered by the programming language used to implement it (i.e., Java).

1(j).i JADE and the multi-agent systems developed with it are written by using Java.

1(j).ii The agents of a JADE multi-agent system can interact with software written in other programming languages by using either special agent wrappers (in the case of non-agentized software) or messages exchange (in the case of other FIPA compliant agents).

2(a).i JADE provides a rich set of documents (manuals and tutorials) and code examples to help the user to install and use it. They are all available from the official JADE Web site (http://jade.tilab.com).

2(a).ii JADE is written in Java. Therefore JADE multi-agent systems may run on the operating systems for which a Java virtual machine is available. In particular, the JADE run-time can be compiled for different

Java profiles allowing the execution of JADE multi-agent systems on a wide class of devices ranging from servers to cell phones.

2(b) JADE is FIPA compliant.

2(c) The whole JADE source code is distributed under the LGPL open source licence. Therefore both the extension of the platform and its use in commercial products are allowed.

2(d).i JADE users can manage an agent platform through the Remote Management Agent and debug their agents through the Dummy Agent, the Sniffer Agent, the Introspector Agent and the Log Manager Agent. All these agents interact with their users through a graphical user interface.

2(d).ii JADE provides a rich documentation to help the user to install and use it.

2(d).iii JADE users can manage an agent platform through the Remote Management Agent interacting with it through a graphical user interface.

2(e) JADE permits an easy integration of external software and it was done with success allowing, for example, the integration of JADE with: rules engines (JESS and DROOLS), Web technologies (servlets, JSP and applets) and ontology management tools (Protege and Jena).

2(f) JADE multi-agent systems must be written using Java, the only constraint for the operating system is the availability of a Java virtual machine.

2(g).i Given its architecture and the different communication mechanisms used, JADE multi-agent systems may contain thousands of agents exchanging a huge amount of messages.

2(g).ii The different releases of the JADE software (including the last one: 3.2) are stable and used in different research and application projects in different part of the world. JADE is distributed under the LGPL open source licence.

2(h).i JADE allows the realization of open systems through the dynamic federation of agent platforms. Agents of such federations may be heterogeneous with the only constraint of being FIPA compliant.

2(h).ii Following the FIPA standard, JADE multi-agent systems use a centralized control: each agent platform is controlled by the AMS. However, JADE offers a fault tolerance mechanism that allows an agent platform to survive the failure of its AMS.

2(h).iii Given that JADE agent system are realized by using Java, all its components are reusable. Moreover, the JADE framework and its comunity of users made available different software libraries and "add-ons" that may be useful to realize agent systems in different application sectors.

3(a) JADE has been used to realize both real and industrial applications.

3(b) JADE applications cover different domains: collaborative work support, e-learning, e-tourism, network management, entertainment, knowledge management, manufacturing and supply-chain management and simulation.

Appendix G: Jadex Summary

1(a) Reactive and deliberative behaviour is supported based on the BDI model and the corresponding mental attitudes. In addition to the basic BDI interpreter known from PRS systems, an explicit representation of goals is provided.

1(b) FIPA-compliant speech-act based communication is provided by the underlying JADE platform.

1(c) Weak mobility is provided by the underlying JADE platform. When developing mobile agents, some features of the system (e.g. thread-based plans) are not available.

1(d) The language is easy to learn, as it is based on well-known technologies such as Java and XML. Experiments with students have shown that new users are quickly able to develop their first agents.

1(e) No formal semantics is available.

1(f) The language is very general and allows creating different kinds of agent applications.

1(g) The system does not define a new language for programming agent behaviour, but instead makes BDI-specific agent facilities available as application program interface (API). Hence, the BDI feature set can be easily extended.

1(h) No path to formal verification is provided.

1(i) The XML language enforces strong typing. The plan language inherits the software engineering and programming language principles of Java. In addition, reusability is supported by the definition of agent-modules called capabilities.

1(j).i Embedding the agent language into a general-purpose language is not necessary, because the system cleanly separates the definition of an agent's structure and the definition of agent behaviour. The structure of an agent is defined in a system specific XML dialect following a BDI-metamodel, while the agent behavior is realized as plans coded directly in the general-purpose programming language Java.

1(j).ii The default plan language is Java and therefore allows accessing any other application code or third party library written in Java. In addition, it is possible to define wrappers that allow executing plans written in other (e.g. visual) languages.

2(a).i The documentation includes an introductory tutorial, a user guide, which also serves as a reference manual, and a guide to the available tools. Javadocs of the plan programming API, and a reference to the metamodel defined in XML Schema are provided, and the distribution includes several example applications with source.

2(a).ii The system is based on Java 1.4, and requires a host agent platform such as JADE (which is currently supported best). The distribution includes the third party packages JBind for XML databinding, Apache Velocity for generating the content of some tool dialogs, and the TouchGraph GraphLayout component for visualizing traces of agent execution.

2(b) The system complies with the FIPA-standards as implemented by JADE.

2(c) The system is Open Source and carefully designed and documented to allow easy and flexible extension of the provided functionality.

2(d).i In addition to the tools provided by the JADE platform such as Sniffer and Dummy Agent, the system supplies an introspector tool to inspect an agent at runtime, and to execute agents step-by-step. A logger agent allows to collect, filter, and view logging outputs and a tracer agent visualizes event traces produced by the different agents of a multi-agent application. The Jadexdoc tool generates documentation for an agent application.

2(d).ii Apart from the documentation material included in the distribution (e.g. user guide and tutorial), there are publicly available web forums for discussion and support requests, a database for bug-reports and feature requests, and a general mailing list with online archives.

2(d).iii No additional tools (apart from those provided by JADE) are yet available, but a tool for multi-agent system deployment is currently in development.

2(e) All kinds of tools and libraries with a Java API can be used within Jadex. For example, in a larger project the Cayenne database-mapping framework was used to connect agents to a relational database.

2(f) Although its current implementation is targeted to run on top of JADE, the reasoning engine provides a general integration mechanism, and is designed to be used on top of any existing middleware. Therefore, it can be easily ported to other FIPA-compliant agent platforms such as CAPA or ADK and to other middleware environments such as J2EE or .NET.

2(g).i The performance of the system regarding the number of agents and messages is bounded by the performance of the underlying platform (e.g. JADE). The computation cost induced by the reasoning engine highly depends on the complexity of the agents.

2(g).ii The system is available as stable Open Source distribution and has already been used in several 3rd party projects. Nevertheless, the set of features is continuously evolving, and compatibility between releases is not guaranteed.

2(h).i The system realizes a specific internal agent architecture, and therefore itself does not address heterogeneity, but it is possible to run Jadex agents on the same platform as other JADE agents. Openness is supported in principle through FIPA-compliant communication, but not especially facilitated by the design of the system.

2(h).ii Jadex agents use the distributed or centralized control structures provided by the underlying platform (e.g. JADE). A hierarchical structure of agents is not supported, but agents can be decomposed into hierarchically structured modules, which are similar to agents, but do not have their own reasoning process.

2(h).iii The system includes a ready-to-use module for communication with a directory facilitator (DF) and for using simple FIPA interaction protocols (e.g. request).

3(a) The system has been used mainly in research projects and teaching courses, e.g. to realize a multi-agent application for market-based negotiation of patient treatment dates, as well as for the simulation of a hospital model. The system has also been applied in mobile environments and to some well-known AI problem domains such as blocksworld and cleanerworld.

3(b) The system is general purpose and not bound to a particular application domain.

Appendix H: JACK Summary

1(a) The JACK language supports BDI style practical reasoning as well as forward-directed inference reasoning, and allows for various agent concepts such as mental attitudes, deliberation, adaptation, reactive and proactive behaviour. There is a JACK extension towards a Cognitive Architecture, for inclusion of cognitive parameters and variations to the reasoning processes, and for modelling of cognitive influences by behaviour moderators.

1(b) JACK provides high-level primitives for communication between agents. Communication is peer-to-peer, and does not include broadcast or multi-cast addressing.

1(c) JACK is not intended for mobile agents.

1(d) JACK is an easy-to-use programming language in the BDI family, and the tool suite includes graphical programming tools both for program design and for decision logic.

1(e) The JACK language has clear and precise (but not formal) semantics.

1(f) JACK is a full programming language well suited for a variety of agent applications.

1(g) JACK allows new program elements to be defined in a systematic way, through compiler plugins.

1(h) This has not been investigated.

1(i) The JACK language is a full-flavoured programming language that combines the logic oriented BDI style with the object-oriented Java style, and it further includes programming elements providing increased support for abstraction, modularisation, information hiding and generic programming.

1(j).i JACK is fully integrated with Java, and it also includes integration mechanisms for combining JACK agents with C++ programs.

1(j).ii JACK is fully integrated with Java.

2(a).i JACK is well documented through a range of manuals and practicals, and is easily installed via the downloadable installer.

2(a).ii JACK runs on all Java platforms from 1.1.3, and has been run on PDAs (Psion 5mx and an HP iPAQ).

2(b) The JACK platform is itself proprietary, but includes the standard architectural elements, and there are FIPA wrapper extensions.

2(c) JACK is built to be open, with a range of "hooks" at various levels to simplify extensions. JACK is not open source.

2(d).i JACK comes with several mechanisms for logging and debugging of JACK agent execution.

2(d).ii The JACK package includes manuals in PDF and HTML format.

2(d).iii JACK includes a development tool.

2(e) JACK is fully integrated with Java and all Java tools can be used.

2(f) JACK is not tied to any specific operation environment.

2(g).i A single process can host thousands of JACK agents.

2(g).ii JACK is a fully supported commercial product.

2(h).i JACK supports open multi-agent systems and heterogeneous agents.

2(h).ii JACK includes a language extension for team-oriented programming, which simplifies coordinated activity and distributed control. The JACK Teams model includes role declarations and hierarchical, dynamic teams.

2(h).iii JACK does not include any pre-programmed libraries of JACK code.

3(a) JACK is being used for several real-world, industrial applications.

3(b) The BDI style programming is well suited to strategic robot control, as used in manufacturing plants, autonomous vehicles, and simulation, as well as business logic applications, including application of analytical procedures, compliance processes, and situated decision making.

References

[1] Agentcities Web Site. http://www.agentcities.org.

[2] J. F. Allen. The TRAINS project: A case study in building a conversational planning agent. *Journal of Experimental and Theoretical AI (JETAI)*, 7:7–48, 1995.

[3] J. Alves-Foss, editor. *Formal Syntax and Semantics of Java*. Springer LNCS 1523, 1999.

[4] D. Ancona, V. Mascardi, J. F. Hübner, and R. H. Bordini. Coo-AgentSpeak: Cooperation in AgentSpeak through plan exchange. In N. R. Jennings, C. Sierra, L. Sonenberg, and M. Tambe, editors, *Proceedings of the Third International Joint Conference on Autonomous Agents and Multi-Agent Systems (AAMAS-2004)*, pages 698–705. ACM Press, 2004.

[5] K. Apt and O. E.-R. *Verification of Sequential and Concurent Programs*. Springer Verlag, 1991.

[6] K. Arisha, F. Ozcan, R. Ross, V. Subrahmanian, T. Eiter, and S. Kraus. IMPACT: A Platform for Collaborating Agents. *IEEE Intelligent Systems*, 14:64–72, March/April 1999.

[7] J. Austin. *How to do things with words*. Springer Verlag, 1962.

[8] H. Becker. Realisierung eines metamodellbasierten Entwurfswerkzeuges für BDI-Agentensysteme. Diplomarbeit, Distributed Systems and Information Systems Group, Computer Science Department, University of Hamburg/Germany, 2005. (in German).

[9] M. Beelen. Personal Intelligent Travelling Assistant: a distributed approach. Master of science thesis, Knowledge Based Systems group, Delft University of Technology, 2004.

[10] F. Bellifemine. Special Issue on JADE. *EXP in Search of Innovation*, 3(3), 2003.

[11] F. Bellifemine, G. Caire, A. Poggi, and G. Rimassa. JADE - A White Paper. *EXP in Search of Innovation*, 3(3):6–19, 2003.

[12] F. Bellifemine, A. Poggi, and G. Rimassa. Developing multi-agent systems with a FIPA-compliant agent framework. *Software Practice and Experience*, 31(2):103–128, 2001.

[13] F. Bergenti, M.-P. Gleizes, and F. Zambonelli, editors. *Methodologies and Software Engineering for Agent Systems*. Kluwer Academic Publishing (New York), 2004.

[14] M. Berger, S. Rusitschka, D. Toropov, M. Watzke, and M. Schlichte. The Development of the Lightweight Extensible Agent Platform. *EXP in Search of Innovation*, 3(3):32–41, 2003.

[15] M. Berler, J. Eastman, D. Jordan, C. Russell, O. Schadow, T. Stanienda, and F. Velez. *The Object Data Standard: ODMG 3.0*. Morgan Kaufmann Publishers Inc., 2000.

[16] B. Berney and E. Ferneley. CASMIR - A Community of Software Agents Collaborating in Order to Retrieve Multimedia Data. In *Proc. of the third annual conference on Autonomous Agents*, pages 428–429, 1999.

[17] BlueJADE Web Site. http://sourceforge.net/projects/bluejade.

[18] R. H. Bordini, A. L. C. Bazzan, R. O. Jannone, D. M. Basso, R. M. Vicari, and V. R. Lesser. AgentSpeak(XL): Efficient intention selection in BDI agents via decision-theoretic task scheduling. In C. Castelfranchi and W. L. Johnson, editors, *Proceedings of the First International Joint Conference on Autonomous Agents and Multi-Agent Systems (AAMAS-2002)*, pages 1294–1302. ACM Press, 2002.

[19] R. H. Bordini, M. Fisher, C. Pardavila, and M. Wooldridge. Model checking AgentSpeak. In J. S. Rosenschein, T. Sandholm, M. Wooldridge, and M. Yokoo, editors, *Proceedings of the Second International Joint Conference on Autonomous Agents and Multi-Agent Systems (AAMAS-2003)*, pages 409–416. ACM Press, 2003.

[20] R. H. Bordini, M. Fisher, W. Visser, and M. Wooldridge. Model checking rational agents. *IEEE Intelligent Systems*, 19(5):46–52, September/October 2004.

[21] R. H. Bordini, M. Fisher, W. Visser, and M. Wooldridge. State-space reduction techniques in agent verification. In N. R. Jennings, C. Sierra,

L. Sonenberg, and M. Tambe, editors, *Proceedings of the Third International Joint Conference on Autonomous Agents and Multi-Agent Systems (AAMAS-2004)*, pages 896–903. ACM Press, 2004.

[22] R. H. Bordini, J. F. Hübner, et al. *Jason: A Java-based agentSpeak interpreter used with saci for multi-agent distribution over the net*, manual, version 0.6 edition, Feb 2005. http://jason.sourceforge.net/.

[23] R. H. Bordini and Á. F. Moreira. Proving the asymmetry thesis principles for a BDI agent-oriented programming language. In J. Dix, J. A. Leite, and K. Satoh, editors, *Proceedings of the Third International Workshop on Computational Logic in Multi-Agent Systems (CLIMA-02)*, Electronic Notes in Theoretical Computer Science 70(5). Elsevier, 2002. http://www.elsevier.nl/locate/entcs/volume70.html.

[24] R. H. Bordini and Á. F. Moreira. Proving BDI properties of agent-oriented programming languages: The asymmetry thesis principles in AgentSpeak(L). *Annals of Mathematics and Artificial Intelligence*, 42(1–3):197–226, Sept. 2004. Special Issue on Computational Logic in Multi-Agent Systems.

[25] R. H. Bordini, F. Y. Okuyama, D. de Oliveira, G. Drehmer, and R. C. Krafta. The MAS-SOC approach to multi-agent based simulation. In G. Lindemann, D. Moldt, and M. Paolucci, editors, *Proceedings of the First International Workshop on Regulated Agent-Based Social Systems: Theories and Applications (RASTA'02)*, number 2934 in LNAI, pages 70–91, Berlin, 2004. Springer-Verlag.

[26] R. H. Bordini, W. Visser, M. Fisher, C. Pardavila, and M. Wooldridge. Model checking multi-agent programs with CASP. In W. A. Hunt Jr. and F. Somenzi, editors, *Proceedgins of the Fifteenth Conference on Computer-Aided Verification (CAV-2003)*, number 2725 in LNCS, pages 110–113. Springer-Verlag, 2003. Tool description.

[27] M. Bratman, D. Israel, and M. Pollack. Plans and resource-bounded practical reasoning. *Computational Intelligence*, 4(4):349–355, 1988.

[28] M. E. Bratman. *Intention, Plans, and Practical Reason*. Harvard University Press, Cambridge, MA, 1987.

[29] L. Braubach, A. Pokahr, K.-H. Krempels, and W. Lamersdorf. Deployment of Distributed Multi-Agent Systems. In *Fifth International Workshop on Engineering Societies in the Agents World (ESAW 2004)*, 2004.

[30] L. Braubach, A. Pokahr, and W. Lamersdorf.   Jadex: A Short Overview. In *Net.ObjectDays 2004: AgentExpo*, 2004.

[31] L. Braubach, A. Pokahr, W. Lamersdorf, K.-H. Krempels, and P.-O. Woelk. A Generic Simulation Service for Distributed Multi-Agent Systems. In *From Agent Theory to Agent Implementation (AT2AI'04)*, 2004.

[32] L. Braubach, A. Pokahr, D. Moldt, and W. Lamersdorf. Goal Representation for BDI Agent Systems. In *Proceedings of the Second Workshop on Programming Multiagent Systems: Languages, frameworks, techniques, and tools (ProMAS04)*, 2004.

[33] P. Bresciani, F. Giorgini, F. Giunchiglia, J. Mylopoulos, and A. Perini. Tropos: An agent-oriented software development methodology. Technical Report DIT-02-0015, University of Trento, Department of Information and Communication Technology, 2002.

[34] P. Bretier. *La communication orale coopérative : contribution à la modélisation logique et à la mise en oeuvre d'un agent rationnel dialoguant.* PhD thesis, University of Paris XIII, 1995.

[35] P. Bretier and D. Sadek. A rational agent as the kernel of a cooperative spoken dialogue system: Implementing a logical theory of interaction. In J.P. Müller, M.J. Wooldridge and N.R. Jennings eds. *Lecture Notes in Artificial Intelligence "Intelligent Agents III" Proceedings of ATAL'96*, pages 189–203, Budapest, Hungary, 1997.

[36] R. Brooks. How to build complete creatures rather than isolated cognitive simulators. In K. VanLehn, editor, *Architectures for Intelligence*, pages 225–240. Lawrence Erlbaum Associates, Hillsdale, New Jersey, 1991.

[37] P. Buckle, T. Moore, S. Robertshaw, A. Treadway, S. Tarkoma, and S. Poslad. Scalability in Multi-agent Systems: The FIPA-OS Perspective. In M. d'Inverno, M. Luck, M. Fisher, and C. Preist, editors, *Proc. Foundations and Applications of Multi-Agent Systems*, volume 2403 of *LNCS*, pages 110–130. Springer, 2002.

[38] M. H. Burstein, A. M. Mulvehill, and S. Deutsch. An approach to mixed-initiative management of heterogeneous software agent teams. In *HICSS*, page 8055. IEEE Computer Society, 1999.

[39] P. Busetta, N. Howden, R. Rönnquist, and A. Hodgson. Structuring BDI agents in functional clusters. In *Agent Theories, Architectures,*

and Languages (ATAL-99), pages 277–289. Springer-Verlag, 2000. LNCS 1757.

[40] P. Busetta, R. Rönnquist, A. Hodgson, and A. Lucas. JACK Intelligent Agents - Components for Intelligent Agents in Java. Technical report, Agent Oriented Software Pty. Ltd, Melbourne, Australia, 1998. Available from http://www.agent-software.com.

[41] L. Cardelli and A. Gordon. Mobile ambients. *Foundations of Software Science and Computational Structures, LNAI*, 1378:140–155, 1998.

[42] C. Castelfranchi and R. Falcone. Principles of trust for MAS: Cognitive anatomy, social importance, and quantification. In Y. Demazeau, editor, *Proceedings of the Third International Conference on Multi-Agent Systems (ICMAS'98), Agents' World, 4-7 July, Paris*, pages 72–79, Washington, 1998. IEEE Computer Society Press.

[43] Cattell, R. G. G., et al., editor. *The Object Database Standard: ODMG-93*. Morgan Kaufmann, 1997.

[44] L. Cernuzzi and G. Rossi. On the evaluation of agent oriented modeling methods. In *Proceedings of the OOPSLA 2002 Workshop on Agent-Oriented Methodologies*, pages 21–30, Seattle, November 2002.

[45] P. Cohen and H. Levesque. Intention is choice with commitment. *Artificial Intelligence*, 42(2-3):213–262, 1990.

[46] P. Cohen and H. Levesque. Rational interaction as the basis for communication. In P.R. Cohen, J. Morgan and M.E. Pollack eds. *Intentions in Communication*. MIT Press, 1990.

[47] P. R. Cohen and H. J. Levesque. Teamwork. *Nous*, 25(4):487–512, 1991.

[48] E. Cortese, F. Quarta, and G. Vitaglione. Scalability and Performance of JADE Message Transport System. In *Proc. of AAMAS Workshop on AgentCities*, Bologna, Italy, 2002.

[49] J. W. Crandall, C. W. Nielsen, and M. A. Goodrich. Towards predicting robot team performance. In *SMC*, 2003.

[50] K. H. Dam and M. Winikoff. Comparing agent-oriented methodologies. In P. Giorgini, B. Henderson-Sellers, and M. Winikoff, editors, *Agent-Oriented Information Systems (AOIS 2003): Revised Selected Papers*, pages 78–93. Springer LNAI 3030, 2004.

[51] M. Dastani. 3APL platform: User guide. http://www.cs.uu.nl/3apl/download.html.

[52] M. Dastani, F. de Boer, F. Dignum, and J.-J. Meyer. Programming agent deliberation: An approach illustrated using the 3APL language. In *Proceedings of The Second Conference on Autonomous Agents and Multi-agent Systems (AAMAS'03)*, pages 97–104, Melbourne, 2003.

[53] M. Dastani, J. van der Ham, and F. Dignum. Communication for goal directed agents. In M.-P. Huget, editor, *Communication in Multiagent Systems · Agent Communication Languages and Conversation Policies*, pages 239–252. Springer, LNCS, 2003.

[54] M. Dastani, M. B. van Riemsdijk, F. Dignum, and J.-J. Ch. Meyer. A programming language for cognitive agents: goal directed 3APL. In *Programming multiagent systems, first international workshop (Pro-MAS'03)*, volume 3067 of *LNAI*, pages 111–130. Springer, Berlin, 2004.

[55] L. P. de Silva and L. Padgham. A comparison of BDI based real-time reasoning and HTN based planning. In *17th Australian Joint Conference on Artificial Intelligence*, 2004.

[56] K. Decker and K. P. Sycara. Intelligent adaptive information agents. *Journal on Intellent Information Systems*, 9(3):239–260, 1997.

[57] S. A. DeLoach, M. F. Wood, and C. H. Sparkman. Multiagent systems engineering. *International Journal of Software Engineering and Knowledge Engineering*, 11(3):231–258, 2001.

[58] D. C. Dennet. *The Intentional Stance*. The MIT Press, Cambridge, MA, 1987.

[59] M. d'Inverno, D. Kinny, M. Luck, and M. Wooldridge. A formal specification of dMARS. In M. Singh, A. Rao, and M. Wooldridge, editors, *Intelligent Agents IV: Proceedings of the Fourth International Workshop on Agent Theories, Architectures, and Languages*, pages 155–176. Springer-Verlag LNAI 1365, 1998.

[60] M. d'Inverno and M. Luck. *Understanding Agent Systems*. Springer-Verlag, 2001.

[61] J. Dix. A Computational Logic Approach to Heterogenous Agent Systems. In T. Eiter, M. Truszczyński, and W. Faber, editors, *Logic Programming and Non-Monotonic Reasoning, Proceedings of the Sixth International Conference*, LNCS 2173, pages 1–21, Berlin, September 2001. Springer.

[62] J. Dix and T. Eiter. Theoretical foundations and practical applications of heterogenous agent systems. Technical report, Working Notes of the *14th annual European Summer School in Logic, Language and Information*, Trento 2002, 2002.

[63] J. Dix, S. Kraus, and V. Subrahmanian. Temporal agent reasoning. *Artificial Intelligence*, 127(1):87–135, 2001.

[64] J. Dix, S. Kraus, and V. Subrahmanian. Agents dealing with time and uncertainty. In C. Castelfranchi and W. L. Johnson, editors, *Proceedings of the First International Joint Conference on Autonomous Agents and Multi-Agent Systems*, pages 912–919. New York: ACM Press, July 2002.

[65] J. Dix, S. Kraus, and V. Subrahmanian. Heterogenous temporal probabilistic agents. *ACM Transactions of Computational Intelligence*, 2005. to appear.

[66] J. Dix, U. Kuter, and D. Nau. Planning in answer set programming using ordered task decomposition. In R. Kruse, editor, *Proceedings of the 27th German Annual Conference on Artificial Intelligence (KI '03), Hamburg, Germany*, LNAI 2821, pages 490–504, Berlin, 2003. Springer.

[67] J. Dix, H. Munoz-Avila, and D. N. an Lingling Zhang. Theoretical and Empirical Aspects of a Planner in a Multi-Agent Environment. In G. Ianni and S. Flesca, editors, *Proceedings of Journees Europeens de la Logique en Intelligence artificielle (JELIA '02)*, LNCS 2424, pages 173–185. Springer, 2002.

[68] J. Dix, H. Munoz-Avila, D. Nau, and L. Zhang. Planning in a multi-agent environment: Theory and practice. In C. Castelfranchi and W. L. Johnson, editors, *Proceedings of the First International Joint Conference on Autonomous Agents and Multi-Agent Systems*, pages 944–945. New York: ACM Press, July 2002.

[69] J. Dix, H. Munoz-Avila, D. Nau, and L. Zhang. IMPACTing SHOP: Putting an AI planner into a Multi-Agent Environment. *Annals of Mathematics and AI*, 37(4):381–407, 2003.

[70] J. Dix, M. Nanni, and V. S. Subrahmanian. Probabilistic agent reasoning. *ACM Transactions of Computational Logic*, 1(2):201–245, 2000.

[71] J. Dix, F. Öczan, and V. Subrahmanian. Improving performance of heavily loaded agents. *Annals of Math and AI*, 41(2-4):339–395, 2004.

[72] J. Dix, V. Subrahmanian, and G. Pick. Meta Agent Programs. *Journal of Logic Programming*, 46(1-2):1–60, 2000.

[73] G. Dorais, R. Bonasso, D. Kortenkamp, P. Pell, and D. Schreck-enghost. Adjustable autonomy for human-centered autonomous systems on mars. In *Mars*, 1998.

[74] J. Doran and N. Gilbert. Simulating societies: An introduction. In N. Gilbert and J. Doran, editors, *Simulating Society: The Computer Simulation of Social Phenomena*, chapter 1, pages 1–18. UCL Press, London, 1994.

[75] J. Doyle. Rationality and its role in reasoning. In *Proceedings of AAAI'90*, Boston, MA, 1990.

[76] M. Duvigneau, D. Moldt, and H. Rölke. Concurrent Architecture for a Multi-agent Platform. In F. Giunchiglia, J. Odell, and G. Wei, editors, *Agent-Oriented Software Engineering III. Third International Workshop, AOSE 2002, Bologna, Italy, July 2002. Revised Papers and Invited Contributions*, volume 2585 of *LNCS*, pages 59–72, Berlin Heidelberg New York, 2003. Springer.

[77] T. Eiter and V. Subrahmanian. Heterogeneous Active Agents, II: Algorithms and Complexity. *Artificial Intelligence*, 108(1-2):257–307, 1999.

[78] T. Eiter, V. Subrahmanian, and G. Pick. Heterogeneous Active Agents, I: Semantics. *Artificial Intelligence*, 108(1-2):179–255, 1999.

[79] T. Eiter, V. Subrahmanian, and T. Rogers. Heterogeneous Active Agents, III: Polynomially Implementable Agents. *Artificial Intelligence*, 117(1):107–167, 2000.

[80] A. El Fallah Seghrouchni, S. Haddad, T. Melitti, and A. Suna. Interopérabilité des systèmes multi-agents à l'aide des services web (in french). In *Proceedings of JFSMA'04*, Paris, 2004.

[81] A. El Fallah Seghrouchni and A. Suna. Claim: A computational language for autonomous, intelligent and mobile agents. *Proceedings of ProMAS'03 Workshop of AAMAS, LNAI*, 3067:90–110, 2003.

[82] A. El Fallah Seghrouchni and A. Suna. An unified framework for programming autonomous, intelligent and mobile agents. *Proceedings of CEEMAS'03, LNAI*, 2691:353–362, 2003.

[83] A. El Fallah Seghrouchni and A. Suna. Programming mobile intelligent agents: an operational semantics. In *Proceedings of IAT'04*, Beijing, China, 2004. IEEE Press.

[84] O. Enseling. Build your own languages with JavaCC. World Wide Web page.

[85] R. Evertsz, M. Fletcher, R. Jones, J. Jarvis, J. Brusey, and S. Dance. Implementing industrial multi-agent systems using JACK™. In M. Dastani, J. Dix, and A. E. Fallah-Seghrouchni, editors, *First International Workshop, PROMAS 2003, Melbourne, Australia, July 15, 2003, Selected Revised and Invited Papers*, pages 18–48. Springer LNAI 3067, 2004.

[86] L. Fariñas del Cerro. Resolution modal logic. *Logique et Analyse: Special issue on Automated reasoning in Nonclassical Logics*, 110-111:152–172, 1985.

[87] D. Fensel, S. Decker, M. Erdmann, and R. Studer. Ontobroker in a Nutshell. In *Proc. of the European Conference on Digital Libraries*, pages 663–664, 1998.

[88] D. Fensel and R. Studer, editors. *Knowledge Acquisition, Modeling and Management, 11th European Workshop, EKAW '99, Dagstuhl Castle, Germany, May 26-29, 1999, Proceedings*, volume 1621 of *LNCS*. Springer, 1999.

[89] FIPA Specifications. http://www.fipa.org.

[90] M. Fletcher and J. Brusey. The story of the Holonic packing cell. In *Agents at Work: Deployed Applications of Autonomous Agents and Multi-Agent Systems*, July 2003.

[91] M. Fletcher, R. Rönnquist, N. Howden, and A. Lucas. Enigma variations – simulating changes in behaviour of British military personnel. In *SimTecT*, pages 21–26, May 2004.

[92] T. Fong, C. Thorpe, and C. Baur. Multi-robot remote driving with collaborative control. *IEEE Transactions on Industrial Electronics*, 2002.

[93] F. Gandon, A. Poggi, G. Rimassa, and P. Turci. Multi-Agent Corporate Memory Management System. *Applied Artificial Intelligence*, 16(9-10):699–720, 2002.

[94] G. Garson. Quantification in modal logic. In D. Gabbay and F. Guetner eds. *Handbook of philosophical logic, Volume II: Extensions of classical Logic*, pages 249–307. D. Reidel Publishing Company, 1984.

[95] M. R. Genesereth and S. P. Ketchpel. Software Agents. *Communications of the ACM*, 37(7):49–53, 1994.

[96] M. Georgeff, B. Pell, M. Pollack, M. Tambe, and M. Wooldridge. The Belief-Desire-Intention Model of Agency. In J. Müller, M. Singh, and

A. Rao, editors, *Proceedings of the 5th International Workshop on Intelligent Agents V: Agent Theories, Architectures, and Languages (ATAL-98)*, pages 1–10. Springer-Verlag: Heidelberg, Germany, 1999.

[97] M. P. Georgeff and A. L. Lansky. Procedural knowledge. *Proceedings of the IEEE Special Issue on Knowledge Representation*, 74:1383–1398, 1986.

[98] M. P. Georgeff and A. L. Lansky. Reactive reasoning and planning: An experiment with a mobile robot. In *Proceedings of the Sixth National Conference on Artificial Intelligence (AAAI'87), 13–17 July, 1987, Seattle, WA*, pages 677–682, Manlo Park, CA, 1987. AAAI Press / MIT Press.

[99] J. Gosling, B. Joy, G. Steele, and G. Bracha. *The Java Language Specification*. Addison-Wesley, second edition, 2000.

[100] G. Gottlob and T. Walsh, editors. *Proceedings of the Eighteenth International Joint Conference on Artificial Intelligence (IJCAI-03)*. Morgan Kaufmann, 2003.

[101] M. Greenberg, J. Buyington, and D. Harper. Mobile agents and security. *IEEE Comunications Magazine*, 36(7):76–85, 1998.

[102] H. Grice. Logic and conversation. In P. Cole and J. Morgan eds. *Syntax and semantics 3/ Speech acts*, pages 41–58. Academic Press, 1975.

[103] J. Halpern and Y. Moses. A guide to the modal logics of know-ledge and belief: a preliminary draft. In *Proceedings of IJCAI'85*, Los Angeles, CA, 1985.

[104] M. Harbeck. BDI-Agentensysteme auf mobilen Geräten. Diplomarbeit, Distributed Systems and Information Systems Group, Computer Science Department, University of Hamburg/Germany, 2004. (in German).

[105] B. Henderson-Sellers and P. Giorgini, editors. *Agent-Oriented Methodologies*. Idea Group, 2005 (to appear).

[106] R. Hill, J. Gratch, S. Marsella, J. Rickel, W. Swartout, and D. Traum. Virtual humans in the mission rehearsal exercise system. In *KI Embodied Conversational Agents*, 2003.

[107] K. Hindriks, F. de Boer, W. van der Hoek, and J.-J. Ch. Meyer. Agent programming in 3APL. *Int. J. of Autonomous Agents and Multi-Agent Systems*, 2(4):357–401, 1999.

[108] K. Hindriks, F. de Boer, W. van der Hoek, and J.-J. Ch. Meyer. Agent programming with declarative goals. In N. Jennings and Y. Lesperance, editors, *Intelligent Agents VI - Proceedings of ATAL'2000*, LNAI-1757. Springer, Berlin, 2001.

[109] D. C. Ho Mok Cheong. An empirical investigation of teamwork infrastructure for autonomous agents, October 2003. Honours Thesis, available as RMIT Computer Science technical report TR-03-2.

[110] G. Holzmann. The SPIN model checker. *IEEE Transactions on Software Engineering*, 23(5):279–295, 1997.

[111] E. Horvitz. Principles of mixed-initiative user interfaces. In *Proceedings of ACM SIGCHI Conference on Human Factors in Computing Systems (CHI'99)*, pages 159–166, Pittsburgh, PA, May 1999.

[112] N. Howden, J. Curmi, C. Heinze, S. Goss, and G. Murphy. Operational knowledge representation– behaviour capture, modelling and verification. In *SimTecT*, May 2003.

[113] N. Howden, R. Rönnquist, A. Hodgson, and A. Lucas. JACK intelligent agents: Summary of an agent infrastructure. In *Workshop on Infrastructure for Agents, MAS, and scalable MAS*, 2001.

[114] M. J. Huber. JAM: A BDI-Theoretic Mobile Agent Architecture. In O. Etzioni, J. Müller, and J. Bradshaw, editors, *Proceedings of the Third International Conference on Autonomous Agents (AGENTS-99)*, pages 236–243, New York, May 1–5 1999. ACM Press.

[115] J. F. Hübner. *Um Modelo de Reorganização de Sistemas Multiagentes*. PhD thesis, Universidade de São Paulo, Escola Politécnica, 2003.

[116] U. Hustadt, C. Dixon, R. Schmidt, M. Fisher, J.-J. Ch. Meyer, and W. van der Hoek. Verification within the KARO agent theory. In *Proceedings of the First Goddard Workshop on Formal Approaches to Agent-Based Systems (FAABS'00)*, LNAI, pages 33–47. Springer, Berlin, 2001.

[117] J. Hutchison. Agent team programming: An evaluation of JACK teams, October 2002. Honours Thesis, available as RMIT Computer Science technical report TR-02-7.

[118] F. F. Ingrand, M. P. Georgeff, and A. S. Rao. An Architecture for Real-Time Reasoning and System Control. *IEEE Expert*, 7(6):34–44, 1992.

[119] JADE Web Site. http://jade.tilab.com.

[120] JADEX Web Site. `Http://vsis-www.informatik. uni-hamburg.de/projects/jadex`.

[121] J. Jarvis. JACK Intelligent Agents JACK Teams Manual, March 2004. Available with the JACK distribution.

[122] N. Jennings and M. Wooldridge. Applications of intelligent agents. In Jennings and Wooldridge [124], chapter 1, pages 3–28.

[123] N. R. Jennings. An agent-based approach for building complex software systems. *Communications of the ACM*, 44(4):35–41, 2001.

[124] N. R. Jennings and M. J. Wooldridge, editors. *Agent Technology: Foundations, Applications, and Markets*. Springer, 1998.

[125] T. Juan, A. Pearce, and L. Sterling. ROADMAP: Extending the Gaia methodology for complex open systems. In *Proceedings of the First International Joint Conference on Autonomous Agents and Multi-Agent Systems (AAMAS 2002)*, pages 3–10. ACM Press, 2002.

[126] D. Kinny. The distributed multi-agent reasoning system architecture and language specification. Technical report, Australian Artificial Intelligence Institute, Melbourne, Australia, 1993.

[127] D. Kinny and R. Phillip. Building Composite Applications with Goal-Directed(TM) Agent Technology. *AgentLink News*, 16:6–8, December 2004.

[128] H. Kitano, S. Tadokoro, I. Noda, H. Matsubara, T. Takahashi, A. Shinjoh, and S. Shimada. Robocup rescue: Search and rescue in large-scale disasters as a domain for autonomous agents research. In *IEEE SMC*, volume VI, pages 739–743, Tokyo, October 1999.

[129] G. Klein, A. Suna, and A. El Fallah Seghrouchni. A methodology for building mobile multi-agent systems. In *Proceedings of SYNACS'04*, Timisoara, Romania, 2004.

[130] K. Konolige. *A deduction model of belief*. Pitman, Morgan Kaufman Publisher, London, 1986.

[131] R. Krafta, D. de Oliveira, and R. H. Bordini. The city as object of human agency. In *Fourth International Space Syntax Symposium (SSS4), London, 17–19 June*, pages 33.1–33.18, 2003.

[132] D. Lam and S. Barber. Debugging agent behavior in an implemented agent system. In *Second International Workshop on Programming*

Multi-Agent Systems at the Third International Joint Conference on Autonomous Agents and Multi-Agent Systems, pages 45–56, 2004.

[133] LEAP Web Site. http://leap.crm-paris.com.

[134] J. Lee, M. J. Huber, P. G. Kenny, and E. H. Durfee. UM-PRS: An implementation of the procedural reasoning system for multirobot applications. In *Proceedings of the Conference on Intelligent Robotics in Field, Factory, Service, and Space (CIRFFSS'94)*, pages 842–849, 1994.

[135] J. A. Leite. *Evolving Knowledge Bases: Specification and Semantics*, volume 81 of *Frontiers in Artificial Intelligence and Applications, Dissertations in Artificial Intelligence*. IOS Press/Ohmsha, Amsterdam, 2003.

[136] F. Levi and D. Sangiori. Controlling interference in ambients. In *Proceedings of the 27th ACM SIGPLAN-SIGACT Symposium on Principles of Programming Languages*, pages 352–364. ACM Press, 2000.

[137] E. Liao, P. Scerri, and K. Sycara. A framework for very large teams. In *AAMAS'04 Workshop on Coalitions and Teams*, 2004.

[138] V. Louis. *Conception et mise en oeuvre de modèles formels du calcul de plans d'action complexes par un agent rationnel dialoguant*. PhD thesis, University of Caen, 2002.

[139] A. Lucas, P. Corke, R. Rönnquist, P. Sikka, M. Ljungberg, and N. Howden. Teamed UAVs – A new approach with intelligent agents. In *AIAA Unmanned Unlimited*, 2003.

[140] A. Lucas, R. Rönnquist, N. Howden, P. Gaertner, and J. Haub. Intelligent battlespace awareness and information dissemination through the application of BDI intelligent agent technologies. In *SPIE - The International Society for Optical Engineering: Digitization of the Battlespace V and Battlefield Biomedical Technologies II*, April 2000.

[141] M. Luck, P. McBurney, and C. Preist. Agent technology: Enabling next generation computing: A roadmap for agent-based computing. AgentLink report, available from www.agentlink.org/roadmap, 2003. ISBN 0854 327886.

[142] M. Luck, P. McBurney, and C. Preist. A manifesto for agent technology: Towards next generation computing. *Autonomous Agents and Multi-Agent Systems*, 9(3):203–252, November 2004.

[143] R. Machado and R. H. Bordini. Running AgentSpeak(L) agents on SIM_AGENT. In J.-J. Meyer and M. Tambe, editors, *Intelligent Agents*

282

VIII – *Proceedings of the Eighth International Workshop on Agent Theories, Architectures, and Languages (ATAL-2001)*, number 2333 in LNAI, pages 158–174. Springer-Verlag, 2002.

[144] E. Mangina. Review of Software Products for Multi-Agent Systems. http://www.agentlink.org/resources/software-report.html, 2002.

[145] F. Marc, A. E. Fallah-Seghrouchni, and I. Degirmenciyan-Cartault. Coordination of complex systems based on multi-agent planning: Application to the aircraft simulation domain. In R. H. Bordini, M. Dastani, J. Dix, and A. E. Fallah-Seghrouchni, editors, *Second International Workshop on Programming Multi-Agent Systems: Languages and Tools (ProMAS 2004)*, pages 115–128, July 2004.

[146] M. Mari, A. Negri, A. Poggi, and P. Turci. Agent-Based Remote Assistance for Software Programming Activities. In *Proc. AI*IA Workshop on Artificial Intelligence & E-Learning*, Perugia, Italy, 2004.

[147] P. Marrow. The DIET project: building a lightweight, decentralised and adaptable agent platform. *AgentLink News*, 12:3–6, April 2003.

[148] T. Martinez, P. Bretier, and V. Louis. Artimis : assistant de voyage et médiateur intelligent dans un système multi-agent. In *Proceedings of JFSMA'03*, Hammamet, Tunisia, 2003.

[149] I. Mathieson, S. Dance, L. Padgham, M. Gorman, and M. Winikoff. An open meteorological alerting system: Issues and solutions. In V. Estivill-Castro, editor, *Proceedings of the 27th Australasian Computer Science Conference*, pages 351–358, Dunedin, New Zealand, 2004.

[150] J.-J. Ch. Meyer. Agent-oriented programming: Where do we stand? (invited talk). In C. Rattray, S. Maharaj, and C. Shankland, editors, *Proceedings of the 10th International Conference on Algebraic Methodology And Software Technology (AMAST04)*, volume 3116 of *LNCS*, pages 23–26. Springer-Verlag, 2004.

[151] D. Milojicic, M. Breugst, I. Busse, J. Campbell, S. Covaci, B. Friedman, K. Kosaka, D. Lange, K. Ono, M. Oshima, C. Tham, S. Virdhagriswaran, and J. White. MASIF, the OMG mobile agent system interoperability facility. In *Proceedings of the Second International Workshop on Mobile Agents*, number 1477 in LNAI, pages 50–67. Springer-Verlag, 1998.

[152] Á. F. Moreira and R. H. Bordini. An operational semantics for a BDI agent-oriented programming language. In J.-J. C. Meyer and M. J.

Wooldridge, editors, *Proceedings of the Workshop on Logics for Agent-Based Systems (LABS-02), held with KR2002, April 22–25, Toulouse, France*, pages 45–59, 2002.

[153] Á. F. Moreira, R. Vieira, and R. H. Bordini. Extending the operational semantics of a BDI agent-oriented programming language for introducing speech-act based communication. In J. Leite, A. Omicini, L. Sterling, and P. Torroni, editors, *Declarative Agent Languages and Technologies, Proceedings of the First International Workshop (DALT-03)*, number 2990 in LNAI, pages 135–154, Berlin, 2004. Springer-Verlag.

[154] H. Muñoz-Avila, D. Aha, D. Nau, R. Weber, L. Breslow, and F. Yaman. SiN: Integrating case-based reasoning with task decomposition. In *IJCAI-2001*, August 2001.

[155] D. Nau, Y. Cao, A. Lotem, and H. Muñoz-Avila. Shop: Simple hierarchical ordered planner. In *Proceedings of IJCAI-99*, 1999.

[156] A. Newell. The knowledge level. *Artificial Intelligence*, 18:87–128, 1982.

[157] E. Norling. Folk psychology for human modelling: Extending the BDI paradigm. In *Proceedings of the Third International Joint Conference on Autonomous Agents and Multiagent Systems (AAMAS 2004)*, pages 202–209, New York, July 2004.

[158] E. Norling and F. E. Ritter. Embodying the JACK agent architecture. In M. Stumptner, D. Corbett, and M. Brooks, editors, *AI2001: Advances in Artificial Intelligence. 14th Australian Joint Conference on Artificial Intelligence*, pages 368–377. Springer LNAI 2256, December 2001.

[159] E. Norling and F. E. Ritter. Towards supporting psychologically plausible variability in agent-based human modelling. In *Proceedings of the Third International Joint Conference on Autonomous Agents and Multiagent Systems*, pages 758–765, New York, July 2004.

[160] H. S. Nwana, D. T. Ndumu, L. C. Lee, and J. C. Collis. ZEUS: a toolkit for building distributed multiagent systems. *Applied Artificial Intelligence*, 13(1-2):129–185, 1999.

[161] J. J. Odell. Objects and agents compared. *Journal of Object Technology*, 1(1):41–53, May-June 2002.

[162] F. Y. Okuyama, R. H. Bordini, and A. C. da Rocha Costa. ELMS: an environment description language for multi-agent simulations. In

D. Weyns et al., editors, *Proceedings of the First International Workshop on Environments for Multiagent Systems (E4MAS)*, number 3374 in LNAI, pages 91–108. Springer-Verlag, 2005.

[163] L. Padgham and M. Winikoff. Prometheus: A methodology for developing intelligent agents. In *Agent-Oriented Software Engineering III: Third International Workshop (AOSE'02)*. Springer, LNAI 2585, 2003.

[164] L. Padgham and M. Winikoff. *Developing Intelligent Agent Systems: A Practical Guide*. John Wiley and Sons, 2004. ISBN 0-470-86120-7.

[165] F. Panaget. *D'un système générique de génération d'énoncés en contexte de dialogue oral à la formalisation logique des capacités linguistiques d'un agent rationnel dialoguant*. PhD thesis, University of Rennes I, 1996.

[166] T. O. Paulussen, N. R. Jennings, K. S. Decker, and A. Heinzl. Distributed Patient Scheduling in Hospitals. In Gottlob and Walsh [100].

[167] T. O. Paulussen, A. Zöller, A. Heinzl, A. Pokahr, L. Braubach, and W. Lamersdorf. Dynamic Patient Scheduling in Hospitals. In M. Bichler, C. Holtmann, S. Kirn, J. Müller, and C. Weinhardt, editors, *Coordination and Agent Technology in Value Networks*. GITO, Berlin, 2004.

[168] C. Perrault. An application of default logic to speech act theory. In P.R. Cohen, J. Morgan and M.E. Pollack eds. *Intentions in Communication*. MIT Press, 1990.

[169] G. D. Plotkin. A structural approach to operational semantics. Technical report, DAIMI-FN 19, Department of Computer Science, Aarhus University, Aarhus, Denmark, 1981.

[170] A. Pokahr and L. Braubach. *Jadex User Guide, Release 0.931*, 2005.

[171] A. Pokahr, L. Braubach, and W. Lamersdorf. Jadex: Implementing a BDI-Infrastructure for JADE Agents. *EXP – in search of innovation*, 3(3):76–85, 2003.

[172] S. Poslad and P. Charlton. Standardizing Agent Interoperability: The FIPA Approach. In M. L. et al., editor, *9th ECCAI Advanced Course, ACAI 2001 and Agent Links 3rd European Agent Systems Summer School, EASSS 2001, Prague, Czech Republic, July 2001*, pages 98–117. Springer-Verlag: Heidelberg, Germany, 2001.

[173] D. Poutakidis, L. Padgham, and M. Winikoff. Debugging multi-agent systems using design artifacts: The case of interaction protocols. In *Proceedings of the First International Joint Conference on Autonomous*

Agents and Multi Agent Systems (AAMAS'02), pages 960–967. ACM Press, July 2002.

[174] D. Poutakidis, L. Padgham, and M. Winikoff. An exploration of bugs and debugging in multi-agent systems. In *Proceedings of the 14th International Symposium on Methodologies for Intelligent Systems (ISMIS)*, pages 628–632, Maebashi City, Japan, 2003.

[175] M. Purvis, M. Nowostawski, and S. Cranefield. A multi-level approach and infrastructure for agent-oriented software development. In *Proc. of the first international joint conference on Autonomous agents and multiagent systems*, pages 88–89, Bologna, Italy, 2002.

[176] D. V. Pynadath and M. Tambe. Automated teamwork among heterogeneous software agents and humans. *Journal of Autonomous Agents and Multi-Agent Systems (JAAMAS)*, 7:71–100, 2003.

[177] A. Rabarijoana, R. Dieng, and O. Corby. Exploitation of XML for Corporate Knowledge Management. In Fensel and Studer [88], pages 373–378.

[178] T. Rahwan, T. Rahwan, I. Rahwan, and R. Ashri. Agent-based support for mobile users using AgentSpeak(L). In P. Giorgini, B. Henderson-Sellers, and M. Winikoff, editors, *Agent-Oriented Information Systems (AOIS 2003): Revised Selected Papers*, pages 45–60. Springer LNAI 3030, 2004.

[179] A. Rao and M. Georgeff. An abstract architecture for rational agents. In *Proceedings of KR'92*, Cambridge, MA, 1992.

[180] A. S. Rao. AgentSpeak(L): BDI agents speak out in a logical computable language. In W. Van de Velde and J. Perram, editors, *Proceedings of the Seventh Workshop on Modelling Autonomous Agents in a Multi-Agent World (MAAMAW'96), 22–25 January, Eindhoven, The Netherlands*, number 1038 in LNAI, pages 42–55, London, 1996. Springer-Verlag.

[181] A. S. Rao and M. P. Georgeff. Modeling rational agents within a BDI-architecture. In J. Allen, R. Fikes, and E. Sandewall, editors, *Proceedings of the 2nd International Conference on Principles of Knowledge Representation and Reasoning (KR'91)*, pages 473–484, San Mateo, CA, 1991. Morgan Kaufmann.

[182] A. S. Rao and M. P. Georgeff. BDI agents: From theory to practice. In V. Lesser and L. Gasser, editors, *Proceedings of the First International*

Conference on Multi-Agent Systems (ICMAS'95), 12–14 June, San Francisco, CA, pages 312–319, Menlo Park, CA, 1995. AAAI Press / MIT Press.

[183] A. S. Rao and M. P. Georgeff. Decision procedures for BDI logics. *Journal of Logic and Computation*, 8(3):293–343, 1998.

[184] A. Richardson, D. Montello, and M. Hegarty. Spatial knowledge acquisition from maps and from navigation in real and virtual environments. *Memory and Cognition*, 27(4):741–750, 1999.

[185] R. Ruddle, S. Payne, and D. Jones. Navigating buildings in desktop virtual environments: Experimental investigations using extended navigational experience. *J. Experimental Psychology - Applied*, 3(2):143–159, 1997.

[186] S. Russel. Rationality and intelligence. In *Proceedings of IJCAI'95*, Montreal, 1995.

[187] D. Sadek. Logical task modelling for Man-machine dialogue. In *Proceedings of AAAI'90*, pages 970–975, Boston, MA, 1990.

[188] D. Sadek. *Attitudes mentales et interaction rationnelle: vers une théorie formelle de la communication*. PhD thesis, University of Rennes I, 1991.

[189] D. Sadek. A study in the logic of intention. In *Proceedings of KR'92*, pages 462–473, Cambridge, MA, 1992.

[190] D. Sadek. Communication theory = rationality principles + communicative act models. In *Proceedings of AAAI'94 Workshop on Planning for Interagent Communication*, Seattle, WA, 1994.

[191] D. Sadek. Towards a theory of belief reconstruction: Application to communication. *Speech Communication Journal, special issue on Spoken Dialogue*, 15:251–263, 1994.

[192] D. Sadek. Design considerations on dialogue systems: from theory to technology. The case of Artimis (invited talk). In *Proceedings of IDS'99 (ETR Workshop on Interactive dialogue for multimedia systems)*, pages 173–187, Kloster Irsee, Germany, 1999.

[193] D. Sadek. Dialogue acts are rational plans. In M.M. Taylors, F. Neels and D.C. Bouhuis eds. *The structure of multimodal dialogue (II)*. John Benjamins publishing company (From the Venaco II Workshop, Italy, 1991), 2000.

[194] D. Sadek. De nouvelles perspectives pour l'ergonomie des interfaces personne-machine : dialogue naturel et agents intelligents dialoguants (invited talk). In *Proceedings of ERGOIA'04*, Biarritz, France, 2004.

[195] D. Sadek, P. Bretier, and F. Panaget. Artimis: Natural dialogue meets rational agency. In *Proceedings of IJCAI'97*, pages 1030–1035, Nagoya, Japan, 1997.

[196] D. Sadek, P. Bretier, and F. Panaget. Submission for standardization of component of France Telecom's Artimis technology - Arcol interagent communication language, MCP, CAP and SAP agent's cooperativity protocols, 1997. *Response to FIPA call for proposals.*

[197] D. Sadek and H. Brouchoud. Intelligent agents. In D. Hardy, G. Malleus and J.-N. Mereur eds. *Networks: Internet, telephony, multimedia - Convergences and complementarities.* De Boeck University, 2002.

[198] D. Sadek, A. Ferrieux, A. Cozannet, P. Bretier, F. Panaget, and J. Simonin. Effective human-computer cooperative spoken dialogue: The AGS demonstrator. In *Proceedings of ICSLP'96*, Philadelphia, 1996.

[199] D. Sadek and R. D. Mori. Dialogue systems. In *Spoken dialogs with computers*, pages 523–561. Academic Press, London, UK, 1998.

[200] G. Salton. *Automatic Text Processing - The Transformation, Analysis, and Retrieval of Information by Computer.* Addison–Wesley, 1989.

[201] P. Scerri, E. Liao, Y. Xu, M. Lewis, G. Lai, and K. Sycara. *Theory and Algorithms for Cooperative Systems*, chapter Coordinating very large groups of wide area search munitions. World Scientific Publishing, 2004.

[202] P. Scerri, D. Pynadath, and M. Tambe. Towards adjustable autonomy for the real world. *Journal of Artificial Intelligence Research*, 17:171–228, 2002.

[203] P. Scerri, D. V. Pynadath, L. Johnson, P. Rosenbloom, N. Schurr, M. Si, and M. Tambe. A prototype infrastructure for distributed robot-agent-person teams. In *AAMAS*, 2003.

[204] T. Schubert. Normen zur Überwachung und Steuerung autonomer Multi-Agenten Systeme. Diplomarbeit, Institut für Programmstrukturen und Datenorganisation, Fakultät für Informatik, Universität Karlsruhe (TH), 2004. (in German).

[205] J. Searle. *Speech acts.* Cambridge University Press, 1969.

[206] Y. Shoham. Agent-oriented programming. *Artificial Intelligence*, 60:51–92, 1993.

[207] J. Siegal. *CORBA Fundementals and Programming*. John Wiley & Sons, New York, 1996.

[208] A. Sturm and O. Shehory. A comparative evaluation of agent-oriented methodologies. In Bergenti et al. [13], chapter 7.

[209] V. Subrahmanian, P. Bonatti, J. Dix, T. Eiter, S. Kraus, F. Özcan, and R. Ross. *Heterogenous Active Agents*. MIT-Press, 2000.

[210] J. Sudeikat, L. Braubach, A. Pokahr, and W. Lamersdorf. Evaluation of agent-oriented software methodologies: Examination of the gap between modeling and platform. In P. Giorgini, J. Müller, and J. Odell, editors, *Agent Oriented Software Engineering (AOSE)*, 2004.

[211] A. Suna and A. El Fallah Seghrouchni. A mobile agents platform: architecture, mobility and security elements. In *Proceedings of Pro-MAS'04 Workshop of AAMAS, LNAI*, volume 3346, pages 126–146, New-York, 2004.

[212] A. Suna, G. Klein, and A. El Fallah Seghrouchni. Using mobile agents for resource sharing. In *Proceedings of IAT'04*, Beijing, China, 2004. IEEE Press.

[213] A. Suna, C. Lemaitre, and A. El Fallah Seghrouchni. E-commerce using an agent oriented approach. In *Proceedings of the Iberagents Workshop*, Puebla, Mexico, 2004.

[214] U. N. Suya You, Jinhui Hu and P. Fox. Urban site modeling from lidar. In *Proc. 2nd Int'l Workshop Computer Graphics and Geometric Modeling (CGGM)*, pages 579–588, 2003.

[215] M. Tambe. Agent architectures for flexible, practical teamwork. *National Conference on AI (AAAI97)*, pages 22–28, 1997.

[216] M. Tambe and W. Zhang. Towards flexible teamwork in persistent teams: Extended report. *Journal of Autonomous Agents and Multi-agent Systems*, 3:159–183, 2000. Special issue on "Best of ICMAS 98".

[217] E. ten Hoeve, M. Dastani, F. Dignum, and J.-J. Meyer. 3APL platform. In *Proceedings of the 15th Belgium-Netherlands Conference on Artificial Intelligence, BNAIC'03*, 2003.

[218] J. Thangarajah and L. Padgham. An empirical evaluation of reasoning about resource conflicts. In N. R. Jennings, C. Sierra, L. Sonenberg,

and M. Tambe, editors, *Proceedings of the Third International Joint Conference on Autonomous Agents and Multiagent Systems*, pages 1298–1299, July 2004.

[219] J. Thangarajah, L. Padgham, and J. Harland. Representation and reasoning for goals in BDI agents. In *Australasian Computer Science Conference*, 2002.

[220] J. Thangarajah, L. Padgham, and M. Winikoff. Detecting and avoiding interference between goals in intelligent agents. In *Proceedings of the 18th International Joint Conference on Artificial Intelligence (IJCAI 2003)*, 2003.

[221] J. Thangarajah, L. Padgham, and M. Winikoff. Detecting and exploiting positive goal interaction in intelligent agents. In *Proceedings of the Second International Joint Conference on Autonomous Agents and Multiagent Systems (AAMAS 2003), Melbourne, Australia*, pages 401–408. ACM Press, 2003.

[222] J. Thangarajah, M. Winikoff, L. Padgham, and K. Fischer. Avoiding resource conflicts in intelligent agents. In F. van Harmelen, editor, *Proceedings of the 15th European Conference on Artificial Intelligence (ECAI 2002), Lyon, France*. IOS Press, 2002.

[223] J. A. Torres, L. P. Nedel, and R. H. Bordini. Autonomous agents with multiple foci of attention in virtual environments. In *Proceedings of 17th International Conference on Computer Animation and Social Agents (CASA 2004), Geneva, Switzerland, 7–9 July*, pages 189–196, 2004.

[224] W. van der Hoek, B. van Linder, and J.-J. Ch. Meyer. An integrated modal approach to rational agents. In M. Wooldridge and A. Rao, editors, *Foundations of Rational Agency*, Applied Logic Series 14, pages 133–168. Kluwer, Dordrecht, 1998.

[225] R. van Eijk, F. de Boer, W. van der Hoek, and J.-J. C. Meyer. Process algebra for agent communication: A general semantic approach. In M.-P. Huget, editor, *Communication in Multiagent Systems — Agent Communication Languages and Conversation Policies*, number 2650 in LNCS, pages 113–128. Springer-Verlag, Berlin, 2003.

[226] M. B. van Riemsdijk, F. S. de Boer, and J.-J. Ch. Meyer. Dynamic logic for plan revision in intelligent agents. In J. A. Leite and P. Torroni, editors, *Proceedings of the fifth international workshop on computational logic in multi-agent systems (CLIMA'04)*, pages 196–211, 2004.

[227] M. B. van Riemsdijk, J.-J. Ch. Meyer, and F. S. de Boer. Semantics of plan revision in intelligent agents. In C. Rattray, S. Maharaj, and C. Shankland, editors, *Proceedings of the 10th International Conference on Algebraic Methodology And Software Technology (AMAST04)*, volume 3116 of *LNCS*, pages 426–442. Springer-Verlag, 2004.

[228] M. B. van Riemsdijk, W. van der Hoek, and J.-J. Ch. Meyer. Agent programming in Dribble: from beliefs to goals using plans. In *Proceedings of the second international joint conference on autonomous agents and multiagent systems (AAMAS'03)*, pages 393–400, Melbourne, 2003.

[229] R. Vieira, A. Moreira, M. Wooldridge, and R. H. Bordini. On the formal semantics of speech-act based communication in an agent-oriented programming language. *Submitted article, to appear*, 2005.

[230] A. S. Vivacqua and H. Lieberman. Agents to assist in finding help. In *Proc. of the Conference on Human factors in computing systems*, pages 65–72, The Hague, The Netherlands, 2000.

[231] P. Vrba. JAVA-Based agent platform evaluation. In V. Mařík, D. McFarlane, and P. Valckenaers, editors, *Holonic and Multi-Agent Systems for Manufacturing (HoloMAS 2003)*, pages 47–58. Springer, LNCS 2744, 2004.

[232] D. Watts and S. Strogatz. Collective dynamics of small world networks. *Nature*, 393:440–442, 1998.

[233] D. Weerasooriya, A. Rao, and K. Ramamohanarao. Design of a concurrent agent-oriented language. In *Intelligent Agents: Theories, Architectures, and Languages, LNAI*, volume 890, pages 386–402. Springer, 1995.

[234] G. Weiss. Agent orientation in software engineering. *The Knowledge Engineering Review*, 16(4):349–373, 2001.

[235] S. Wilmott, O. Rana, K.-H. Krempels, P. McBurney, and G. Weichart. Networked agents: Towards large-scale deployment of agents in open networked environments (NET AGENTS). *AgentLink News*, 16:16–17, December 2004. Available from http://www.agentlink.org/newsletter/.

[236] M. Winikoff, L. Padgham, J. Harland, and J. Thangarajah. Declarative & procedural goals in intelligent agent systems. In *Proceedings of the Eighth International Conference on Principles of Knowledge Representation and Reasoning (KR2002)*, Toulouse, France, 2002.

[237] M. Wooldridge. *Reasoning about Rational Agents*. The MIT Press, Cambridge, MA, 2000.

[238] M. Wooldridge. *An Introduction to MultiAgent Systems*. John Wiley & Sons, 2002.

[239] M. Wooldridge and N. R. Jennings. Agent Theories, Architectures, and Languages: A Survey. In *ECAI Workshop on Agent Theories, Architectures, and Languages*, pages 1–39, 1994.

[240] M. Wooldrige and N. Jennings. Towards a theory of cooperative problem solvings. In *Proceedings of MAAMAW'94*, Odense, Denmark, 1994.

[241] K. Yoshimura. FIPA JACK: A plugin for JACK Intelligent Agents, 2003. Available from http://www.cs.rmit.edu.au/agents/protocols/.

[242] F. Zambonelli, N. Jennings, and M. Wooldridge. Developing multiagent systems: The Gaia methodology. *ACM Transactions on Software Engineering and Methodology*, 12(3):317–370, July 2003.

[243] F. Zambonelli and A. Omicini. Challenges and research directions in agent-oriented software engineering. *Autonomous Agents and Multi-Agent Systems*, 9(3):253–283, November 2004.

[244] L. Zhang. Documentation for ASHOP 1.0. Technical Report CSC-TR 2102, University of Maryland, 2002. Master Thesis.

Index